Religions of India

RELIGIONS OF INDIA

Hinduism, Yoga, Buddhism

THOMAS BERRY

COLUMBIA UNIVERSITY PRESS   *New York*

Cover photo by Dick Waghorne

Columbia University Press
Publishers Since 1893
New York   Chichester, West Sussex
Copyright © 1992 by Thomas Berry
Columbia University Press edition, 1996

Library of Congress Cataloging-in-Publication Data

Berry, Thomas Mary, 1914—
Religions of India : Hinduism, Yoga, Buddhism / Thomas Berry.
p.   cm.
Includes bibliographical references and index.
ISBN 0-231-10781-1
1. India–Religion. 2. Hinduism. 3. Yoga. 4. Buddhism.
I. Title.
BL2001.2.B4   1996
294–dc20   96-28515
CIP

∞

Printed in the United States of America
p 10 9 8 7 6 5 4 3 2

Acknowledgements

The author and publisher wish to express their thanks for the use of quoted materials taken from the following:

R. D. Ranade, *Pathway to God in Marathi Literature* (Bombay, India: Baratiya Vidya Shavan, 1961); J. J. Jones, *Sacred Books of the Buddhists-Mahavastu*, 3 vols. (London: Pali Text Society, 1949, 1952, 1956); C. and H. Jesudasan, *A History of Tamil Literature* (New Delhi, India: YMCA Publishing House, 1961); Kingsbury and Philips, *Hymns of the Tamil Saivite Saints* (New Delhi, India: YMCA Publishing House, 1921); H. Kern, trans., "The Lotus Sutra," in *The Saddharma-Pundarika* or *Lotus of the True Law* (Oxford, England: Clarendon Press, 1909); T. W. Rhys Davids, trans., "The Milinda Panha," in *Questions of King Milinda*, 2 vols. (Oxford, England: Clarendon Press, 1890, 1894); E. B. Cowell, trans., "Buddhacarita of Asvaghosha," in *Buddhist Mahayana Texts* (Oxford, England: Clarendon Press, 1894); H. C. Warren, trans., "The Jataka," in *Buddhism in Translations* (Cambridge, Mass.: Harvard University Press, 1896); Justin E. Abbott, trans., *Stotramala* (Poona, India: Scottish Mission Industries Co., 1929); Justin E. Abbott, trans., *Tukaram* (Poona, India: Scottish Mission Industries Co., 1930).

Contents

Foreword

The relevance of this book is enhanced rather than diminished by the years since its original publication. The human situation has become even more critical. We are moving from a period of industrial plundering of the planet into a more intimate way of relating to the planet. We can no longer violate the integrity of Earth without becoming a destructive force for both the surrounding world and for ourselves.

Too frequently we have based our spiritualities simply on divine-human relations and inter-human relations while neglecting any concern for the role that the natural world has in this process. What strikes us immediately is the extent to which the experience of the divine is inseparable in India from the experience of the natural forms that surround us throughout the universe. Absolute transcendence requires total immanence. We read in the Upanishads that the divine is the numinous presence within every visible form. Especially in the Epic tale of Rama and Sita narrated in the *Ramayana* and celebrated throughout the Asian world we find this human intimacy with the flowering plants and with every living form, all of which become a protective and healing presence to the two exiles in their long journey through the fields and woodlands of this vast subcontinent.

As with the divine so with the human mode of being. We also have an intimate presence within the natural world, a presence that began in paleolithic times and continued on through the neolithic and into the classical civilizations, until recent centuries when we in the western world began to see the natural world simply as mechanism, devoid of any vital principle or spirit presence enabling the natural world to establish a communion relationship with ourselves. Because of this spiritual degrading of the natural world we began our physical plundering of the Earth until now every living creature on the earth is experiencing a degraded mode of existence. Most of all the human is experiencing a devastation that we seem not to understand or be able to remedy.

As we seek to heal this situation we turn to earlier spiritual traditions to guide us in restoring our sense of the sacred as a pervasive presence manifested in the dawn and sunset, in the wind and rain and thunder and lightning, in the dark forests and the snow-covered mountains, in the flow of the river, the soaring of the eagle, in the song of the mockingbird, and in the evening chorus of the cicada. In all these manifestations of the world about us we spontaneously bow our heads in a gesture of reverence for the presence of the sacred, for the deep mysteries of existence, for the fearsome as well as the fascinating qualities of the surrounding universe.

Strangely in this late twentieth century even when we witness all these astounding manifestations of the world of the sacred, they make very little impression on us. Our cultural fixations do not permit us to see what is simply there before us. Thus there is a need for traditions not afflicted with our pathology to assure us that it is quite proper to let the spontaneities within our own souls respond to the resplendent universe in which we live. The strange mental fixations that close off our deepest spontaneities need the examples of the poets and artists and spiritual personalities of other times and places to once again awaken us to the realities there before us.

Such is the role that India can fulfill in these times. Influences from India have been present throughout the spiritual traditions of the western world ever since the closing decades of the 18th century when our modern discoveries of India, the Sanskrit and vernacular languages and literatures and spiritual traditions took place. Since then our association with India and its religions has passed through a scholarly period of acquaintanceship, into the period of spiritual practitioners, to our present understanding of the intimate spiritual mode of the physical universe as this is revealed to us in this closing decade of the twentieth century when the dominant issue confronting us is how to establish a mutually-enhancing mode of human presence to the Earth.

In India we find a unique sensitivity to the pathos not simply of the human but of the entire natural world rooted deep within the religious experiences that have given its inner shape to the soul of India. One of the most profound doctrines of India is the doctrine of Ahimsa (non-injury) a term that can be understood as a negative way of expressing a positive all-embracing love or affection for every being in the universe. This teaching of Ahimsa is prior to the coming of the Aryan peoples and the Sanskrit tradition. It belongs to the primordial orientations not only of the conscious life of India but even to the unconscious depths of the Indian psyche.

These deeper spontaneities within the soul of India have been a transforming element throughout the intellectual, emotional, moral, religious, and aesthetic teachings handed down in India from earliest times. An all-pervading reverence for life was especially prominent in the teachings of the Buddha who had a profound experience of the sorrow of things and a corresponding sympathy whereby he sought to alleviate the pain not simply of the human but of all beings. This unwillingness to consider the suffering of humans apart from the suffering of the natural world led Buddha, in one of the stories of his prior existences, to throw himself over a cliff to give himself as food for a mother tiger and her cubs who were at the time starving to death. This rings quite authentic in the traditions of India, although it would generally be totally unacceptable to western religious or moral or humanist thinking. So too there is the example of Shanti Deva who offered to take upon himself the sufferings of all beings. He considered it more appropriate that he himself should suffer the pain of every other being rather than that other beings should suffer.

While in this book we are presenting our interpretation of India mainly through its spiritual and religious literature, a verification of what is suggested here can be found throughout the artistic and literary productions of the tradition. The intimate rapport of India's peoples with the natural world can be seen from its early period of sculptured columns in the time of Asoka in the 3rd century BC. Again it is seen in the Buddha images, in the Hindu temples of South India, in the Murals of Ajanta. In all of these presentations we find an immense delight in all forms of earthly existence. The universe entire seems to come to itself in an integral moment of self-fulfillment.

We see this especially in the remarkable sculpture at Mamallapuram on the eastern shores of the Indian sub-continent portraying the Descent of the Ganges. Here all of nature is depicted in a reverent presence to the divine river coming down from heaven upon earth. All the animals as well as the humans and the devas bow in a hushed silence in gratitude for this wondrous gift. Such intimate presence of the divine throughout is expressed in the miniature paintings of the 16th and 17th centuries, especially in the tenderness of the Rajput paintings of this period. Rarely do we see such intimacy with the natural world. This is a sublime folk art where play and delight and sensuous joy in existence all resonate together.

We in the western world are not without our artists and poets and mystics who express their sense of intimacy with the natural world. But somehow we have not been able to carry over our emotional, aesthetic, and spiritual perceptions into the habits of daily living. The demands for materials to build our industrial civilization have overwhelmed us. Somehow we have become frightened by the rigors of life, by the violence often experienced in nature, experiences that have caused us to withdraw into our cities, to build barriers between ourselves and the surrounding world. We have shaped for ourselves a mechanistic wonderworld that we seem determined to build even when we are obviously reducing the entire planet to a condition of waste and ruin.

In a kind of mental fixation we have become autistic in relation to the natural world. We have closed it out as an unacceptable world. We impose our mechanistic systems on our surroundings until we have attained an abiding beatitude beyond all contact with the natural life communities to which we belong and without which we cannot survive. The world about us has become a collection of objects to be exploited for comfort and commercial gain rather than a universe of subjects to be communed with. It is this communion with the natural world that is so infinitely important in any form of survival, economic or aesthetic or spiritual.

We need to hear the voices of the natural world, the voices of the mountains and rivers, the voices of the ocean and the sky and the wind and all natural phenomena. The traditions of India can assist in teaching us this, if only we will first enter into its deepest experience of the divine as expressed in its great spiritual heritage. This experience first articulated in the Vedic hymns and the mystical teachings of the Upanishads, was later expressed even more intimately in the Hindu devotional hymns to the deities Vishnu and Shiva and the great diversity of regional names under which these deities were worshiped. It is also communicated to us through the Buddhist sensitivity to the pain of the universe, a pain akin to that expressed in the Aeneid of Virgil where he speaks of the lachrymae rerum, the "tears of things."

It is precisely this pathos of temporal existence that leads to an ever-deepening delight in existence. Because of its transience, existence becomes

Foreword

infinitely precious. For time bears eternity within itself. That these are dimensions of each other is entirely clear to the spiritual traditions of India. Yet only now are we in the West becoming aware of these two modes of each single reality. The fragility of things needs the presence of the absolute while the absolute can reveal itself only in the fragile formations of time.

The final term of all existence is "Celebration." This is the origin, purpose, and destiny of every form of being. Indeed we can say that the universe throughout its vast extent in space and its long sequence of transformations in time is a single, multiform celebratory event. Humans already in the paleolithic period had discovered that the proper role of the human was to integrate human activity with the activity of the universe, to participate in the Grand Liturgy of the seasonal transformations. Such is India a single vast multiform celebration in itself. Such is the literature of India from the Vedic hymns through the mystical literature of the Upanishads, the great devotional writers, and especially the great Mahayana Buddhist Sutras the Lotus Sutra, the Vimalakirti Nirdesa Sutra, and the Awakening of Faith in the Mahayana Sutra. The culmination of joy finds special expression in The Great Surprise when the promise of Nirvana in the earlier Buddhist scriptures is fulfilled in becoming a Buddha Being. The universe entire finds a new level of exaltation. In this manner India offers a comprehensive way of human fulfillment within the ultimate liturgy of the universe itself.

Under the Great Red Oak
at Riverdale
Spring 1992

The Spiritual Aspect of Asian Civilizations

This study is concerned with the spiritual formation of man in the Asian world. This spiritual formation has provided the Asian peoples with a bond of communion between the divine and the human worlds; it has established the ideals of perfection toward which human life is directed; it has enabled Asian peoples to manage the human condition in a creative manner; it has inspired the arts and sciences that have characterized the Asian civilizations up to modern times. These spiritual traditions of Asia are so highly developed that they frequently attain a level that corresponds more with the higher mystical traditions of the West than with its ordinary levels of religious and moral life.

Some traditions, such as Hinduism, are principally concerned with the response of man to divine reality and to the final consummation of human life within this divine reality. Others, such as Buddhism, are less attracted to religion in its ordinary manifestations; rather, they are immediately concerned with forming a spiritual life that will enable men to master the human condition and eventually attain total release from the sorrowful aspect of life. But whatever the point of emphasis, these sacred traditions have been the supreme dynamic forces in structuring the civilizations of Asia. They are all keenly aware of a transphenomenal dimension of reality, whether this be the Brahman of the Hindu, the Nirvana of the Buddhist, the Kaivalya experience of the Yogin, or the Tao of the Chinese.

Man is most truly himself when he shares in this higher dimension of reality. There is a surprising variety in these experiences. Yet all attain a higher fulfillment of man's being; they give to human life divine significance. If the sorrows of life are not perfectly healed in this experience, they are at least given depth of meaning. A constructive process is set in motion to remove the limitations of man's earthly condition, to give man a transformed existence in a higher order of reality. Differences and similarities in these traditions are both significant, yet the differences are especially striking and need to be studied with some care. The variety in his spiritual formation is among the most fascinating aspects of man's historical development. The differences of cultural expression that distinguish the various peoples of earth come largely from these differences in their experience of the divine order of reality and their efforts to elevate human life to a greater participation in this higher order.

Rituals, beliefs, and ways of perfection became more and more complex as these traditions developed through the centuries. At first the ritual development was of primary importance. Ritual on a grand scale provided the basic structure within which human life attained its greatest significance. Man's ritual life included everything from sacrifices and prayers offered to the divine, to the customs governing marriages, to the manner in which people greeted each other on the street. Through ritual a profound intercommunion was established between all three realms of reality: the divine, the natural, and the human. Human life was seen as a single compact order in which the spiritual and the secular were inseparably associated with each other. Ritual was the main instrument through which man found his place within the larger human community and within the cosmic order beyond.

Along with this ritual development came development of the higher thought traditions. Great systems of belief were evolved concerning divine reality and the relation between the divine and the earthly realms. Narratives set forth the manner in which things came into existence at the beginning. Explanations were given of the inner nature of things, their significance, and their proper function in the universe. Hinduism was deeply concerned with the inner life of the divine, its ineffability, its creative power, its omnipresence. Other traditions, such as Confucianism, were intellectually oriented toward a comprehension of man and his place in the cosmic order and his proper perfection as a human being. Yet both these traditions remained within a basic religious context throughout their formative periods. Neither in Asia nor elsewhere has man in the traditional societies attained any deep comprehension of the world of time except in relation to some higher reality that is both above and present in the world of constantly changing phenomena. Only in relation to the higher reality do things of this lower realm have reality, value, or truth.

The intellectual situation in both India and China differs from that of Plato, who saw the realities of time as reflections of the ideal realities that transcend time and space and have eternal and absolute existence. In Hindu India there is a more absolute division and a closer identity. The higher and lower orders are linked by a mysterious power, that of Maya. Only the absolute order is truly real; the phenomenal order is manifestation. Yet there is here a coincidence of opposites. The phenomenal and the absolute are totally different, yet totally identical. In the final analysis, however, the lower is derived from the higher, is contained in the higher, and is directed toward a transformation in the higher. In China, the mysterious Tao is beyond the phenomenal order yet present in it and manifested through it. Here also there is a coincidence of opposites, although in this case the phenomenal as such is much more real than in India. A doctrine of archetypes is indicated but not fully developed.

While the ritual and intellectual developments of Asia are of primary importance in any study of the Asian religions, the present work is focused not so much upon these aspects of the Asian traditions as upon their spiritual meaning—the way in which these peoples subjectively experienced the divine, the ways through which they sought salvation from the human condition, the ideals of human perfection toward which they directed their efforts. The ritual forms of worship were not the main points of emphasis in the later stages of the Asian traditions. Attention was focused upon a better comprehension of man himself, on how to manage life so that man would attain to the most perfect expression of himself. This quest for a life discipline was even more universal in Asia than was the creation of ritual expressions of worship. From their inception, some of the higher traditions of Asia were more directly concerned with the salvation of man than with the worship of God. They were religious only to the extent that the final goal of this spiritual effort was release from the phenomenal world into the world of the infinite. The Yoga tradition, one of the most unique and most influential forms of Asian spirituality, had in itself a minimum of religious content. Yet through its association with other Indian traditions, especially Buddhism, its spiritual influence was felt throughout the entire Far-Asian world.

Although the spiritual disciplines must be distinguished from the ritual and intellectual aspects of the religious life of Asia, it should be noted that they were intimately related to man's intellectual understanding of the divine and to the manner in which ritual communion with the divine takes place. If ritual was the earliest way in which form and structure were given to the spiritual life of these peoples, the spiritual disciplines, as a distinct aspect of man's life, led more directly to the fulfillment of human existence. This spiritual development brought to fulfillment the salvation to which all else was subordinated. It contained the quintessence of religion as this was expressed in daily life.

As these societies developed, the importance of human spiritual formation loomed more significant. Ritual itself was ineffective if any failure in the human personality was associated with it. If ritual served for a time as the principal spiritual guide of man, this inner spiritual development gave vital content to the ritual. While these two were mutually implicated, the spiritual transformation of man remained the primary concern. This was religion in its highest expression. This inner human transformation was the true ritual, the true sacrifice, the true response to divine presence, the true perfection of man, his way of attaining his final destiny, his only way of achieving his true, his real self.

Moreover, the main intellectual developments were centered on establishing a way of spiritual perfection by which final release from the human condition was obtained. The main function of Vedantic philosophy was the curing of man's illusions about the external world in order to lead man toward spiritual release into the Supreme Reality. Thus the intellectual life itself must be viewed less as a rational process than as a way of salvation. One of the most important reasons for the high development of the spiritual traditions of Asia is that the Asian peoples saw with extraordinary clarity that man in his original state was only the crude material of his real self. Man was an unfinished being who must give higher form and substance to his own existence. The very purpose of the higher Asian cultures was to develop a setting in which the real man could be formed, a setting that would bring man into conscious accord with the larger realms of the divine and natural worlds with which he is intimately associated and upon which his perfection depends.

Introduction

Intense preoccupation of Asian peoples with the spiritual formation of the human personality led them to insights that have great significance for the religious and spiritual life of all mankind. The Buddhist tradition has much to offer precisely because it is a spiritual discipline more than a ritual tradition. Confucianism, also, is of universal value because of its teaching concerning the formation of the human personality in the full range of its faculties. The ritual aspect of these and the other Asian traditions is almost totally incommunicable. The intellectual insights and the efforts toward a higher spiritual development of man—these are the things that come through to other societies across the expanse of space and time. These spiritual traditions are important not only because they enrich man's understanding of how to achieve a status of perfection; they also indicate how man has dealt with the sorrows, tensions, frustrations, and limitations to which he is subject both from the external world about him and from the inner constitution of his own being.

The similarity of the human condition throughout the ages is one of the forces that brings together all the spiritual traditions of mankind and enables them to communicate with one another on the most profound level, even in present times. Modern man has become increasingly conscious of the agonies inherent in the human condition. Intellectual and mechanical progress have not cured man of the inner limitations to which he is subject. Indeed, we are more highly sensitized to the human condition than the peoples who have preceded us. Other peoples, knowing that they could do little to alter the human condition externally, built up a spiritual capacity to sustain themselves as they worked toward final triumph over this condition. Modern man seeks to remove the painful elements of the human condition by the control he exercises over the natural world and over the inner functioning of his own physical and psychic organism. But in neither case has modern man eliminated the personal agonies or the larger terrors inherent in his historical situation. In many ways he has only aggravated his life tension while lowering his spiritual capacity to absorb the afflictions inseparable from his existence as man.

It is within this salvation context that the higher thought traditions arose in Asia. Philosophy, there, is an effort to understand and deal with both the transphenomenal and the infraphenomenal, both divine splendor and human sorrow. Such monumental challenges call for a response from the depth of a man's being rather than from the top of his mind. In a special manner, however, philosophy arose from within the urgencies of human life itself, from the agonies associated with the human condition, from the effort to establish an intellectual-spiritual response that would comprehend and then control this situation. Philosophy in Asia did not arise from curiosity concerning the nature of things, as Aristotle suggested, it was the expression of a spirituality rather than the expression of an abstract intellectual insight. Until recently, we in the modern West were inclined to give spirituality a place in the lower emotional life of man rather than in his higher intellectual life. Thus it is still difficult to place the thought traditions of Asia within Western philosophical and theological categories. While this effort at philosophical understanding has not been entirely satisfactory, it is beginning to achieve some impressive results. The designation of Asian writings either as philosophy or as theology cannot be completely dismissed, for they contain many philosophical and theological discussions such as we have in the West. Yet there is a wider spiritual context which is quite different from the rational context of most modern Western philosophy.

The Asian works fit best in a category that is neither philosophy nor theology. They belong in the realm of spirituality, the realm in which much of St. Augustine's work was done, the realm of Dionysius, of Bonaventure, Eckhart, John of the Cross, and more recently of Nietzsche and to some extent Heidegger. This is true particularly of the Indian traditions, which are directly concerned with the higher spiritual development of man, not with intellectual enlightenment within the rational order. In fact, they are principally transrational or even antirational. They intend to make man truly man by carrying him beyond himself to a participation in divine existence, for only there is man fully what he should be, only there are the sorrows of life totally healed, only there is the full vision of truth.

Thus the classical writings of Asia are spiritual treatises that have for their purpose the guiding of man along the path of salvation. This is found in the Hindu Upanishads, but especially in the greatest of India's spiritual classics, the *Bhagavad-Gita*. The Buddhist scriptures, especially the *Dhammapada (Way of Perfection)*, offer spiritual guidance rather than philosophical insight. In China this is especially clear in the *Book of History*, the *Book of Changes*, and the *Book of Ritual*, as well as in the writings of Confucius and Mencius. In all these works the entire civilizational structure is seen as a way of spiritual perfection. The *Tao Te Ching* of Lao Tzu and the writings of Chuang Tzu are primarily spiritual classics. Thus, these Asian classics should be considered not only as ritual guides and as speculative doctrines, but even more as outlines of a way of salvation. This is true even of such highly developed scholastic writings as those of Shankara and Ramanuja, the greatest Hindu theologians, and of Chu Hsi, who created the most impressive and most influential synthesis of Confucian thought. They instruct man in the manner in which he should respond to the higher order of reality that governs the world, how he should manage the afflictions of human life, how he should attain his higher perfection as a man, how he comes finally to a divine transformation.

This preoccupation with the spiritual cannot be considered as strange in that the more significant Western philosophers were themselves spiritual writers rather than rational thinkers, just as were many of the philosophers of later times. In its more lively moments, philosophy, even in the West, is primarily a spiritual quest for salvation. The pre-Socratic philosophers such as Pythagoras and Parmenides present spiritual vision rather than rational philosophy. Greek philosophy of the later period is less rational in its finer examples than is generally thought. This can be seen especially in Plato, whose philosophy is clearly a way of salvation, a spiritual discipline. That this is also true of Plotinus can be seen from the mystical content of his thought and from his vision of the One. Yet, certainly, Western philosophy has inquired into the nature of things more than did the Asian writers generally. Since the medieval acceptance of Aristotelianism there was in the West a growing tendency toward rational, logical thought as the ideal of man's intellectual life. The historical trend in India, however, moved in the opposite direction; there was a progressive attraction toward a saving spiritual vision.

Asian education, too, must be seen as primarily spiritual initiation. In all traditional civilizations the bearer of wisdom was the spritual personality in the society. This is true of the Brahman class of India, of the scholar class of China, of the Buddhist monks throughout Asia. The intellectual leaders of India and China were primarily spiritual guides who carried the learning of these societies and provided its proper explanation. These spiritual guides were the teachers of the young, whose education was a training for spiritual perfection, and not the inculcation of facts or a preparation for some mundane occupation. This too was done, but it was not primary. It was not the basic educational process. Education was primarily an initiation into the expansive realms of the spiritual; thus it had a sacred character. This is true even of Chinese education, which emphasized the humanities but always with profound spiritual implications.

THE SEVERAL TRADITIONS

There is no one, universal Asian religious or spiritual tradition. Neither is there any ideal norm of Asian spirituality, just as there is no ideal flower or ideal tree. There is simply the variety, at times an interrelation and derivation within the variety. Within the Asian traditions it is difficult to designate each of them as spiritual traditions in the same sense of the word. This is a serious problem in any study that includes the multiplicity of traditions within the same frame of reference. Indeed, at first sight there seems to be more contradiction than agreement within Asia. At times the Asian traditions differ more among themselves than the individual traditions differ from the basic traditions of the West.

The first step in a study of Oriental religions must be to accept the diversity of man's spiritual traditions as historical fact. This comes hard for us in the West; we are extremely sensitive to differences in man's spiritual life. Because we have difficulty in accepting this differentiation we lack the interest needed to understand it. A common attitude is that it should not be, or, if it is, that it should be eliminated as soon as possible. Antagonism to spiritual diversity is so great that the spiritual traditions of Asia have often been considered a catastrophe for them and a danger for us. This attitude does no credit to intelligent persons, much less Christians. In reality these traditions are the glory of these peoples, a support for our own traditions, and a treasure for all mankind. Once this is realized we can begin a sound approach to these traditions.

In an effort to understand, caution must be taken not to listen first to what Western writers have said about these traditions, but to listen first to their own expressions of their thoughts and ideals, which are found in their sacred writings, in their genuine traditions, and in their present religious thinking. These sacred scriptures, traditional writings and present teachings are all available and wonderfully instructive. They are neither mysterious nor seductive. The earlier sacred writings, especially, are inspiring documents that for centuries have guided Asian peoples along the path of virtue and the avoidance of vice, illumined them concerning the final realities of human existence, instructed them concerning the ineffable nature of that supreme reality upon which the visible world depends, explained to them the sorrows of life, and given them hope for salvation from this sorrow through divine aid and human effort.

In recent years the most fundamental of these spiritual writings have been collected and translated into the Western languages. Excellent anthologies have been compiled from the traditions individually and from the various traditions collectively. Encyclopedias have excellent articles on these subjects. Introductory studies abound. Books giving detailed historical background on Asian religious development have been done by highly trained scholars. Reference works have been improved. Translations from the best of the sacred writings of Asia are printed in popular editions that can be read with little difficulty.

Even more important than the newly available study material is the new intellectual attitude in the West, where secular traditions feel the need of a more spiritual interpretation of life. Modern man, experiencing anew the limitations of the human condition, the general frustrations of life, the burdening complexity of a highly technological civilization, is embarking once more on his perennial quest for spiritual salvation. This quest has been rising in spiritual intensity ever since the time of Nietzsche, at the end of the nineteenth century. Secular man is presently fascinated with the lofty spiritual visions that can be found throughout the entire world. There is a feeling that something splendid is happening in the universal spiritual life of mankind.

In a particular manner there is a new awareness within the Christian tradition that it should enter more fully into the spiritual life of the world, that it should seek not the destruction but the preservation and development of all that is precious in the spiritual heritage of the peoples of the earth, especially in the traditions of Asia, which are more highly developed than the traditions of most other parts of the world. We are now sufficiently mature in understanding our own religious traditions that we can appreciate and learn from other traditions even while bringing to these traditions the divine communication that has entered the world through our own traditions. Exciting possibilities will exist when Christianity and the Asian religions begin to understand each other in some depth and bestow upon each other the special treasures so long confined within each.

The basic proposition to be set forth is that the spiritual traditions of man are complementary, not contradictory. Indeed, we will not fully understand any of the spiritual traditions of man until we understand them all. For none of them will have attained its full development until it has entered profoundly into communion with all the traditions of mankind. Just as the pieces of a mosaic cannot be understood apart from the whole, neither can the spiritual development of any single world tradition be fully understood until it is seen in the context of the whole. The basic values of the various spiritual traditions are not mutually destructive. They rather so enhance one another that the total picture of man's spiritual development will eventually be seen as a far greater splendor than anything one can behold in the present divided state of man's spiritual traditions.

Diversity itself is a principle of unity rather than of conflict. Diverse things need each other, for each has something that the others do not have. Identical things exclude each other because there is nothing one has that the others do not have. This was to some extent appreciated in Asia in an earlier period. Asia was aware that man's spiritual development required a rich and complex background composed of various traditions. Thus in Japan there was no difficulty in simultaneous appreciation of Shinto, Buddhism, and Confucianism. Each supplied something lacking to the others. Each needed the others, as Christianity and Hellenism needed each other for their full development in the earlier phases of Western history. In the future, mankind will need all the spiritual resources that are available from his total historical experience.

Before proceeding with this study of the larger complex of Asian religious traditions, some insight into each of these traditions is necessary. Each is founded in a unique experience of reality. Each has something that is irreducible and irreplaceable. Each is founded in some primordial experience that has provided the major determinant for the rich traditions that developed later. None of these primordial experiences can be dispensed with in the complete story of man's spiritual development without producing serious distortions in our view of man and his historical development. Each of these traditions is a revelation of the capacity of man for responding in unique fashion to the world that surrounds him. This is immediately evident in such traditions as Hinduism, Buddhism, Confucianism, and Shinto. Each has an insight that is startling in its distinctive qualities and in its total impact on later civilizational developments. Until we meet the reality we could never have guessed that such a thing as the Buddhist experience of the emptiness of the phenomenal world could exist or that such amazing intellectual vision could have been developed such as we find in Nagarjuna (second century) and Vasubandhu (fifth century), or the remarkable insight of the *Tao Te Ching* into the power of the weak and lowly things of the earth. After an acquaintance with the Hindu vision of the world of absolute divine reality it is amazing to find in Asia a tradition as humanist, as interested in the temporal life of man, as committed to the natural world as that of Confucianism. Nor, once we come to know Confucianism, would we expect to discover such efforts at inner withdrawal as we find

Introduction

in the Yoga tradition. Each of these is absolutely extreme in relation to the others, yet each is needed in the larger pattern of the total human experience. In his earliest period a total experience of reality was impossible to man. The total experience must emerge from diverse experiences, each of which must be developed separately. Each has its place in the larger pattern of the total human experience. Until now there have been severe limitations in the phases of reality experienced by a single society or by a single spiritual tradition.

The spiritual traditions that have given shape and substance to human life in the individual societies of Asia have also, to some extent, isolated these societies from one another. Only one of these traditions, Buddhism, has influenced practically all of Asia east of Persia (or Iran). This tradition stands unique among the Asian traditions as the only one that has entered into and profoundly modified all the other major traditions that have emerged in this region. Buddhism is the first multicultural spiritual tradition in the higher history of mankind. Thus, any study of the Asian spiritual traditions must give a special place to Buddhism as the most universal of Asian spiritual traditions. It is also significant that Buddhism is the Asian tradition that is most appreciated in the West.

Only by virtue of this new comprehension of Asian cultural development can the full range of spiritual insight that is possible to human nature be understood. But even with all the experience of the centuries, we find it difficult to enter into a vital appreciation of this total spiritual heritage. These are the most precious experiences that mankind has known and the highest treasures that man possesses. Only when we understand these traditions will we understand the peoples whose lives have been formed in their uttermost depths by these traditions. Because the reconciliation between the Oriental religions and the Western religions is of such magnitude, it is best to study first the manner in which the Asian religions mutually identify and complete each other. Then the larger problem of the differences and identities of the Oriental and the Western traditions can be considered.

THE RELIGIOUS COMPLEXITY OF INDIA

India is the most complex of the higher civilizational areas of the world in its peoples, its languages, its cultural and spiritual traditions, its social and political functioning. In a special manner India is the land of religions.

Within this subcontinent of Asia are found religions which are among the most primitive and the most advanced of all religions known to man.

Yoga and Jainism represent two of the primordial spiritual disciplines that have survived to date. Both reach far back into the earliest days of India's development. Yoga particularly has been an all-pervading spiritual influence in India and in the other parts of Asia influenced by India. Buddhism, the greatest spiritual movement known to Asia east of Persia, developed in India in the sixth century B.C. and flourished there for some sixteen centuries before it finally faded from that country. From an early period, possibly as early as the first century, Christianity found a home in India. St. Thomas the Apostle may have brought the Gospel to this region. While this has never been satisfactorily demonstrated, it is at least true that Christianity was in India by the fourth century, long before it reached many parts of Europe. The influence of Christianity on the religious life of India during these early centuries has never been adequately studied, although Christianity has had a continuous tradition in India until the present day.

A new addition to the complex of Indian religious traditions came with the introduction of the Parsis in the eighth century when they fled from Persia on the arrival of the Islamic forces. The Parsis have been in the regions of the west coast of India ever since. They are found mostly in the Bombay region, although their numbers in India have never been very large. Presently they number over a hundred thousand. The Parsis represent the Zoroastrian religious tradition. By coming into India they are to some extent rejoining the common Aryan tradition of which the Persian and the Indian Vedic developments are branches.

Islam came into India in the eleventh century, although its highest development took place during the eighteenth and nineteenth centuries. The greatest of the Mogul rulers, especially Akbar (1542–1605), fostered a spiritual understanding between Islam and the other religions of India. Of all the religions that entered the country from without, Islam prospered most, was the greatest spiritual influence over the country, and attained most followers. The intimate association of Islam with Hinduism produced the Sikh religion, one of the great religious-spiritual developments of the modern world. It has a great richness in its spiritual teaching and represents the greatest single product of Western and Hindu religious meeting.

In the sixteenth century Roman Catholicism was established in India, principally under the influence of the Jesuits, who were welcome at the court of Akbar and were effective for a while in communicating with both the upper and lower classes of the people. In the eighteenth century Protestant Christianity was established in India, principally through the effort of Danish missionaries. Then through the efforts of the English Baptist, William Carey (1761–1834), and his successors in the nineteenth century, a new social and spiritual movement swept over India that led eventually to the modernization of the country. The new influence of Protestant Christianity was more decisive than the other forms of Christianity, which included the Oriental, largely Syrian Christianity of the early period and the Roman Christianity of the sixteenth century. In particular it was the influence of Protestant reform movements that evoked a revitalization within Hinduism itself by giving to Hinduism a new sense of its identity. India awakened to a new sense of the reality of the world and the need for achieving certain social and human goals never before really appreciated or intently sought after in the Hindu world.

These religions all belong to the higher spiritual development of India, to the more literate traditions with an extensive thought development. But there are other religions of India. Especially to be noted are the multitude of local deities, cults, ceremonies, and beliefs, which belong to the people in a very special way. They have not yet been adequately identified or described even in modern studies of the religious life of India. They are so many, so varied, so constantly renewed, so creative in response to new circumstances, that they can be only partially observed and imperfectly described. The experience of these religions among the people, however, is powerful and most effective in bestowing meaning, value, and direction to the life process. While they have contributed much to the higher religions, they have never been fully absorbed into them.

A final significant influence on the religious development of India has been the introduction of modern secularism. This all-pervading influence has done much to counterbalance the excessive religiosity of the people. It has brought about a new intellectual experience of reality that is both shattering and refreshing. It has produced a helpful critique of the past religious preoccupations, focused attention upon man and his human welfare, and initiated a quest for relief from the needless misery caused by an oppressive caste system. It is desirable, of course, that secularism make its benefits available without damaging the basic spiritual values of the Indian people. To date there have been difficulties in achieving this, but it can be said that India remains a people with a powerful and all-pervading spiritual orientation toward life.

With this simple listing of religious developments in India across the last four thousand years, India is seen to be a veritable forest of spiritual growth, a forest so dense that it is difficult to identify and explain in detail. Yet even before an examination of the more important of these religious traditions we should be aware of India's intense preoccupation with the religious-spiritual aspect of life. This is so all-pervading that it is disconcerting to a modern Westerner. It is completely foreign to our present secularist life attitude. Amid this religious diversity there are differences and tensions but seldom such antagonism as religious diversity has evoked in the West. These differences in India concerned especially the way of salvation. Some depended principally on ritual, some on knowledge, others on ascetic practices or Yogic techniques, many on devotion to a personal deity. There were also extensive doctrinal divergencies, especially between Buddhism and Hinduism. Buddhism refused to give name and identity to any absolute reality as Hinduism had done. Buddhists in turn were frequently, but mistakenly, considered nihilists by Hindu theologians.

Despite this conflict and frequent misunderstandings, mutual influences radiated back and forth among all these religions of the Indian subcontinent. Yet along with these mutual influences there was a strong tendency toward independent development. India is still creating new forms of spirituality, as is seen in such moderns as Ramakrishna and Vivekananda, in Tagore and Gandhi. India develops every doctrine to its extreme implication. Even contradictory doctrines are pushed to their extremes without rejection of either alternative. This is the baffling element in any study of India. There is insistence on extreme immanence and extreme transcendence at the same time. The two, it is felt, implicate each other and finally identify with each other. Absolute immanence and absolute transcendence must eventually be the same. So with all oppositions. Extreme intellectualism exists in India along with extreme devotionalism; extreme sensualism, along with an unbelievable asceticism. There is no wish to extinguish one in favor of the other. There is a certain ease within these manifold, opposing traditions, a feeling that everything has its proper place, that nothing should be excluded.

Part One:

Hinduism

Chapter One

General Considerations

THE CENTRAL TRADITION

Amid the complex of spiritual developments in India, Hinduism holds the dominant position. It controls the life of India more than any other tradition. Hinduism is simultaneously a higher religion, a developed cultural tradition, and a social structure. In each of these aspects Hinduism is exceedingly complex. A luxuriant growth in all directions, Hinduism has an amazing capacity for holding together a variety of spiritual, cultural, and social extremes. For Hinduism holds together not only the diversity of movements within its own spiritual tradition; it also holds together, in the unity of a single civilizational complex, the spiritual and civilizational developments of the entire subcontinent. This is a massive work that should be fully appreciated in any study of Hinduism.

All traditions within India are in some manner related to the Hindu social order. Hinduism encompasses all, finds a place for all, and establishes the functional relations between diverse traditions. Those who are not Hindu in their spiritual orientation still find their place in India by virtue of the Hindu arrangement. In accord with the social order of Hinduism a balance is maintained among the religions of India. Hinduism is itself so complex a spiritual tradition that there is no such thing as Hindu doctrinal orthodoxy. So long as a person accepts the authority of the Vedas and the basic elements of Hindu social order in his conduct he may believe anything and remain within the pale of Hinduism. He must, however, follow with the greatest strictness the prescriptions that govern the life and activities of the subgroup of which he belongs. In Hinduism we find an orthopraxy rather than an orthodoxy.

HINDUISM AS PROCESS

To this cultural complexity of Hinduism is added a historical diversity of expression. For this reason Hinduism must be studied not as a fixed and integrated body of doctrines, but as a developing tradition that has changed considerably throughout the centuries and which is still changing in a creative direction. Everything in India makes sense in the light of this changing process. Nothing makes sense without it. To give lists of Hindu beliefs or descriptions of Hindu practices without identifying the period and area in which they took place is to present a static picture of something very different from Hinduism as it has actually existed. The basic unity is the unity of a changing life process, not the unity of a fixed pattern. Even though Indian civilization was thoroughly ahistorical, even though the people were not aware of the historical significance of the changes through which their religious-spiritual traditions were passing, it remains true to say that there can be no understanding of Hinduism except that which is based on the developmental process that has been taking place in India during the whole of India's recorded and unrecorded history.

Thus, in this study we do not present a list of fixed doctrines, rituals, or modes of conduct as though these constituted a fixed and integral system which could be designated by the term "Hinduism." We present rather a process which had a beginning and which has gone through several main phases of development up to the present time. Hinduism is still a living, changing process and must be seen as such.

The three most significant changes were: (1) that effected by the arrival of Aryan peoples into India around 2000 B.C.; (2) that which occurred just before the beginning of the Christian era, which led to the rise of the theistic sectarian religions of Vaishnavism and Shaivism; (3) that which occurred in the nineteenth century when Western influences poured into India. The entire development of Hinduism has been determined by these three experiences.

The creative impetus of the early period resulted from the interaction of two traditions, the Aryan and the non-Aryan, which are the two basic components of Hinduism. The non-Aryan represents the primordial tradition of India. Little was known of this pre-Aryan development until the discovery in the 1920s of the prehistoric Indus Valley civilizations. Until then, scholars generally traced the entire development of Hinduism and of Indian civilization itself from the Sanskrit records written by the Aryan peoples who came into India after 2000 B.C. There were indications that any account of Hinduism based entirely on these records was not adequate. These records themselves noted that a prior native tradition existed and had powerfully influenced the total development of Hinduism. They also gave some indication of the characteristics of this prior tradition. This was not fully appreciated, however, until archaeological research brought to light the extent of India's development in the pre-Aryan period. After the discovery of early sites at Harappa and Mohenjo-Daro had shown the development of Indian culture prior to the arrival of the Aryans, the Sanskrit records were examined anew and a deeper understanding was attained of this earlier tradition. The development of Hinduism is now seen as a progressive Indianization of the incoming tradition. By Indianization is meant that the non-Aryan native elements gradually modified the Aryan elements and, over the centuries, achieved an ever-larger place in the total pattern of cultural and spiritual interaction. This indicates how important it is to know the distinctive spiritual orientation of India prior to the coming of the Aryans, for only this can explain the later developments that must be traced to the reassertion within an Aryan context of elements present in India from the earliest times.

Told very simply, the historical development and intellectual expression of Hinduism is the meeting and fusion of Aryan and non-Aryan elements, with a general tendency toward the predominance of the native non-Aryan over the incoming Aryan elements in the creative process that emerged from this meeting.

A parallel can be drawn here with Western cultural development, which has as its central feature the meeting of two basic components, the Christian and the Hellenic traditions. There has been an extensive interaction of these two in the West with a tendency at different times for one to overcome the other. As Western civilization carries the Christian tradition in union and constant tension with Hellenic tradition, as Chinese tradition carries the union and tension of Taoism and Confucianism, so Hinduism carries the tension of the Aryan and non-Aryan forces within itself. The difference is that the Aryan and non-Aryan elements of Hinduism have greater spiritual complexity than those in the examples given. Thus these comparisons give only a slight indication of the real process taking place within Hinduism.

Because the Aryan peoples from an early period produced extensive literary compositions in the Sanskrit language that have been preserved through the centuries, more is known about the Aryan Vedic developments of the early period of India than of the non-Aryan native developments, especially those prior to the coming of the Aryans. Developments that took place after the coming of the Aryans have attained rather complete expression in Sanskrit literature. This is apparent in the Sanskrit documents, especially those composed during the period of the Upanishads (a special type of intellectual-mystical literature which attained its most brilliant expression between 1000 and 600 B.C.). Many of the ideas found there that seem to be alien or opposed to the spirit of the Vedic Hymns may be attributed at least in part to the non-Vedic and non-Aryan foundations of India.

The earliest, most direct, and clearest information on the non-Aryan elements of the early period comes, however, from the civilizations which existed in the Indus Valley between 2800 and 1700 B.C. and which were discovered in modern times by Sir John Marshall in the 1920s. Of the principal sites so far excavated, Mohenjo-Daro, Harappa, and Chanhu-Daro are especially important. In these sites were discovered engraved seals and statuettes that indicate something of the religious life of the people of those times—image worship, veneration of a deity apparently with the characteristics later attributed to Shiva, phallic worship, veneration of animals, Yogic meditation. When the information from these seals and other art products is combined with other information obtained about the aboriginal inhabitants of India at the time, as this is recorded in the early and later Sanskrit compositions, these sources are seen to have exerted a massive influence over the whole course of India's spiritual development.

It is important to recognize that the non-Aryan element was much more complex than simply the Indus Valley tradition. In other regions—in the Tamil territory of the South and in the Bengal region of the East, for instance—there were native forces at work from the beginning that survived throughout the entire course of Hindu history and profoundly modified the tradition. Thus there has been a profusion of influences rather than a single united influence with strong inner consistency. This complex of native traditions, though, was a still undefined group of traditions that gradually came to be associated with and gathered into a vast current of religious-spiritual developments that defies clear delineation and even modest comprehension.

Sometimes this entire complex of pre-Aryan and non-Aryan elements in Hinduism is referred to as "Dravidian," a term applied to the people of southern India. This use of the term supposes that the people of southern India today (properly referred to as Dravidian) are descended from the peoples of the early Indus Valley civilizations. Yet there is no satisfactory evidence that the pre-Aryan peoples of India were racially the same as the present Dravidians. They may have been pre-Dravidian or even non-Dravidian. Certainly, however, the Dravidians as they are now known have supplied a major part of this native non-Aryan influence within Hinduism.

While this discussion of the Aryan and non-Aryan elements of Hinduism has not directly revealed anything of the specific doctrinal orientation of Hinduism, it is a necessary discussion, for without it the whole tradition of Hindu teaching becomes unintelligible and inexplicable.

THE NON-ARYAN COMPONENT

Because of the profound mutual influences of the two elements in the Hindu tradition, it is not possible to list in full detail the contributions of each, as if the later developments were due exclusively to one or the other. There are, however, some instances in which strong influences from one or the other of these elements can be identified. Thus it might be well from the beginning to learn the basic concepts of Hinduism in relation to one or the other of these traditions.

World-negating attitude. There is in Hinduism a world-negating aspect that seems clearly to derive from non-Aryan Indian sources. This attitude is so opposed to the delight in life which is found in the Vedic Hymns that it would be difficult to see how this pessimistic attitude could derive from that source. There were undoubtedly historical incidents that strengthened the original native critique of life, but this is not found anywhere else in the Indo-European world. There must have been a strong determinant already present and operating independently of the Aryan Vedic tradition.

This devaluation of the world as non-being, as confinement, as meaning-less, as a source of *moha* (confusion), even as *duhkha* (suffering) may be the most significant aspect of the entire spiritual development of India. More than anything else it has determined the course of Indian spiritual traditions. Strongly felt in Hinduism, it is even more strongly felt in the Buddhist and Jain traditions, which are much closer than Hinduism to the non-Aryan elements of India. Nowhere else in the higher civilizations of the Eurasian world was the objective world experienced so consistently as unreal, as oppressive, as an alienating force in human life. This resulted from an exceptional awareness of the human condition. Man is affected not only by the afflictions of the external world but even more by the structure and inner limitations of his own being. This experience has a depth and intensity that is uniquely Indian. It separates India's spiritual experience not only from the Western experience but also from the religious experi-ence of China and Japan. Since this experience is not found in the earliest of the Vedic Hymns composed by the incoming Aryans, we may properly conclude that it arises from the non-Aryan elements of the Indian tradi-tion. This is not, however, the only evidence that this experience of sorrow comes from the non-Aryan elements of the tradition. There is also the fact that almost all the traditions that arise within India have at the basis of their life attitude an extraordinary experience of life as painful, as the result of ignorance, and finally as unreal and unacceptable. This feeling was so intense that it was soon accepted by the Aryans themselves and entered profoundly into the complex of religious thought that came to be known as Hinduism.

Extreme asceticism. One of the strongest influences that emerged from the non-Aryan backgrounds of India is the strong emphasis on asceticism. Ascetical attitudes can be found in the Vedic Hymns, but there is no great emphasis on the type of personal deprivation that characterizes much of later Hinduism. The extremes of asceticism in India can be found no-where else in the Indo-European world. The Vedic Hymns, the earliest productions of Sanskrit literature that have survived, speak of certain native, strangely clad spiritual personalities wandering about India when the Ary-ans first arrived. These wanderers were known as *Munis* (the silent ones), a type of person still found in India. From the *Munis* developed the *San-nyasis* and the entire complex of wandering mendicants, men who live the homeless life, without wife, children, or possessions of any sort except robe, staff, begging bowl, and drinking cup. These wandering saints of India are destitute, yet honored by all.

The ascetic orientation was so strong in India that it came to be integrated into the basic life pattern of Hinduism as the fourth and final stage. After the early years as a student, the Hindu, in the ideal life pattern, becomes a householder. Then after a third stage of withdrawal and meditation, before the close of life, a person should, in a fourth stage, disengage himself completely from ordinary social life and become a wandering mendicant. This final stage is clearly an ascetic extreme added to the other stages. It brings man into a final phase of spiritual disengagement from life before the physical phase of the death experience is upon him. This came to be considered the natural, the desirable fulfillment of life, even though in fact the total giving up of personal relations could seldom be carried out.

Puja: worship, especially image worship. Worship is shown to divine beings throughout the history of Hinduism, yet the special type of image worship developed in later Hinduism is not found in the Vedic period. The typical act of Vedic worship was *Yajna* (sacrifice), a ceremony carried out in the open air or in the home. There was no need of temples. Thus there is a long period in the history of Hinduism when there were neither temples nor images. In the pre-Aryan religions of the Indus Valley, however, images were already in use. This use of images remained undeveloped for almost fifteen hundred years after the arrival of the Aryans in northern India. Then at a time corresponding to the last centuries of the pre-Christian era, a significant change took place in the entire Hindu tradition, a transformation in which personal devotion to a supreme deity, veneration of images, and the building of temples became intensive preoccupations. Later, in the opening centuries of the Christian period, these were fostered by regional rulers throughout India who patronized the new theistic cults.

Yoga techniques of meditation. Among the most unique of all the contributions of primordial India to the spiritual life of Hinduism and the world was the development of the Yoga technique of meditation. This tradition was later associated with most of the native spiritual disciplines of India, although the Yoga tradition developed also with a certain independence as an integral spiritual discipline and way of salvation. Thus Yoga merits the consideration given it in Part Two of this volume.

Atheism. Surprisingly enough there is a strong current of atheism in early Hindu thought, a current that can be clearly identified with the non-Aryan elements of Hinduism. This came to expression in one of the earliest and most influential of the systems of Hindu thought, the Sankhya. It is also found in the heterodox traditions of the Jains and Buddhists. Of the high intellectual traditions of Hinduism only some of the Vedanta systems, especially those of Ramanuja (twelfth century), Madhva (fourteenth century), and Vallabha (sixteenth century), are strongly theistic.

THE ARYAN COMPONENT

Although many spiritual and cultural influences have flowed into India during the past four millennia, the most significant was the incoming of the Aryan peoples shortly after 2000 B.C. These peoples brought with them an extensive cultural development that immediately began to influence and even at times to control the spiritual development of India. The existing accounts of the incoming Aryan tribes were compiled mainly from the early Vedic literature. Although the historical details are not at all clear, it is known that they came in through the northwest passage into the upper regions of the Indus Valley and settled there where five tributary rivers that form the Indus flow southwest from the lower Himalayan regions. This was their first home in India. Later, around 1200 B.C., the Aryans moved to the central Ganges region known as *Madhyadesa* (the Middle Region), where they settled mainly between the Himalaya mountains and the Ganges River. Here the later Vedic developments took place, especially the composition of the Upanishads, which comprise the last part of the Vedic literature and which were the foundation of the later Vedanta philosophies. During the course of succeeding centuries the Aryan influence spread over the whole of India.

Sanskrit. The first contribution of the Aryans to the development of India was the gift of a sacred language, Sanskrit. This language became in time one of the most beautiful, most precise, and most expressive of all the languages of the higher civilizations of the Eurasian world. It also became the canonical language of the Hindu scriptures. Because this Indo-European language (of the same origin as the Greek, Latin, Slavic, Teutonic, and English languages) was used by the Aryans in the composition of the Hindu scriptures, the Aryan character was deeply impressed upon the entire tradition, even to the extent that Hinduism was for a long time studied as the creation solely of the Aryan peoples. As previously mentioned, however, this is not true. Yet the importance and extensive influence of the Aryan traditions should never be minimized. Even the fundamentals of the native traditions were modified considerably under Vedic influence. The two became one in the larger tradition of Hinduism.

Yajna: sacrifice. Although Puja, that is, worship of a personal deity through veneration of images, is characteristic of the non-Aryan element of the Hindu tradition, Yajna, worship through sacrifice, is characteristic of the Aryan peoples especially in their earlier period. The most common sacrifice was that of a fermented drink *(soma).* There were also other sacrifices, especially the great Horse Sacrifice, which was performed by the rulers who took upon themselves the title of World Sovereign. A most elaborate sacrifice, it took years to perform, required a large number of priests, and was carried out with astounding precision in every detail. Sacrifice became so central to the early religion of the Vedic period that the sacrifice itself was divinized and then the sacrificial formula under the designation "Brahman" was divinized. Later Brahman was used to designate the absolute reality beyond the entire phenomenal world. Although present within all particular forms, Brahman was transcendent to all. Transition from sacrificial act to ontological absolute was possible because the sacrifice was considered the dynamic whereby the entire cosmic-human order was sustained in existence.

Theological thought. The Aryans were responsible for much of the higher theological thought of India during the earlier period. This can be seen in the development of the Vedic Hymns, which began as simple nature poems addressed to the deities as these were perceived through natural phenomena. Even before the identification of the sacrifice as the supreme reality there was a growing perception of some one reality behind the entire range of phenomena. This awareness of an abiding support behind phenomena and present in phenomena developed into awareness of an ontological absolute whence all things attained their existence and inner dynamism. This was expressed first in terms of the Maker of All Things *(Visvakarman)* or as the Lord of Creatures *(Prajapati).* Then came the amazing insight of the 129th hymn in the tenth book of the *Rig-Veda* in which there is mention of That One *(Tad Ekam),* a designation that remained in constant point of reference in the later intellectual life of India. From all of this it is clear that, from the Hymns on, the speculative intellect of the Aryan people was busily at work inquiring into the existence, distinctive characteristics, and creative power of the final reality upon which all things depend.

Atman-Brahman: inner self of all things, Supreme Reality. Both Atman and Brahman designate the final reality, the inner support of beings, the One behind all multiplicity. Each has its origin, however, in a different aspect of man's experience of reality. Atman indicates the absolute support of being, experienced subjectively as the support of a person's own existence. Brahman came to designate the absolute reality as this is experienced objectively as the support of the visible world. It was a great moment in the history of Hindu thought when the identity of these two was perceived: "Thou art that," meaning that the deepest subjective reality is identical with the absolute manifested objectively in the world without.

THE UNION OF TRADITIONS

Even though the dominant contributions of each of the two principal components of Hinduism have been indicated, it must be remembered that these aspects of Hinduism developed together over a long period of time with intimate and extensive mutual influences. The Hindu people in later times found little difficulty in accepting all these beliefs, attitudes, institutions, ways of thinking, and patterns of salvation as the multiple aspects of a single tradition. Everything fitted within the one tradition. Of course, there occurred historical moments which placed greater emphasis on one aspect or another, but the entire complex remained a functioning whole. Each of the spiritual teachings mentioned were developed in terms of the total complex. After the very early period there was no independent development of any single aspect of the tradition. The fascinating extremes within Hinduism originated principally from the meeting of these two very different traditions. The oppositions were not destructive but creative tensions. They mutually affirmed each other and evoked the creative activity of each other. Out of the meeting of these traditions the following principal doctrines emerged.

Maya: the world of change. When the supreme wisdom came to be the recognition of Brahman as the supreme reality and indeed as the only true reality, then the phenomenal world became extremely thin, so thin that it began to lose its opaque quality. It was seen as a veil hiding the true reality from the eyes of those who saw only the surface of things. Then, this phenomenal world came to be spoken of as unreal, as the realm of death and of nothingness. Thus the term "Maya," which originally referred to the creative power of Brahman, came to mean the insubstantial nature of the visible world. At different times this word has meant different things, but generally it must be reallized that Maya means simply the realm of change as distinct from the realm of the absolute. If it is designated as illusory, insubstantial, and unreal, this is only in relation to that which is supremely and absolutely real. Maya is one of the most difficult words in all of Hinduism to understand correctly. It has a threefold reference: to the phenomenal world itself, to the "mysterious power" of Brahman in producing the world, and to the human mind which attributes more reality to the phenomenal world than it possesses.

Samsara: the world conceived as constant, endless, cyclic process of change, of birth and death and rebirth. This concept of Hinduism was powerfully influenced by the early pre-Aryan traditions of India, yet it could not fully develop until the later period when the concept of an absolute reality had more fully evolved. Thus in the end it is the result of the meeting of both traditions. Its repercussions on Indian thought were all-pervading. *Samsara* (change) affected not only the surface of things in the visible world, but also the natural and the human worlds to their very depths. From earliest times India has felt trapped in this cycle of painful, unending change. Death itself brings no relief. At the time of death, one form gives way to another form according to a process designated as reincarnation. Another body of the human, subhuman, or suprahuman succeeds the dissolution of the body. It, too, enters on a path of decline and death shortly after it appears. This constitutes the salvation problem of Hinduism. How does man escape this unending cycle, this constant agony, of birth-death-rebirth?

Karma: the law of moral causality. Every deed, good or evil, has an inevitable consequence leading either toward final release from the birth-death cycle, or toward further immersion in the painful cycle of unending change. The law of Karma is sometimes known as the law of sowing and reaping. Whatever a person sows, that he will reap. So with the deeds of men, whatever a person does, for good or for evil, has consequences in the very nature of things that are absolutely inevitable. This provides an explanation for the present condition in which each person finds himself. The entire order of things becomes eminently reasonable. If a person is suffering from some evil, he must deserve this in virtue of some deed performed either in this life or in a former life. A certain fatalism is involved. In another sense, however, this is the opposite of fatalism since according to the doctrine of Karma a person is always free to perform deeds that will lead to salvation or at least to an improved state of existence. The law of Karma enabled the people of India morally and psychologically to accept the human condition in which they found themselves individually. Any affliction was bearable under the conviction that it was merited and that faithful acceptance of the life situation resulting from one's own deeds would assist toward final salvation. Not to accept one's earthly condition would be to worsen the condition, to lengthen the time prior to salvation. In all this, as in Indian life disciplines generally, there is a severe spiritual individualism.

While it cannot be said that the law of Karma in its developed form was singularly derived from the non-Aryan element of the Indian tradition, it can be said that the doctrine has no evident foundations in the earlier Vedic writings. On the other hand it does seem quite consonant with the general life orientation of the non-Aryan traditions. It became one of the all-pervading elements in Indian spiritual life, occurring in heterodox traditions, such as Buddhism and Jainism, as well as in orthodox Hinduism in its every division.

Moksha: salvation by union with Brahman. Salvation is thought of in India as a liberation from the limiting, confining world of time and an emergence into the more expansive world of the eternal and infinite. It is the extinction of phenomenal existence and absorption into Brahman. Clearly a later conception in Hinduism, it supposed a powerful attraction toward the absolute world and a feeling of discontent with the world of change. Attraction toward the absolute came with the Vedic development of the abiding reality beyond the phenomenal; discontent with the world of time came mainly from the non-Vedic and non-Aryan feeling of oppression with the visible and changing world of matter and time. Here the two traditions could meet and complement each other in a powerful fashion and seal the unity of the two traditions.

Bhakti: intimate devotion to a personal deity. In the centuries just prior to the Christian era Hinduism developed an amazing awareness that the supreme way of salvation was that founded in the love of God. This devotional attitude was known as Bhakti. The first extensive presentation of this doctrine is found in the *Bhagavad-Gita*, the supreme religious work of the entire Hindu tradition. This devotion to a personal god came to exercise an extraordinary influence during the early centuries of the Christian era. Found in the North and South, it produced a long succession of saints who spent their lives proclaiming the graciousness of the Lord and the mystical devotion they experienced toward him. Similar expressions of devotion to God are found in other traditions—the mystical traditions of Christianity, the Sufi traditions of Islam, the Amidist tradition of Buddhism—but it would be difficult to find anywhere more intense expressions of divine love than those found in the ecstatic songs and sermons of the medieval saints of the Hindu tradition.

The Bhakti tradition of Hinduism derives from both the Aryan and the non-Aryan elements, but it is difficult to identify the aspects of the devotional tradition which come from each of these sources. In the Vedic Hymns a most intimate relationship is established between the heavenly deities and earthly humans. This is expressed mainly through the concept of loving faith (*shraddha*). This sense of intimate devotion is also found in the later writings, the Upanishads. There is, however, a new intensity in the devotional life of Hinduism that emerges at the beginning of the Christian period when the larger tradition of the Vedic period is joined with the local cults of the primordial traditions of India. Since this new intensity found its first full expression in southern India and in the parts of the country least influenced by the Sanskrit Vedic tradition, it is clear that there was a major contribution to the devotional tradition of Hinduism from its non-Aryan elements.

THE LITERATURE

After indicating that Hinduism must be studied as a developmental process, and after identifying the two basic components that entered into the historical process of Hinduism, the next concern will be with the stages through which Hinduism passed from its origins up to the present time. This must be studied through Hindu literature. In quality, in quantity, in significance for man's intellectual, cultural, and spiritual life, this literature in its totality is unsurpassed among all other literary traditions of the world. It belongs with the literary traditions of the classical Mediterranean world, of China, of Islam, of Buddhism, of Western civilization itself. In the strictly spiritual-religious order it is among the great literary traditions of mankind.

This survey of the great volume of Hindu literature cannot be complete, yet it can suggest the vast range of spiritual experience that took place within the Hindu tradition. From the different periods certain types of literature are selected to present the stages through which Hinduism has passed in the thirty-five centuries of its development. The earliest compositions that still exist probably go back as far as 1500 B.C. This literature, the oldest extant literature composed in the Indo-European languages, provides a vivid account of the religious life, the ritual, thought, and spirituality that existed during this early period. It is important to note that information received from these earliest compositions of Hinduism must, in studying the historical reality of the tradition, be supplemented by information from archaeological, historical, sociological, and artistic sources which help to verify, to complement, and often to modify the information obtained from the literature. Yet the greatest single source of information on Hinduism must be the literary records of this tradition. A list of the religious literature of Hinduism would include the following:

Vedic Hymns, Brahmanas, Aranyakas, Upanishads
Codes of conduct: Laws of Manu, Dharma Sutras, Grihya Sutras
Epics: *Mahabharata, Ramayana*
Bhagavad-Gita
Philosophical Sutras: Sankhya, Yoga, Vaishesika, Nyaya, Mimamsa, Ve-
    danta
Puranas, Agamas, Tantras
Writings of Vedanta theologians
Hymns and writings of the saints
Modern spiritual and theological writings

The main division in this literature has been made between the *Sruti* and the *Smriti* (what is heard and what is remembered). The *Sruti* (what is heard) includes the Vedas, the *Brahmanas* (Ritual Books), the *Aranyakas* (Forest Meditations), and the Upanishads, the highest form of intuitive vision in the Hindu tradition. The *Smriti* (what is remembered) includes the codes of conduct: Laws of Manu, Dharma Sutras, and Grihya Sutras; the Epics: *Mahabharata* and *Ramayana*; the *Bhagavad-Gita*; the Puranas, and the Sutra collections. The division between the Sruti and the Smriti is most important, for it separates the canonical literature from the traditional literature. The Sruti includes what amounts to the infallible revelation itself, received by the saintly seers *(Rishis)* of the early period. All theological discussion within orthodox Hinduism must be settled directly or indirectly from the Sruti, the highest communication made to man from the realm of Absolute Truth. The Sruti literature is the infallible source of the wisdom that leads to salvation. Later ages, especially the Vedanta theologians, based their reasoning directly on the revealed teaching of the Sruti, especially on those Upanishads which are also called the *Vedanta* (the end of the Veda). So basic is this Sruti literature that future writers explained their thought mainly in the form of commentaries on these sacred scriptures and on the Sutra collections.

Another significant division in Hindu religious literature has been made between the literature prior to the Puranic period (the fourth to the tenth century A.D.) and that after this period. The Epics, especially the *Mahabharata*, can be considered the connecting link between these two periods. With the Puranas a new devotional, theistic religious development took place that henceforth dominated the religious-spiritual life of the people. The two most prominent deities in the Puranas are Vishnu and Shiva. From the fourth century on, the main body of worshippers in traditional Hinduism has been divided into two sects:—one devoted to Vishnu, and the other to Shiva. Numerically and in terms of total influence the Vaishnava tradition is probably the greater.

Selected for special consideration are several phases of Hinduism as expressed in this literature, arranged roughly in chronological order. The works considered in detail from the earlier literature (prior to the Puranas) are the *Rig-Veda*, the Upanishads, and the *Bhagavad-Gita*; and from the later literature, the Puranas, the writings associated with the devotional cults and individual theologians, and modern writings.

Chapter Two

Early Development

THE VEDIC HYMNS

The Vedic Hymns contain some of the most ancient compositions of the entire body of Indo-European literature, as well as the earliest known speculative efforts of the human mind in the Indo-European tradition. These hymns tell how men in this period experienced divine reality and how they responded to this experience with exuberant joy, with confidence, and with a feeling of intimacy with gods who had brought into existence and who controlled the lower order of the natural and human worlds. No one knows just when these hymns were composed, although at the latest they should be dated between 1200 and 900 B.C. Possibly the earliest hymns go back as far as 1500 B.C. This hymnal literature is not "primitive." It is highly developed in its literary form, in its intellectual insight, and in its questioning attitude. The glory of this literature, however, is its imaginative and emotional qualities. There is a deeply religious mood in the longer hymns to

Varuna, an awareness of divine might in the hymns to Indra, a special radiance and loveliness in the hymns to Usas.

Of the four collections of these hymns—the *Rig-Veda, Sama-Veda, Yajur-Veda,* and *Atharva-Veda*—the most important are the *Rig-Veda* and the *Atharva-Veda.* The *Sama-Veda* is a collection of verses from the basic hymns recited at the sacrifices by a special group of priests, especially at the Soma Sacrifice. Almost all the verses of the *Sama-Veda* are contained in the *Rig-Veda.* The *Yajur-Veda* is also an important ritual book containing a collection of verses to be recited at various sacrifices. It contains much that is found in the *Rig-Veda,* although a decided development had taken place by the time of its composition. Next to the *Rig-Veda* the *Atharva-Veda* is most important because it carries the rich popular tradition of the period, both Aryan and non-Aryan. Although it was composed later than the other collections and was added to these as the fourth, it contains much that is very early in the religious life of India. It is less concerned with the public and solemn sacrifices than with the home rituals, popular prayer, and spells to ward off evil and obtain blessings. Nor should it be thought that this collection in the *Atharva-Veda* is lacking in intellectual content; it expresses some of the most profound thought of this early period.

Yet the core collection of Vedic Hymns is that found in the *Rig-Veda.* This is especially significant because it carries the basic mythology that dominated Hindu tradition from its earlier formative period down to the present, although much has been added to this mythology in succeeding centuries. Hindu mythology was always developing, always drawing more of the local traditions of the people into association with the larger tradition. This mutual influence was quite strong in the Puranic period (the fourth to the tenth century A.D.), when many additions were made to the mythology of Hinduism. Yet the mythology of the Vedic Hymns remained for the more literate and intellectual traditions of Hinduism the basic background of Hindu development.

According to Vedic mythology there are some thirty-three gods. This is not meant to be a precise figure, but it came to be the standard number used in referring to the Vedic deities. Traditionally these deities are divided into the heavenly, the atmospheric, and the earthly. Indra, the most powerful atmospheric deity, also a warrior figure, is the most prominent of the Vedic deities in terms of the number of hymns devoted to him in the *Rig-Veda.* Of the more than one thousand hymns in the collection, some two hundred and fifty are addressed to Indra. Two hundred more are addressed to Agni, the god of priests and priest of the gods. Agni is the mediator between man and the other deities. He is frequently invoked and prayers to him generally enter into all sacrifices. There are over a hundred hymns to Soma, the fermented drink offered in sacrifice. But while these numbers give some idea of the significance of these particular deities in the *Rig-Veda*, the importance of the various deities in the entire Hindu tradition at this time cannot be judged by these numbers, for the *Rig-Veda* was a collection especially related to the Soma Sacrifice. Other great and important deities, such as Varuna, had only a few hymns devoted to them in this collection, but they are in the whole tradition much more important than this would indicate.

Indra. Both a warrior deity and a storm deity, Indra is the master of lightning and thunder. He is moved by passions similar to man. The most clearly delineated personality of the Vedic deities, he often appears as a powerful hero of the human order rather than a sublime deity of the divine order. His ways are rough. Sometimes he is depicted as being drunk with the fermented drink offered to him in sacrifice. His primary attribute is power; he is able to shake the world to its foundations. He is frequently considered the creator of things, although this attribute of creator is assigned to all the major Vedic deities. Indra can be compared with Zeus of the Greeks or with Jupiter of the Romans as a storm deity, also possibly with Thor of the Teutonic world. Above all he is the conqueror of Vitra, the personification of evil. The slaying of Vitra is related to the slaying of some primordial monster found in many traditions. Thus the salvation motif is introduced, in that a principle of evil is destroyed by a beneficent deity or heroic figure. In the figure of Indra these elements exist together.

> I will set forth the mighty deeds of Indra, deeds performed by him who hurls the thunderbolt; he shattered the dragons, revealed the waters, cut pathways for the streams in their course.
> He slew the dragon there atop the mountains; Tvashtar forged his celestial thunderbolt. The streams, as lowing cows returning, move downward to the sea.
> Unrestrained as a bull, he took the soma, drank the threefold offering. Maghavan seized his weapon, the thundershaft, and struck the firstborn of the dragons with a fatal blow.
> After this mortal stroke, Indra, you destroyed the deceiving forces. Then bringing forth the sun, the dawn, the heavenly vault, you had no longer anyone opposed.
> Indra with the fatal might of his thunderbolt struck the dark one, Vitra.

As a tree trunk cut down with an ax lies abandoned on the ground, so Vitra lies upon the earth.
Defiant Vitra, as though unequalled, challenged Indra, mighty hero, destroyer of the wicked; Vitra then, himself falling, overwhelmed the rivers.
Indra, the Thundergod, is king of whatever moves or does not move, of beings with or without horns. Monarch of men, he contains within him all things, as the rim contains the spokes of a wheel.

—Rig-Veda, I, 32

Varuna. While Indra had a large place in the Hinduism of this period, Varuna is without question the highest conception of deity at this time. The guide and support of all beings, the upholder of order, Varuna is the one from whom forgiveness is obtained after breaking the established norms of conduct. As creator, custodian, and restorer of order both in the cosmological and human spheres, he is guardian of *rita* (the sacred order of the universe).

As men everywhere, O divine Varuna, we daily offend you by our faults.
Yet give us not over to death through thy wrath when so provoked.
With our praises, O Varuna, we seek to obtain thy favor, to bind your heart as a driver binds his horse.
He knows the pathway of the birds soaring through the sky; he knows the ships that sail across the sea.
He knows the pathway of the lofty, swift, powerful wind, and the deities there above.
Listen, O Varuna, to this prayer of mine. Grant us joy.
To thee I cry out for thy protection.
Set us free from the upper bond, undo the bond between and that below, that we may live.

Rig-Veda, I, 25

Rudra. Although now a deity of outstanding importance in the hymnal literature, Rudra is significant as the Vedic prototype of the deity who later appeared as Shiva. He is also the wielder of lightning and the thunderbolt, as is Indra. Rudra, however, is more fierce and destructive. In this he differs from Indra, who has a massive strength but whose total conduct is more protective toward men. Indra's force is used in beneficent fashion. In Rudra there is a primitive wildness that is carried over to the later period. Rudra becomes especially important in the period after the Hymns were written, in the period of the Brahmanical rituals. From that time on he seems to enter into alliance and assimilation with a pre-Aryan deity. Then, later, when sectarian Hinduism arose in the beginning of the Christian period, this figure as Shiva became one of the two major deities that have dominated Hinduism from that time until the present.

Vishnu. Although of little significance in the Vedic Hymns, Vishnu must be given serious attention because he later became the supreme deity of Hinduism in the sectarian tradition known as Vaishnavism, the largest of the sectarian traditions. In the Hymns the most distinctive element of his mythology is the taking of three steps whereby he attains control over the entire universe. Later Vishnu appears on earth in various forms, known as Avatars. The most important of these are Vishnu's manifestations as Rama and as Krishna. The divine communication to man takes place largely through Krishna. The legends concerning Krishna are an expression of the mystical love relationship between God and man.

Surya, Savitri, Usas. Other attractive and significant deities are Surya, the Sun, and Savitri, a solar deity to whom the beautiful morning prayer of the Hindu people has been offered through the centuries and is still offered at this time. "Let us think upon the god Savitri, that he may inspire our thoughts" (*Rig-Veda*, III, 62/10). This is the most famous single verse in the entire collection and the one most recited. Of the hymns to the minor deities, those to Usas, the Dawn, are especially beautiful. Some of the loveliest nature poetry of this period is dedicated to her, depicted as a young maiden who comes to mankind in the special characteristics of the dawn. Dawn brings a feeling of hope and refreshment, of entering into the activity of the universe. These hymns to dawn should be appreciated just as they stand without symbolic or mystical interpretation. Usas equates with Aurora in the Roman world.

> *This light, most radiant of lights, has come; this gracious one who illumines all things, is born. As night is removed by the rising sun, so is this the birthplace of the dawn.*
> *The fair-shining dawn has come, bringing forth the sun. The darkness of night has given up her domain. Related to each other, immortal, succeeding one another, mutually exchanging appearances, they move across the heavens.*
> *Munificent dawn awakens men curled up asleep; one of enjoyment, another for devotion, another to seek for wealth; they who could scarcely see, now see clearly. All living beings are now awakened.*
> *We behold her, daughter of the sky, youthful, robed in white, driving forth the darkness. Princess of limitless treasure, shine down upon us throughout this day.*
> —*Rig-Veda*, I, 113

In addition to these deities associated with natural phenomena there are the deities formed from more abstract notions. Faith personified is addressed as a deity. Also there are such conceptions as the Lord of Creatures (*Prajapati*) and *Visvakarman* (Maker of All Things). These represent a tendency toward the higher intellectual conceptions of deity. Finally there is one hymn, unique in depth and in significance, that deserves special attention:—the famous "Creation Hymn" of the tenth book of the *Rig-Veda*.

At that time there was neither the non-existent nor the existent,
Neither the air nor the sky beyond,
What did it inclose? Where? Protected by whom?
Was water there of unmeasured depth?
At that time there was neither death nor immortality
No indication of day or of night.
That One without wind breathed by its own resources.
Other than that One was nothing at all.
Darkness infolded in darkness, such the beginning.
In a state beyond comprehension as primal waters.
Out of that status, emerging into being, inclosed in emptiness
That One came forth through the power of heat.
In that moment of beginning desire arose,
The earliest impulse of mind
Seers with wise seeking in their own thoughts
Discovered the bond of the existent within the non-existent.
Their cord stretched across
Was there a beneath, an above
There were begetters, powers,
Below energy; above, impulse.
Who really knows? Who can say?
Whence it emerges, whence comes this creation?
Only after this creation do the gods appear.
Who then understands its origin?
Whence comes this creation?
Whether he brought it forth or not
He who beholds it from the highest point of heaven,
Only he knows, or perhaps even he does not know.
                                                    —*Rig-Veda*, X, 129

THE UPANISHADS

The Upanishads are a group of mystical-intuitional writings that were inspired by an amazing intellectual experience of the absolute reality beyond the phenomenal world. Although there are devotional expressions in the

Upanishads, these works are for the most part highly intellectual and intuitional in character. They seek liberation from the human condition through a saving vision. This enables man to realize his identity with Brahman, the Absolute Reality, Supreme Truth, Complete Bliss. Thenceforth man has no isolated existence of his own; his true life is lived in this higher order. The Hymns provide the imaginative insight, the Brahmanas provide the ritual experience, the Upanishads provide the intellectual intuitions. The poetic experience, the sacrificial experience, and the intellectual experience are equally exalted, each in its own way. In the present aritualistic age one could scarcely enter into the same experience of sacrifice which is the central activity of this entire period. The Hymns provide the language of the sacrifice; the Brahmanas, the ritual form; the Upanishads, the spiritual interpretation. It is difficult for modern men to appreciate just how central the sacrificial, ritualistic experience of the Hindu tradition was at this period; even the concept of Absolute Reality arose from the search into the meaning of the sacrifice. This is found especially in the earlier Upanishads, the *Brihadaranyaka* and the *Chandogya*. In a later period the Upanishads were disengaged from immediate concern for sacrifice, and it is then that we can appreciate in a more direct manner the insights that they offer.

There are fourteen Upanishads that might be called the principal Upanishads. They have been selected for their special significance from more than one hundred works written in this form. The selection was made principally by Shankara in the eighth century. The central figure in the post-Vedic period, Shankara, brought the entire Hindu tradition to integral expression in an orderly manner for the first time. He also gave to the tradition its first thorough metaphysical exposition. The Upanishads that Shankara chose as the foundation references of his own thought have, ever since that time, been considered the basic source of higher speculative thought in the dominant Vedanta tradition within Hinduism.

The early Upanishads, composed between 800 and 500 B.C., contain all the more important Upanishadic teaching. The later Upanishads, containing specific answers to problems that arose later, were written for some particular school or tradition in order to defend or explain certain sectarian teachings. Within the Upanishads there is a wide differentiation in style, content, terminology, and processes of reasoning. Among the earliest of the Upanishads are the *Brihadaranyaka* and the *Chandogya*. These provide the first sublime insights of the intuitional powers of India. Known as the

Great Upanishads, they are both quite long. Others are very short: *Mandukya* has only twelve verses; *Isa*, only eighteen; *Kena*, only thirty-four. *Svetasvatara*, one of the more significant because of its new presentation of a theistic approach to reality, is of substantial length, having some one hundred thirteen verses in six chapters.

The phrase whose resonance is felt throughout all Upanishadic literature is *Tat tvam asi* ("Thou art that"). The deepest subjective reality of man is identical with the final objective reality. This is the unity of the Upanishads, the unity of a quest for this final identification experienced either subjectively as Atman, the true Self, or objectively as Brahman, the absolute support of all phenomenal reality, indeed the only true reality behind the world of appearances. This awareness of Brahman is found in all the Upanishads, although nowhere is there any effort in these works to form an integral synthesis concerned with the nature, attributes, and functioning of this Absolute Reality. The experience was too vast, too highly differentiated, too vital. As a live, developing, enduring thought experience it was not to be confined within the set expression. Yet all the Upanishads agree in their quest for understanding the nature of Brahman, his transcendence and his immanence, the identity of Brahman with Atman, the fragile, even illusory quality of the phenomenal world, the difficulty of understanding, the impossibility of expressing the inner nature of the supreme reality, the final mystery of things.

As Brahman came to be identified as the only true, the only absolute reality, there was an increasing desire within Hinduism for liberation from the lower forms of existence to attain this supreme transforming experience that would bring about absorption into Brahman. Thus the prayer of the Upanishads: "Cause me to pass from the unreal to the real, from darkness to light, from death to immortality" (*Brihadaranyaka*, I, 3/28).

Brahman occupies the central place in Hindu thought, as Being is central to Greek thought, as Tao is central to Chinese thought, as God is central to Western thought. It is the supreme reality on which all else depends. It should be of value, then, to examine here the Upanishadic statements concerning the existence and nature along with the entitative and operative attributes of this Atman-Brahman reality, remembering that these two represent the same supreme being experienced subjectively and objectively.

Existence. The existence of Brahman is manifest in everything that exists. The existence of Brahman is known in the very act of consciousness, whereby a person recognizes his own existence. To deny Brahman is to deny a person's own being. Later Shankara said: "The existence of Brahman is known from the fact that it is the Self of everyone. Everyone is aware of the existence of his own Self. No one thinks, 'I am not.' If the existence of the Self were not known everyone would think 'I am not' " (*Commentary on the Vedanta Sutras*, I, 1/1). This is derived from the Upanishadic texts which clearly affirm: "Neither by speech nor by mind, nor even by sight can he be grasped, nor in any way other than by the statement saying, 'He is.' When so apprehended by the thought 'He is' then his true nature manifests itself" (*Katha*, VI, 12–13). So important is this affirmation of Brahman that "Anyone who considers Brahman as non-existent himself becomes non-existent. A person who recognizes that Brahman exists, is himself known as existent" (*Taittiriya*, II, 6/1).

Ineffability. Hindu thinkers, conscious of the sublime character of Brahman, knew that this ultimate truth could not be understood in any adequate manner by human intelligence: "There the eye cannot go, nor speech, nor the mind. We neither know nor can we understand how anyone can attain it. It is other than what is known and beyond the unknown" (*Kena*, I, 3). In another passage it is stated that the divine is of "unthinkable form" (*Mundaka*, III, 7); and furthermore: "It is known by him who knows it not. He by whom it is known knows it not. Not understood by those who understand it, it is understood by those who do not understand it" (*Kena*, II, 3).

Self-existence. While other beings depend upon Brahman for existence this supreme reality is his own existence. This is expressed in the *Isa Upanishad* where many of the basic qualities of the Atman are identified. His presence is everywhere. He is "bright, incorporeal, intangible, without sinews, pure, wise, intelligent, all-pervading, and self-existent" (*Isa*, 8). The entire list of distinguishing qualities of this supreme reality culminates in the attribute of *svayambhu* (self-existence), an expression similar to that of medieval Western theologians who identify absolute being as *esse sui ipsius*, or as *esse subsistens*, subsistent being. He is his own being, a pure flame of life totally fulfilled in itself. He is also depicted as shining by his own light. "There the sun shines not, nor moon, nor stars. From his radiance everything shines. This whole world is ablaze with his light" (*Katha*, V, 15). The Upanishads delight in multiplying the qualities of earthly things that cannot be predicated of Brahman or Atman: "That which cannot be seen or grasped, which is without family and caste, without eyes or ears, hands or feet, the eternal, all-pervading, infinitely subtle, that which is imperishable, this the wise consider to be the source of all beings" (*Mundaka*, I, 1/6). This is indeed the formless source of all forms (*Katha*, III, 15). "Beyond all this is that which is without form, also without sorrow" (*Svetasvatara*, III, 10). This indicates that the absolute reality is beyond limitation and without distortion. It is a fullness uncontained, a radiance undimmed, a purity unsullied.

Divine personality. One of the difficulties with Hindu thought of the Upanishads is its constant emphasis on Brahman simply as the absolute reality without any reference to personality. The words "Brahman" and "Atman" are both of neuter gender. The human experience of the divine at this moment was so overwhelming that attribution of personality seemed to be imposition of some limit or imperfection on this highest reality. There is no explicit or direct denial of personality, but it is not discussed in the terms in which it is discussed outside its own tradition. There is at this time rather little of the "I-Thou" relation that is so important in divine-human relations in Western tradition. Yet if personality receives little recognition in the Upanishads generally, there are two Upanishads in which awareness of personality as the highest and primary category of the divine is realized: the *Isa* and *Svetasvatara Upanishads*. In the *Isa Upanishad* this is clear from the use of the word *Isa* (Lord), a word designating the divine reality as person. The *Svetasvatara Upanishad* speaks of Shiva as "Creator both of existence and non-existence" (*Svetasvatara*, V, 14). "Of lords the supreme great lord, of gods the highest god, of rulers the highest ruler. Thus we know him as god, adorable lord of the universe. There is nothing he needs to do, nor any instrument of his work. There is no one like him, no one greater. . . . No one anywhere is his master, none his ruler; there is no way of designating him. . . . No one brought him forth, no one is his lord" (*Svetasvatara*, VI, 7-9).

Creation. This supreme being, Brahman, is the origin of all things: "Forth from him, all the seas and mountains, forth from him flow all the various rivers, from him come all plants, the very essences of things. Thereby the interior Self dwells in things" (*Mundaka*, II, 1/9). This creation process is most frequently described according to similies or metaphors that indicate a kind of emanationist theory of creation: "As a spider comes forth by means of its thread, as small sparks shower forth from fire, even so from this Atman come forth all life energies, all worlds, all deities, all beings. The inner meaning of this is 'the real of the real.' The life breaths are the real. He is their reality" (Brihadaranyaka, II 1/20).

Yet there are brilliant passages in which creation is described as response to the divine word. "At the word of the imperishable the sun and the moon stand forth, Truly, O Gargi, at the word of the imperishable the earth and sky appear in their distinct form. At the word of that imperishable the minutes, the hours, the days, nights, fortnights, months, seasons, and years stand forth. At the word of that eternal one some rivers flow eastward from the snowy heights, others westward, in whatever direction each flows. At the word of that imperishable men praise those who give, the gods desire a sacrificer, and the fathers desire the sacrifice to the departed" (Brihadaranyaka, III, 8/9).

Supreme ruler of the universe. Associated with the creative power of the supreme being is the sustaining and directing power of the universe. "He who is the supreme lord of lords, the supreme god of gods, the supreme king of kings, above all, him we know as the god to be adored, the Lord of the universe" (Svetasvatara, VI, 7). "He is the guardian of the world in time; supreme lord of all, he is hidden in all being" (Svetasvatara, IV, 15). As the sustaining power in things: "Verily this Atman is the ruling lord of everything, the king of all. As the spokes of a wheel are held together in the hub of a wheel, just so in this Atman all beings, all deities, all worlds, all living things, all these selves are held together" (Brihadaranyaka, II, 5/15).

Transcendence. One of the most famous phrases in Hindu thought is *Neti, neti.* "It is not this, it is not that; unseizable, it cannot be grasped; indestructible, it cannot be shattered; unattached, it does not bind itself; it is unbound; it does not quiver; it is not harmed" (Brihadaranyaka, IV, 2/4). Earlier in this same Upanishad a list of thirty-one negations denies of Brahman any of the qualities or activities that characterize the things of earth. This ends with the significant phrase, "without inside and without outside" (Brihadaranyaka, III, 8/8). This is one of the most direct ways of asserting an absolute simplicity in the divine, the first of the divine attributes, the attribute which belongs only to divine reality, for it alone is a not-put-together reality. This being without inside or outside enables it to be inside and outside all things.

Immanence. Awareness of divine immanence is even more evident in the Upanishads than awareness of transcendence. "This very breathing spirit, the supreme conscious self, has entered this bodily self up to the hair and fingernails. As a razor is contained in a razor-case, or fire in its container, so this supremely conscious self has entered this bodily self up to the hair and the fingernails" (*Kaushitaki,* IV, 20). "The god in fire, in water, the god who has entered into all this universe, the god in plants, in trees, to that god, praise and adoration" (*Svetasvatara,* II, 17). Even more impressive is the passage that occurs in the *Atharva-Veda* and in the *Svetasvatara Upanishad:* "You are man, you are woman; you are boy, you are girl; you are the aged man that totters along on his staff; from birth your face is turned in every direction. You are the dark-blue bee, the green parrot with red eyes; you are the storm-cloud above, the seasons and the seas. Without beginning or end, from you come forth all worlds" (*Svetasvatara,* IV, 3–4).

Immanence and transcendence. Hindu thinkers from the ninth to the sixth century B.C. sought with untiring effort to state correctly the correlative doctrines of immanence and transcendence. This can be seen in the number of passages in which both these attributes of the divine in relation to the created world are stated together. The *Brihadaranyaka Upanishad* is particularly clear on this point: "He who dwells in the earth, yet is other than the earth, whom the earth does not know, of whom the earth is the body; He who rules the earth from within, He is your very Self, the ruler within, the immortal one" (*Brihadaranyaka,* III, 7/3). Then after repeating this same proposition in relation to water, fire, air, wind, sky, sun, heaven, moon and stars, space, darkness, light, all things, breath, speech, eye, ear, mind, skin, the author comes to the inner spiritual aspect of man, the power of understanding: "He, who, present in the understanding is other than the understanding, whom the understanding does not know, whose body the understanding is, who inwardly determines the understanding, He is your absolute Self, the interior ruler, the Immortal" (*Brihadaranyaka,* III, 7/22).

One of the most precise statements of immanence and transcendence together is found in the *Isa Upanishad:* "It moves, it does not move. It is far away, it is nearby. It is within everything, it is outside everything" (*Isa,* 4). The *Katha* says: "He who is bodiless among bodies, steady among the unsteady, the great, all-pervading, aware of him, the wise man grieves not" (*Katha,* II, 22). Even more impressive are these verses: "The one air on entering this world becomes diversified in form according to the variety of things, just so the one Atman within everything becomes varied according to the form of each thing, and yet is outside. As the sun, the eye of the universe, is not affected by the external flaws seen by the eye, even so, the one within all beings is not affected by the sorrow of the world, for he is outside it. . . . That one who is eternal in the transient, conscious among the conscious, the one in the many, who grants their desires, to those who are wise, those who recognize him present in the Self, to them is eternal peace and to no one else" (*Katha*, V, 10–11, 13).

Salvation. Liberation from the sorrows of the human condition is consequent on a saving wisdom by which one knows Brahman; or, as in the *Svetasvatara Upanishad*, it is the result of the wisdom by which one knows God. These may be taken as two aspects of the same reality, the one more impersonal, the other more personal. "By knowing God man is freed from all bonds" (*Svetasvatara*, IV, 16). "His form cannot be seen, no one beholds him with the eye. He is attained by the heart, by thought, by the mind. Those who know this become immortal" (*Katha*, VI, 9). "The inner self of all beings, the one lord, who manifests his unique form in a variety of ways, the wise who are aware of him present within, they alone have everlasting bliss" (*Katha*, V, 12). The bliss of union with Atman is described: "As a man intimately embraced by his devoted wife, is aware of nothing without or within, so is a person intimately embraced by the Self made up of wisdom, aware of nothing without, nothing within. That is his very form in which his desires are satisfied, in which Atman is his desire. There he has neither longing nor sorrow. There a father ceases to be a father, a mother is not a mother any more, conditioned beings are no longer such, deities are not deities, the Vedas are not Vedas. There a robber is not a robber, a slayer is not a slayer, an outcaste not an outcaste, a wandering mendicant no longer a wandering mendicant, an ascetic not an ascetic. He is not followed by good nor by evil, for then he has gone beyond all affliction of heart" (*Brihadaranyaka*, IV, 3/21–22).

Grace. The Upanishads take for granted that man is a sharer in the divine nature even though there is never any clear perception of the manner in which human nature shared in this higher nature without losing the conscious experience of its lower nature. The Upanishads contain no real doctrine of the created world and its limitations. They do not clearly distinguish between the natural and supernatural orders. All things are in a sense caught up in the supernatural. This powerful sense of immanence tends to diminish the need for a doctrine of "sanctifying grace," which is described in Western theology as a formal participation in divine life, a type of deiform brought about within the human person. Already in Hinduism this deiform is there in such a profound way that it is as though a doctrine analogous to that of sanctifying grace were the very substance of the Hindu approach to man. The entire effort of Hindu thought is to evoke in man an awareness of this reality which is closer to man than he is to himself. Indeed it is the true Self of man. In studying this mysterious divine presence and transformation of human nature everything said seems too much or too little. What can be said is that the Hindu scriptural writings taken as a whole defend both immanence and transcendence in such a way that a basis exists in these writings to interpret them in a satisfactory manner on this point. Indeed Hindu thinkers and Christian thinkers may offer much to each other to clarify the thought of both traditions on this subject.

When there is mention of grace in Hinduism it is clearly in the category of what Scholastic theologians would designate as actual grace, that is, a transient divine aid in performing the actions needed for salvation. Hinduism from an early period was aware that attaining salvation required divine help. While this is not often explicitly stated, it is found in the *Katha Upanishad:* "Smaller than the small, greater than the great, is the Atman that is present in the heart of things. One who is without attachment beholds Him, and is free from sorrow; then by the grace of the creator he beholds the grandeur of the Atman. . . . This Atman is not to be attained by teaching, nor by intellect, nor by extensive learning. He is attained only by that one whom He chooses: To him the Atman reveals his own form" (*Katha*, II, 20, 23). This statement was considered of such importance by the writer of the later Upanishad, the *Svetasvatara*, that he repeats this expression, in almost the same words, although he gives it a stronger theistic emphasis: the one granted the vision "through the grace of the creator beholds the Lord and his greatness" (*Svetasvatara*, III, 20).

THE BHAGAVAD-GITA

The *Bhagavad-Gita* is the jewel of all Hindu religious writing. This sacred poem, which appears in the great Hindu epic, the *Mahabharata*, is the quintessence of the Upanishadic teaching. The chief doctrines of the *Bhaga-*

vad-Gita are its theism, its devotionalism, its doctrine of the divine appearance in human form as savior of man, and its teaching of salvation by divine grace. Some of these doctrines were foreshadowed in the later Upanishads, especially in the Isa, the Katha, and the Svetasvatara. Thus there is a continuity of teaching; yet there is also a most significant discontinuity. This was the decisive moment when Hinduism turned away from ritualism and intuitionalism toward devotion as the supreme way of salvation. In the Bhagavad-Gita is found the first clear statement of beatitude as a mutual indwelling of God in man and man in God: "They who with devotion worship me, they are in me and I in them" (IX, 29). The intellectualist trend of the Upanishads was continued in the work of the later Vedanta theologians, but along with this there was henceforth in the Hindu tradition an ever-increasing emphasis on salvation by love of God.

While technically the Bhagavad-Gita does not belong among the revealed literature of the Sruti, it has a special place of its own. Later commentators on the Scriptures have generally felt it necessary to explain their teachings also by references to the Bhagavad-Gita and by commentaries written specifically on this work. It has its own place apart. In this work God speaks to man more intimately and in more detail than anywhere else in the entire tradition. This is the highest moment of meeting of Hinduism with a personal deity after long centuries of effort to clarify and intensify their conscious awareness of the transcendent world beyond all appearances. As the Upanishads lifted up the Hindu mind to a sustained awareness of the absolute realm beyond the world of changing phenomena, so here mankind is lifted up to an affective union with this sublime reality in personal form. This new devotional experience was not a negation but rather an affirmation of the prior mystical insight of the Upanishads. It was an addition and expansion of the earlier tradition, not a retraction or a suppression. Neither the Upanishadic experience nor the Bhagavad-Gita experience have since faded from the Hindu mind. They constitute the two complementary aspects of Hindu tradition.

In structure the Bhagavad-Gita is a poem of some seven hundred verses in eighteen chapters. The setting is the great war described in the Mahabharata, the war that took place prior to 1000 B.C. between the Kaurava and Pandava for succession to the throne. The theme of the poem is the dejection experienced by Arjuna, one of the sons of Pandu, just before the battle as he thinks over the disastrous consequences of war. Should he fight or not fight? In a dramatic move he commands that his war chariot be drawn out between the two opposing forces. The questions then set forth by Arjuna are answered by Krishna, his charioteer, who is identified with the god Vishnu. Most of the dialogue is carried on by Krishna, who explains to Arjuna just why he should fight. The problem is immediately taken much deeper into human life than simply the specific problem of Arjuna. The deeper problem is that of the motivation, determination, and value of any human act. Is any deed worth the doing? Man's deeds only serve to involve him more and more deeply in the confused phenomenal order. From this there seems no escape. The answers given by Krishna are a spiritual analysis and resolution of the entire question of human deeds and how they should be performed to attain salvation, for the problem is ultimately the problem of salvation itself, total release from the limitations and tensions of the human condition. The discussion involves all the most basic theological and spiritual problems of men ancient and contemporary.

Dharma. The first answer given to Arjuna is that he must fulfill his Dharma, that is, the basic obligations of his state in life. Only in this way can his salvation be achieved. He is a warrior. To abandon the field is to betray his fundamental duty: "Aware of the duties of your life-status you should not be upset. For a warrior there is nothing better than a conflict required of him by duty. . . . If you refuse to carry out this battle demanded of you by your life-status, you abandon this obligation and its glory, then you will obtain affliction for yourself" (II, 31–33). The word "Dharma" to which appeal is made here is one of the most important words in the entire Hindu tradition. It signifies life status, duty, but beyond this it has larger implications of the spiritual and religious order. For duty and life status have here a spiritual and religious import. All of life in Hinduism is controlled by Dharma. It is a social, legal, spiritual, religious absolute in Hindu life. It is the basic word used to translate the Western word "religion," meaning a body or structure of religious belief and norms of conduct. This word is of special importance in the *Bhagavad-Gita*, for one of the basic objectives of the work seems to be to draw into full consciousness the importance of Dharma in dealing with any life problem.

Non-Attachment. Yet if Dharma is to be fulfilled, it must be done with total self-detachment. There must be no seeking after success in life, for the fruit-of-action (*karma-phala*). Actions are to be done because they are correct, because they are required by Dharma, not for personal gain. Quest for personal gain involves a person in the temporal order. Eventually it draws all things down to destruction. "Be concerned with the deed alone, not on its profit; let not the consequences of the deed be your motive, nor be you attached to non-action. Perform your deeds in a disciplined way. Bear yourself the same in success and failure; discipline is defined as equanimity" (II, 47–48). Throughout chapters two and three there is a thorough inquiry into the reasons for man's attachment to the sense world and the manner in which release is obtained by turning mentally to the highest reality and most sublime truth. This shows a profound inner awareness that even the doing of good deeds can bind man within the phenomenal order if there is any attachment whatsoever, any individual self-aggrandizement within time. This is what is known in the West as purity of intention: to do things which should be done precisely because they should be done.

Divine appearance in human form. One of the central features of later Hinduism appears first in its full presentation in the *Bhagavad-Gita*, the doctrine of the divine appearance upon earth in human form to communicate divine truth to man, to rescue man from destruction by a threatening tide of evil, to bring man to salvation by union with the supreme deity. In the poem a supreme divine secret is revealed: God considers man his devotee and friend. Of this secret Krishna tells Arjuna: "Communicated to them through successive generations the royal seers knew it. Afterwards in later centuries this discipline was lost. Now finally it is proclaimed once again to you by myself. You are my devoted one, my friend; this is a supreme mystery" (IV, 2–3). This earthly appearance is also for the repression of evil: "Though I am unborn, eternal, the Lord of all things, depending on my own primal nature I come into being by my mysterious power. For whenever a dissolution of the right order appears, Son of Bharata, a rising up of disorder, then I send myself forth. For protection of the good and for destruction of the evil, to establish a firm basis for righteousness, I bring myself forth ::pon earth in age after age" (IV, 6–8).

Multiple ways of salvation. Diverse ways of salvation are recognized in the poem: the way of inner recollection, performance of good deeds, faithful ritual practice, and living without attachment to earthly things. To the questions concerning the best way, the reply is given: "Direct your mind to me alone; cause your inner consciousness to enter me and you will dwell in me thenceforth; of this there is no doubt. Even if you cannot concentrate your thought on me, then seek to gain me by disciplined deeds. If you are without capacity even for this then be entirely devoted to work for me; performing deeds for my sake you will win perfection. But if even this you cannot accomplish, then controlling yourself give up all attachment to the fruit of actions" (XII, 8–11). Put simply the pattern is: "To whomever blame and praise are the same, disciplined in speech, satisfied with whatever happens, without a dwelling place, firm in mind, with a devout attitude, that person is dear to me" (XII, 19).

Vision of God. The climax of the poem is reached in chapter eleven when the vision of God is granted to Arjuna at his own request: "I long to see your form as God, O supreme Spirit! If you judge that it can be seen by me, O Lord, Ruler of unique power, then reveal to me your own immortal Self" (XI, 3–4). Before the vision is granted it is made clear that a special divine power must be conferred upon Arjuna: "Because you cannot see me with your own eye, I give you a divine eye; behold my unique power as God" (XI, 8). Arjuna describes the vision granted: "If the light of a thousand suns in the sky should suddenly burst forth, it would be as the light of that supreme being. The son of Pandu saw the whole world there united and diversified in the body of the god of gods" (XI, 12–13). A further description is given by Arjuna: "Without beginning, middle, or end, of limitless power, of numerous arms, I see you with the sun and the moon as your eyes, your face a blaze of fire that illumines this whole universe with its radiance" (XI, 19). One of the most sublime and comprehensive expressions of praise of God in the Hindu tradition is found in the words of Arjuna concerning the praise given God by the perfected ones: "Why should they not worship you, exalted as you are? You are even greater than Brahman; you are the primordial Creator; O Infinite Lord of Gods, in you the entire universe dwells. You the imperishable one, the existent, non-existent, and beyond both! You are the Primal God, the Ancient Spirit, the supreme abode of this universe; you are the knower, the object known, and the highest dwelling place. By you this universe is pervaded, by you of infinite form!" (XI, 37–38).

Devotion: the supreme way of salvation. Everywhere in the poem there is a sense of the divine compassion for mankind. Krishna is aware that man needs a very simple way of salvation, a way found more in the affective life of man than in his intellectual life. Thus the supreme way of salvation comes as a development of the affective qualities, even though throughout the poem there is also a certain emphasis on knowledge: "Not by Vedic learning nor by ascetic practices, nor by gifts, nor by ritual acts of worship, can I be seen in the manner in which you have beheld me. Only by a steady devotion, Arjuna, can I be so known and seen in reality and entered into. He who does my work, is supremely attached to me, devoted to me, released from desires, without hatred for anyone, he it is who comes to me" (XI, 53–55). The utter simplicity of this way of salvation is seen in this passage: "Whoever with love presents to me a leaf, a flower, a piece of fruit, some water, that offering I accept from the devoted giver. Whatever work you do, whatever you eat, whatever you sacrifice or bestow as a gift, whatever ascetic practices you perform, son of Kunti, do everything as an offering to me" (IX, 26–27). The full intimacy achieved in this life of devotion is felt in the request of Arjuna: "Bending down and prostrating myself I beseech grace of you, revered Lord; as father to son, as friend to friend, as lover to beloved, be gracious, O Lord" (XI, 44).

Grace. Awareness of the need for grace is seen in several passages, but a special emphasis on this need for divine help is found in the closing chapter where the perfect one is described: "Let him perform all actions trusting in me; then, by my grace he attains an eternal abiding status. In thought bestowing all deeds upon me, devoted to me, disciplined in mind, think ever on me. With your mind fixed upon me, you will by my grace overcome all difficulties. But if because of selfishness you refuse to listen, then will you perish" (XVIII, 56–58).

This leads to the final beautiful passage of the closing stanza of the work: "Listen, now, to the most profound of all secrets, to my supreme communication: Because you are dearly loved by me, I will tell you what is best for you. Be ever mindful of me, devoted to me, worshipping me, bowing down before me. Thus to my very self shall you come. In truth I pledge this to you for you are precious to me. Giving up all other obligations, come to me alone as your refuge; I will protect you from every evil. Be not concerned. This must never be told by you to anyone not given to austerity, or to one not devoted to me; not to anyone unresponsive to my voice, or to one antagonistic toward me. Whosoever, supremely dedicated to me, communicates this supreme mystery to those devoted to me, he shall come to me alone, of this there is no doubt. Among men of earth there is no one who does anything more pleasing to me, nor shall there by anyone on earth dearer to me" (XVIII, 65–69).

Chapter Three

The New Hinduism

After the *Bhagavad-Gita*, toward the end of the pre-Christian period, a new development took place in Hinduism that changed the entire mood of the tradition. Although the ritual and the codes of conduct have not been dealt with, they are of fundamental importance for they had an ever-present control over the details of daily living. The Laws of Manu outlined the basic pattern of social life, the Dharma Sutras indicated the manner in which social obligations were to be carried out, the Grihya Sutras regulated the home rituals and the general life pattern of the home.

GENERAL CHARACTERISTICS

Intellectually the life of Hinduism was dominated from above by a high tradition, while below the devotional life of the people had not yet attained an authoritative status or intellectual expression. The entire tradition of this period is known as the Brahmanical tradition. It was presided over by the Brahman class, who performed the rituals, guided the social

38

order, educated the young of the higher classes, provided the intellectual interpretation of life, and explained the way of salvation. All of this was reaching a certain fullness of development in the centuries toward the end of the pre-Christian era and the opening centuries of the Christian era. At the same time the heterodox traditions of Buddhism and Jainism had attained considerable influence. From 200 B.C. to A.D. 200, massive spiritual and cultural forces were at work that had not yet found their proper expression. The forms in which the creative intuitions could be released did indeed evolve from the third to the tenth century. The intellectual life found expression in a Sutra literature containing the foundations of the six philosophical systems that emerged. The aesthetic life found expression in the classical poetic and dramatic forms, in new temple achitecture and sculpture, and in cave paintings. The religious life was expressed in the change from a ritualistic-intellectual tradition to a devotionalism in which popular song and all the arts served as media of expression. The period of the Guptas, from the fourth through the seventh century, can be considered the Periclean period of India, a period of true classical attainment. But while this period was important in every aspect of Hindu life, it was especially important for the new changes that took place in the spiritual mood of the tradition. Expressed in its simplest form, it was a change from a ritualistic-intellectual-legalistic Hinduism to a highly devotional-theistic-religious tradition in which the immediacy of personal religious experience played a new and significant role.

While this change was an expansion rather than a break in the tradition, it can be said that a new Hinduism arose at this time. Of the time between the entry of the Aryans into the country shortly after 2000 B.C. and the arrival of the Western religious influences in the nineteenth century, this is the most significant moment, the period of greatest change in the entire history of Hinduism. It is so significant that the term "Brahmanism" is generally used to designate the tradition prior to this period, and the term "Hinduism" to designate the tradition after this period. There are three main elements that produced this new phase of development: the filling of a devotional void within Hindu tradition, reaction to Jainism and Buddhism, and reassertion within Hinduism of a basic non-Aryan element of the tradition. The ritualism, legalism, and intellectualism previously mentioned seem to have been primarily derived from the Aryan elements of the tradition. The new emphasis on devotion, on image worship, and on personal religious experience seems to be primarily associated with the non-Aryan elements of the tradition.

The key words of the new Hinduism are *Puja* and *Bhakti* (image worship
and loving devotion). Both these activities were directed toward a clearly
perceived theistic deity. Along with Puja came a new material setting for
religious life in the building of the first temples of India. Prior to this
time there had been no need for temples or images; all that was needed
were altars. Then temple-building and image-making spread over the
entire country. Ever since this time India has been covered with religious
sites and religious structures. Many of the ancient temples still survive,
although time and conquest have brought many to destruction.

Even more significant, however, is the devotional (*Bhakti*) tradition that
arose at this time as a vast movement from the deepest realms of the
Hindu soul. Here India found its supreme religious experience in its intense
affective love of God. Undoubtedly the intuitions of the Hindu mind
reached awesome heights and bestowed upon the inquiring faculty of man
the sublime vision of an abiding reality beyond observable phenomena.
This intellectual vision has continued undimmed until modern times; however, it could not be the final religious expression of the peoples of India.
Not only was it too sophisticated in its requirements, but it was also not
complete as a religious experience. It satisfied the mind but not the heart
of India. It did not give adequate expression to the love experience that
was even deeper than the intellectual experience. A response to divine love
was possible as soon as the people were awakened to the existence and
loving qualities of the supreme deity. The Indian people were extreme in
their response. Seldom if ever in man's history has there been another
tradition where the affective life of religion was sustained so consistently
on such a lofty devotional plane. The devotee casts himself in absolute dependence upon the mercy and love of the supreme deity. The Bhakti movement has remained the single most distinguishing characteristic of Hinduism from the opening centuries of the Christian era until the present.

THE NEW SCRIPTURES

The new religious situation required a new body of scriptures. These were
produced in the form of Puranas, Agamas, Tantras, and hymns. These
new scriptures, except for the Tantras, are sectarian documents. Two
principal sects, Shaivism and Vaishnavism, developed during this creative
period, although many local cults existed and continued to thrive throughout the country. But insofar as there can be said to be major deities in

India, they are Shiva and Vishnu. Associated with each of these is a feminine principle, or *Shakti*, who is the creative aspect of the deity. Shakti worship might be considered the third main focus of worship along with Vishnu and Shiva, although in final resolution Shakti worship is most often associated with the deity with which the Shakti is related.

The new elements in the religious life of this period and the new scriptures, while really new, were also in continuity with the past. The new creation was more an addition to and transformation of the older tradition than a denial of it. The spiritual insights of the earlier period, especially, were integrated into this new vision. Among the Upanishadic teaching of primary importance throughout the entire course of Hindu religious development is the doctrine of the transcendence and immanence of Brahman, with emphasis on immanence and identity rather than on transcendence and difference. The distinctive contribution of the Puranas was to identify this final reality as possessing the attributes of personality. Impersonal treatment of Brahman in the Upanishads was continued in the theological writings of the Vedanta schools, but henceforth in the general tradition of Hinduism there was more attention to the personal aspect of this final reality. These two positions continued within the tradition. One must speak, then, of the larger tradition of Hinduism as a diversified unity— a diversity that can only be understood through the various traditions of which the larger unity was composed.

Puranas. Of the forms of writing mentioned as the new scriptures, the Puranas occupy the first place and can most properly be designated the scriptures of the new period. In relation to the earlier literature, the Puranas are most closely related to the Epics, especially to the *Mahabharata*, in their general content and spiritual concern. For, apart from the dramatic narrative itself, the *Mahabharata* seeks to provide an account of how things took place in the past and how the present order of human life came about. The Epics were of special importance in relating the manner in which a divine being assists and guides the course of life. Both the Epics and the Puranas are an effort to situate man in time and space, that is, to relate the present situation to the changing course of human affairs from the beginning and to locate the lower world in its functional relationship with higher powers. The lower and the higher achieve their final unity when time itself, in its origin and sequence, is related to a creative deity who is the origin and end of all and present in all.

Eighteen principal works are known as Puranas. Although more works fall into this category, most are decidedly less significant than the principal eighteen. Composed during a period of eight hundred years, from the fourth to the twelfth century, the Puranas treat the formation of the world, the deeds of the gods, the heroic figures of the past, the descent of royal families, the festivals of the gods, prayer and proper manner of worship, and the duties of caste. Encyclopedic in nature, for the most part they are poorly written collections of information on all that has to do with religious tradition. In them the older Vedic mythology is expanded, transformed, and further enriched. The new mythology is much closer to the popular level of thinking than the older, for this new mythology was absorbed into many of the local traditions and legends of the people. The ancient Vedas were available to instruct and guide the thought and worship of the three higher castes exclusively. The Puranas were available to guide even *Shudras* and women. At this time people other than the upper classes attained some, though limited, spiritual recognition. Nevertheless, Hinduism became closer to the people in a more adequate fashion.

As sectarian documents, the Puranas were directed toward the worship of Vishnu, Shiva, and Brahma. These deities dominate the religious life of Hinduism, though the god Brahma (to be clearly distinguished from the ontological absolute, Brahman) was never of such importance as Vishnu or Shiva. The latter are the two that have presided over the religious life of India for the past fifteen hundred years, along with their Shakti consorts and the innumerable deities of the villages.

Associated with the Puranas of the Vaishnava tradition is the doctrine of Avatar, that is, divine appearance in the form of living beings, both animal and human. This doctrine is now a central feature of the Vaishnava tradition. The Avatar doctrine is of less importance to the worship of Shiva than to the worship of Vishnu, for worship in the Shaivite tradition is directed to the deity himself or to his consort, while worship of Vishnu is most often directed to him in one of his human appearances, either as Krishna or as Rama.

Of the Puranas devoted principally to Vishnu, the *Vishnu, Padma,* and *Bhagavata Puranas* are the most significant. The *Padma* is divided into five books that are concerned with creation, earth, heaven, regions below the earth, and with a last section outlining the devotional life addressed to Vishnu. There the emphasis is not on mental concentration, but on offerings, ceremonies and festival, prayer and pilgrimage as the fundamental way of salvation. The *Vishnu Purana* is the ideal Purana in its compositional form, since it gives in order the stages of creation, the descent of the gods and heroes, the reigns of the ancient rulers and the chronology of historical events. In its legends it provides some of the main subjects of Hindu art of this period. Doctrinally, Vishnu is presented in this Purana as identical with Brahman and as the one and only god, creator and preserver of the world. The historical orientation of the Puranas is revealed strongly in this work.

Of even greater influence on the lives of the people is the *Bhagavata Purana*. This Purana from the South must be considered among the most beautiful religious compositions of India. It ranks with the *Bhagavad-Gita* and the *Ramacarita* of Tulsi Das (1532–1623) for its attractiveness of composition and its influence in the spiritual life of the Hindu people. Knowledge of these three works is absolutely necessary to understand the religious life of Hinduism. The *Bhagavata Purana* is especially important for its tenth book, which gives the account of Krishna, the human manifestation of Vishnu, as a playful child and later as a young man. This story of Krishna and his love relations with the milkmaids, especially with Radha, is interpreted as indicating that the divine-human relation is fundamentally a love relation, that this way of love is the supreme and only effective way of salvation. It is suggestive, in its basic theme, of the *Canticle of Canticles* in the Western Scriptural tradition. This account of Krishna's love for the milkmaids has been the central story in the devotional tradition of Vaishnavism. The Purana itself, popular throughout India, is late in composition, probably belonging to the tenth or eleventh century.

Among the Puranas directed primarily toward worship of Shiva are the *Vayu, Linga*, and *Kurma Puranas*. The *Vayu Purana* is very early, possibly from the fifth century A.D. Its four sections deal with the stages of creation from the earliest period to the final age yet to come. It is particularly clear in its devotion to Shiva as the supreme deity. In the *Kurma Purana* the four basic aims of life in the Hindu tradition are explained: fulfillment of the duties of one's state in life, quest for wealth, pursuit of pleasure, and finally attainment of final liberation. Although this Purana is spoken by Vishnu in the form of a tortoise, it is a work teaching the worship of Shiva. The *Linga Purana*, also prominent among the works dedicated to worship of Shiva, gives great emphasis to the generative power of Shiva.

As a deity Shiva is a complex figure both in historical origin and significance. The study of this deity and the worship rendered him is difficult but rewarding. Shiva is a deity with both creative and destructive powers. In this deity there is apparently a meeting and identification of a prominent non-Aryan deity of primordial India with the Rudra figure of the Vedic

Hymns, a deity presented there as a storm god. This figure appears in the *Svetasvatara Upanishad* as a benign deity who is given the epithet "shiva," which means gracious, kind, bounteous, benign. This descriptive title then becomes the name of the deity. Shiva appears in the *Mahabharata*. From this epic he passes on into the Puranas as one of the two main deities of the entire Hindu tradition. In Shiva opposites are reconciled, even identified. Creation and destruction, unity and diversity, the phenomenal and the noumenal—all is reconciled in this deity. The dance of creation performed by Shiva is also the dance of destruction. These opposed qualities of Shiva correspond with the twofold effect that deity intensively experienced makes upon man; the one is attraction toward divine splendor, the other aversion from overwhelming majesty.

Also associated with Shiva is his feminine consort, who is extremely prominent in the Shaivite tradition. The feminine consort of a deity in Hinduism is his *Shakti* (creative power). The Shakti of Shiva is known as Devi, Uma, Durga, Kali, or Parvati. As does Shiva, she has both benign and terrifying aspects. She is a protecting mother goddess and a fierce deity demanding bloody sacrifice. In the worship of the Shakti tradition this strong awareness of a cosmic feminine principle leads at times to an extreme eroticism associated with worship. This is found both in Shiva worship and in the worship of his Shakti, Kali. The Linga symbol, prominent in the Shaivite temples of India, is a primary objective of worship in this tradition.

Agamas. Associated with the Puranas is a great volume of religious writing in the sectarian traditions known as Agamas. Found in both the Vaishnava and Shaivite traditions, the Agamas give further intellectual, ritual, and devotional development to the traditions. There is some common subject matter in the Puranas and the Agamas, but in general it could be said that the Puranas provide the historical and doctrinal phases of development of the human-divine relations for the new phase of Hinduism, while the Agamas are a guide to worship. Followers of the sects give full canonical authority to the Agamas. The Agamas, which were composed after the Puranas, remain fully within the orthodox tradition of Hinduism since they accept the Vedic tradition as it was handed down with all its Brahmanical prescriptions. There are over two hundred Agamas in each of the two traditions, the Vaishnava and the Shaivite. Written principally in the period from A.D. 500 to 1000, they have as their metaphysical basis the same doctrines of the absolute reality as this is expressed in the Upanishadic writings, although this is adapted to the new theistic context. Their teaching is divided generally into four sections, teachings concerning the proper philosophical knowledge of reality, the Yogic discipline of meditation, the practical side of temple building and erection of representations of deities, and finally the prescriptions for the proper veneration of the deities. They provide guidance for the religious worship and for the proper performance of the Hindu ritual, and they are extremely valuable in any study of the real meaning of the Hindu ritual as it is performed even today.

Tantras. The world of Tantric thought, ritual, and literature is a world of symbolism and involves a vast sacramental order that encompasses the entire cosmic and psychic realms of human experience. The Tantric tradition contains a range of experience that passes from the mystical and the mysterious to the magical. The Tantras fulfill in this new period what the Brahmanical rituals fulfilled in an earlier period. The Tantras provide a technique of managing and harmonizing the divine, cosmic, and human orders. This establishment of man at the absolute center of all being and all reality moves in the opposite direction of Yoga, but in the end accomplishes an equivalent salvation function. Whereas Yoga moves away from all phenomenal experience, Tantrism moves inward toward the center of the phenomenal and there discovers the transphenomenal. The Tantrist places himself at the sacred center wherein he eliminates all the tension and opposition of life and overcomes all evil. To accomplish this, Tantrism uses diagrams in which the psychic, moral, and spiritual conflicts are worked out and resolved. When used effectively, these sacred formulas, signs, symbolic actions, and diagrams all function as so many instruments whereby the divine, cosmic, and psychosomatic identification is attained. In this tradition, the simplest thing in the universe carries within itself the entire order reality; a person need only to be aware of this in order to go beyond the appearances of the inner reality of things. Finally, in attaining this inner and absolute harmony of reality he reaches a state of salvation and eternal blessedness.

The volume of Tantric writings is extremely large. The tradition can be traced back through the entire span of the centuries to the Vedic Hymns themselves which are concerned at times with spells and magical techniques of a Tantric nature. The earlier Vedic scriptures of Hinduism are fully recognized by the Tantric tradition, but only as norms of the past. The new, the fourth age of the world, needs the new vision, the new guidance, the new techniques provided by the Tantras. These provide a new orthodoxy, a new Sruti. The Tantric tradition finds it easy to assimilate into itself all the basic accomplishments of the Indian traditions. In a special manner it is able to incorporate the teaching of the Sankhya and the Vedanta traditions and to reconcile them.

Hymns. While the Puranas, Agamas, and Tantras provided for succeeding centuries the basic historical orientation, the dogmatic beliefs, and the ritual practices of sectarian Hinduism from the fifth century, the hymnal literature expressed the actual religious experience of the people. Unlike the other forms of literature discussed, hymns were composed mainly in the vernacular language spoken by the people, although a sizable number were composed in Sanskrit. Use of the vernacular provided an immediacy of expression and communication lacking even in the exalted language of the *Bhagavata Purana.*

Although these hymns were often composed and sung by *Shudras* and outcastes and although they were expressed in the popular languages of the country, it must not be concluded that they were lacking in depth of intellectual insight. Indeed, one of the amazing characteristics of Hinduism is the universal communication of lofty religious teaching throughout the whole of the society. Thus the hymns carried the sublime intuitions of the Upanishadic thinkers, the lofty insight of the *Bhagavad-Gita,* the voluminous teaching of the Puranas, and a rich mythology derived from all periods. The entire tradition now lived in the radiance of a new devotional experience; the saint-singers of this period gave expression to the spiritual experience that was taking place within their own being. The most decisive difference from the earlier period is that the Brahman experience of the past was reinterpreted in terms of a personal supreme deity. Divine personality permeates the whole range of Hindu consciousness at this time, finding expression in art, architecture, and sculpture, as well as in life and in poetry. Love of God was considered the rich inner nourishment, the cream of the entire Vedic tradition.

The earliest hymns in the vernacular literatures appeared in the South in the Tamil language and were addressed to Shiva. Just slightly later, Tamil hymns of great fervor were addressed to Vishnu. The sixth to the ninth century was the period of the greatest Tamil singers. Their works were collected into new sectarian canons often considered to be the true expression of the Vedas and even to constitute a new Veda, one not opposed to the old but carrying to a new experiential height the Vedic ritual and intellectual experiences. This tradition was later communicated to the western regions of India where new songs appeared in the Kannada literature. By the thirteenth century the Maratha region was filled with devotional songs. The creative period in this region continued through the seventeenth century. In the North, songs of praise to Vishnu and Shiva were rising in the Hindi and Bengali languages by the fifteenth century. In all these regions the creation of sacred song has continued until modern times, when it found new warmth of expression in the lyrics of Tagore (1861–1941).

Chapter Four

Saints and Theologians

SAINTS AND THEIR SONGS

Devotees of Shiva. The hymnal literature of later Hinduism brings us into contact with some of the most impressive personalities in the religious history of India. These personalities emerged first in southern India and were devotees of Shiva, to whom they addressed their songs of praise, petition, and repentance. These early Shaivite poets were later known as *Nayanars*. The first of these saint-singers, Appar, known as the Devout Prince of Song, was active during the seventh century. Born in the Shaivite tradition, but converted to Jainism, he later returned to the worship of Shiva. During the remainder of his life he wandered from one temple to another, singing the verses that arose in his mind in praise of Shiva. Some of his deepest emotions were associated with presence at the feet of the Lord, with being close to them, shadowed by them, embracing them. Among his songs are some that have a special poetic feeling for the natural world.

> *The faultless vina; the twilight moon;*
> *The breeze that blows; the fragrant spring;*

> *Bee-haunted pools like these, the shade*
> *Of my God's, my Father's twin feet.*
> *—History of Tamil Literature* (p. 78)

Other of his poems present deeper emotions of the religious soul, especially the feeling of his own sinfulness that sometimes overwhelms him.

> *In right I have no power to live,*
> *Day after day I'm stained with sin*
> *I read, but do not understand;*
> *I hold Thee not my heart within.*
> *O light, O flame, O first of all,*
> *I wandered far that I might see,*
> *Athihai Virattanam's Lord,*
> *Thy flower-like feet of purity.*
> *—Hymns of the Tamil Shaivite Saints* (p. 43)

Second in the line of Tamil poet-saints of this early period is Sambandar. Less impressive as a poet than Appar, he sang of Shiva in such a way that the heterodox traditions of Buddhism and Jainism, dominant in south India at this time, were considerably reduced in strength. The Hindu revival that came at this time was largely through the songs of Sambandar.

> *Thou Light whom Brahma, being's fount, and Vishnu could not see,*
> *No righteousness have I, I only speak in praise of Thee.*
> *Come, Valivalam's Lord, let no dark fruit of deeds, I pray,*
> *Torment Thy slave who with his song extols Thee day by day.*
> *—Hymns of the Tamil Shaivite Saints* (p. 21)

The intent of this poem is to place Shiva at the height of man's consciousness by placing him above the ontological absolute, the very source of being. Also it places Shiva above Vishnu. This poem is a plea for release from all the stain of Karma, that is the bond that keeps man bound to the world of time and change.

Generally mentioned third among the four great singers of the period is Sundarar, a Brahman who lived in the first part of the ninth century. He was even more direct and spontaneous in his life and in his poetry than the others. From his remarkable poetic talent he threw forth his verses with a defiant abandon. He is especially fierce in his writings against the Buddhists and Jains. Even when he speaks to God it is with a barbed directness that comes from both intimacy and confidence. Speaking of his blindness he cried out to God: "I was sold and bought by you; I am no loan; of my own will I am your slave, I did no wrong. You made me blind! Why, Lord, did you take away my sight? The blame is yours alone! If you will not restore the sight of my other eye, well, may you then live long!" (*History of Tamil Literature*, p. 84). This ending is a curse flung at God in ironic fashion. Such is the type of sharp rebuke to God that is rare indeed in the religious compositions of the saints. In India, however, familiarity with God goes this far. The saints scold and blame God, fight with Him, challenge Him, play with Him, all with perfect assurance that God in his love wishes men to speak with him in this manner. To the Indians, this appeared to be a higher and more honest devotion than that of affected piety, a piety not truly in the soul at the moment. It was also part of the love-play that existed between God and man in India.

The last of the four great singers of Shiva in early Tamiland is Manikka, Speaker of Gems. Generally recognized as the finest of all the *Nayanars*, he was able to express the deepest religious emotions of the human heart. In addition, he possessed a rare depth of philosophical insight that gave rich substance to what he composed. His greatest work is the *Tiru-vasaham*. Manikka was conscious of his burden of guilt in life and this is often mentioned. In deep praise and appreciation he says:

Whether I praise or curse thee, still I'm stained with sin and sorrowing,
   Yet, wilt thou leave me? Splendour shining like the red-hued coral mount,
Master, thou drankest poison black, the humbler beings pitying,
   That I, thy meanest one, might find no poison, but a nectar fount.
               —Hymns Tamil Shaivite Saints (p. 101)

Manikka wrote songs for different groups of the people so that while at work or at their daily duties they might sing of the Lord. Thus he composed *The Grinding Song*:

Grind we the powder gold, that He may bathe;
For He is Scripture, He is sacrifice;
He's being's truth, and being's falsehood too.
Light is He, yea, and He is darkness deep;
He is deep sorrow, and true bliss is He;
He is the half, and He again the whole;
Bondage is He, but He is true release;
He is the alpha, He the omega.
      —Hymns of the Tamil Shaivite Saints (p. 103)

A person could study in detail the religious experience reflected in such poems. There is an intimacy, a confidence, a directness of approach, a feeling that God is present in his own person and is deeply concerned with every smallest aspect of human life, a feeling that nothing can take man from the divine presence. This exalted song to Shiva begun in the Tamil region was communicated shortly afterward to the region of Kannada, where it was taken up by Basavaraja in the twelfth century. From there it passed on to the northern regions of India, where in the fourteenth century in Kashmir, Lalla sang of the ecstatic experience of divine union. She described herself as "drunk in the delight of divine knowledge." From this region the song tradition in praise of Shiva passed on to the eastern regions of Bengal. There, in the eighteenth century, the last of the great Shaivite poets, Ramaprasad, wrote his praise of Kali, consort of Shiva.

Devotees of Vishnu. As did the Shaivite saints, the saintly poets of Vishnu arose first in the Tamil region of the South. While their compositions achieved high poetic expression, the Vaishnava verses do not always have the freedom and the grand spontaneity of emotional expression that characterize the Shaivite works. Yet this is not to deny the significance and nobility of their work. They were called *Alvars* (men immersed in the divine). Their influence was also great in establishing the tradition of Bhakti in the worship of Vishnu. Twelve poets flourished in the South during the seventh to the tenth century, the greatest of whom were Periyalvar, Tirumangai Alvar, and Nammalvar.

Periyalvar was a Brahman who wrote nearly five hundred poems, many of them in praise of Krishna, the incarnation of Vishnu. These poems, however, are concerned more with the childhood of Krishna than with his later life as lover of the milkmaids, especially of Radha. Periyalvar gives delightful descriptions of childhood and deals with the marvel that a deity has appeared on earth as a child in all its simplicity. He speaks of Krishna as a roguish boy:

> *He'll tip over the jar of oil;*
> *He'll pinch and wake the babe,*
> *And roll his eye in mischief.*
> —*History of Tamil Literature* (p. 103)

After him comes Tirumangai Alvar, who produced the greatest volume of compositions of the *Alvars*. He wrote much on the theme of divine love. The last of the *Alvars* is Nammalvar, who is considered by many as the greatest of them all. He had extensive learning which shows throughout all his compositions. But great as these poets were in their influence, they do not evoke the attraction of modern readers the way this attraction and admiration is evoked for the Vaishnava poets of the Maratha region.

It was there in the west-coastal region of India that a vigorous tradition of high spirituality was established in the thirteenth century by Jnanadeva, a person of exceptional ability and of superb spiritual insight. He wrote a commentary on the *Bhagavad-Gita* that is considered one of the greatest of all commentaries on that work, one that may provide a deeper spiritual insight than that provided by any of the other commentators. There he included the following prayer:

> *Victory! Victory! to Thee, Holy Mother,*
> *Well known for Thy generous heart;*
> *Always sending down showers of joy.*
> *When the serpent of sensual desires*
> *Has coiled itself tightly around me,*
> *And pride of heart does not leave me,*
> *By thy compassionate look the serpent loses its venom.*
> *Who can be scorched by the three forms of affliction?*
>   —*Stotramala* (p. 4)

In this passage Jnanadeva is considering the divine under the aspect of a mother, with tender concern for her children. Often quoted is the prayer he wrote at the end of his commentary on the *Bhagavad-Gita*.

> *And now may God, Soul of the Universe,*
> *Be pleased with this my offering of words.*
> *And being pleased may He give me*
> *This favor in return.*
> *That the crookedness of evil men may cease,*
> *And that the love of goodness may grow in them.*
> *May all beings experience from one another*
> *Friendship of heart.*
> *May the darkness of sin disappear.*
> *May the universe see the rising of the Sun of Righteousness.*
> *Whatever is desired, may it be received*
> *By every living being.*
> *And may the Supreme Being be worshipped*
> *For ever and ever.*
>   —*Stotramala* (p. 180)

Jnanadeva was succeeded by a series of impressive spiritual personalities; Namdev (1270–1350), Eknath (1548–1600), Tukaram (1608–1649), and

Ramdas (1608–1681) are the best known and were most influential. Eknath is known as a scholar of some repute who commented on the eleventh chapter of the *Bhagavata Purana*. Also he did a translation of the *Bhagavad-Gita* into Marathi. His writings are too philosophical perhaps to be considered with the other devotional poetry of the period, except for a few of his prayers.

Hasten, hasten, O Ram, Lover of thy Bhaktas,
Through lustful desires I am entangled in worldly things.
In my youth, through pride, I became stiff in my conceit,
Sensual things, especially love of wealth, flourished in me like twigs on a
    tree.
While enjoying sensual things, I ministered to my body,
But I did not remember my true good, and I neglected to think of Thee.
But now I am forsaken by these sensual things, and therefore have come
    as a suppliant to Thee
At Thy feet, I, Eka Janardan, humbly place myself.
                                                    —*Stotramala* (p. 26)

Tukaram (1608–1649) is one of the saints who produced an extraordinary influence on the Maratha world through his poems. He speaks of God as Vitthal, Vithoba, or Pandurang, local names for God applied now to the supreme deity in the Vaishnava tradition, especially to Vishnu in his Krishna incarnation. His life was filled with an unending succession of troubles: family misfortune, social disgrace, loss of possessions. Few have felt the inherent tragedy of the human condition with such sensitivity as Tukaram. All this is expressed in his verse. Although very little of the social situation is discovered in the devotional literature of the Tamil region, this is not true of the devotional literature in the Maratha region, especially in the work of Tukaram. The times and his personal life and emotions show through his poetry with extraordinary clarity. The sorrows of his life were the occasion for spiritual elevation. He considered that his destitution was a needed condition for his higher spiritual achievement, his greater love of God. Perhaps the extensive suffering in his life was the reason for the exceptional influence he had among the people.

At this time the Maratha saints had developed to a high degree an informal ecstatic ritual known as the *kirtan*. This was a combination of song and dance in which the most intense love of God was expressed. Often at night Tukaram led the people in such performances. In one of the accounts of his life we read: "Thus the Vaishnava bhakta began his kirtans after the night had advanced four ghatikas. In pleading tones, and with a feeling of love, Tuka addressed his songs to the Lord-of-pandhari. . . . While Tuka in his love was thus pleading for God's mercy, though still in his body, he became one unconscious of body, and by force of his devotion accompanied with love, the image of Pandurang appeared in his heart. In his love for God he began to dance in the kirtan, and moment after moment he would bow prostrate on the ground. (In his ecstasy) Tuka forgot his relation as bhakta, and Vithoba forgot his relation as God" (*Tukaram*, pp. 174, 175).

These verses by Tukaram are found in Ranade's study of the Maratha saints: "Make me homeless, wealthless, childless so that I may remember Thee. Give no child to me, for by its affection Thou shalt be away from me. Give me not either wealth or fortune, for that is a calamity itself. Make me a wanderer, says Tuka, for in that way alone I may be able to remember Thee night and day. . . . Let me get no food to eat, nor any child to continue my family line; but let God have mercy on me. This is what my mind tells me, and I keep telling the same thing to the people. Let my body suffer all sorts of calamities, or adversities; but let God live in my mind. All these things verily are perishable, says Tuka; for God alone is happiness." (*Pathway to God in Marathi Literature*, p. 223).

Ramdas (1608–1681), last of the five great Maratha saints, wrote in a style that is generally prose in content and expression. Devoted to the Vishnu incarnation in Rama, he lived as a wandering mendicant visiting the temples of the region. One of his most frequent sayings was "Run to my help, Dear Ram. To what extremity are you willing to see me suffer?" Ramdas was spiritual teacher of the greatest of Maratha political rulers, Shivaji. Among the ones composed by Ramdas is the following:

> O dear Ram, in Thy mercy meet me.
> Through separation from Thee my whole being is in distress.
> I cannot free myself from worldly things amongst men.
> In my despondency I know not how to pass my time.
> May the Almighty One not have in mind to reject me.
> May there ever be kindly thought for His bhaktas.
> Union with Thee I have been unable to have. How am I to acquire it?
> In my despondency I know not how to pass my time.
> Victory, Victory to Ram Almighty!
>   —*Stotramala* (pp. 59, 60)

Among those who wrote in the Hindi language is Kabir (1440–1518), one of the most creative of all the saints, a man who was strongly influenced by Islamic mysticism. Kabir was also influenced by the spiritual traditions that came from Jnanadeva and Namadeva. Because of the strong Islamic influence on his work Kabir was strongly monotheistic and sharply opposed to the excessive worship of images found in much of Hinduism. He was also opposed to the caste system. He was the first to express the Bhakti love experience in poetry written in the Hindi language.

Another significant figure who wrote in the Hindi language is Tulsi Das (1532–1623), who translated into Hindi and reinterpreted the epic poem, the *Ramayana*. His work, the *Ramacarita*, is a highly spiritual interpretation which so elevated the message of this epic that it became the Bible of vast numbers of people. Vishnu in his Rama incarnation became for these people of northern India the highest expression of the divine. This exaltation of Rama had begun earlier with the writings of Ramananda (1400–1470), a holy man from southern India who journeyed north and settled at Banaras, where he established the tradition of Rama worship. When Tulsi Das wrote his account of the Rama story a new element was established in the religious life of India. This poem became a new scripture for a large part of the people and even a new integration of the whole of Hinduism. Thereafter, the basic knowledge of the Hindu religion for vast numbers of peoples was achieved through this work.

THEOLOGIANS AND THEIR TEACHINGS

Simultaneous with the devotional development of Hinduism was an extensive intellectual development. Much of this, too, was carried out by men of the South. India's first efforts at intellectual synthesis were expressed in a Sutra literature. Sutras are cryptic expressions grouped together in orderly fashion to express some comprehensive view of reality or some discipline of action. There are six basic Sutra collections of the philosophical-theological traditions which exist in Hinduism and which have dominated Hindu thought from the later pre-Christian period up to the present: the Nyaya, Vaishesika, Sankhya, Yoga, Mimamsa, and Vedanta. Of these six the Vedanta tradition contains the highest thought concerning the nature and attributes of God, the relation of God to the created order, and the way by which man attains salvation from the human condition and a state of lasting bliss in Brahman. The Vedanta is based directly upon the Upanishadic awareness of Brahman as origin, preserver, and end of all things.

The Vedanta Sutras, also known as the Brahma Sutras, were composed by Badarayana and are of exceptional significance in the history of Hindu thought. This Sutra collection was the first extensive effort to bring the great intuitions of the Upanishads into some orderly presentation. Composed at the beginning of the Christian period, this work was the first thorough effort to give intelligible order to the vast realm of thought in the Hindu religious development. It showed an exceptional power of synthesis and provided the impetus for the intellectual clarification so much needed by Hinduism at that time. Without this work and the commentaries that have been written on it there would be much greater difficulty in understanding the entire Hindu tradition. The Vedanta Sutras were primarily directed toward a refutation of the Sankhya tradition of dualism, a view based on the two principles of matter and spirit (*Prakriti* and *Purusha*). The five hundred fifty-five brief statements of doctrine in the Vedanta Sutras are grouped into four sections, each of which is again divided into four chapters, each containing somewhere between twenty and fifty propositions.

Shankara. The first Vedanta theologian whose commentary on the Sutras has been preserved is Shankara who lived during the eighth century. His work is so comprehensive in its scope, so penetrating in its insight, and so influential on later centuries that he may be considered the Aquinas of the Hindu tradition. He wrote commentaries on many of the Upanishads and on the *Bhagavad-Gita*. But his central work, the greatest single work in Hindu theology, is his *Commentary on the Vedanta Sutras*. This work became so central to Hindu theology that it was itself the subject of many commentaries in later centuries. Shankara identified the basic Upanishads and differentiated between those that were the most authentic and most helpful in sustaining the higher vision of Brahman. Ever since the time of Shankara, the Upanishads that he used in his writings and those he commented on have been considered the greater and more significant of these works. Also regarding the principal Upanishads, Shankara identified the more important statements and placed them in proper relief so that henceforth they could stand out clearly from the mass of Upanishadic compositions.

Shankara insisted on the importance of attaining true knowledge. Just as bliss for St. Thomas is primarily a vision of the mind, so for Shankara adjustment of human understanding and doing away with ignorance are primary steps on the way to salvation from the human condition. Fundamentally, ignorance of some kind is frustrating man and keeping him from final fruition of the divine. Removal of this ignorance cannot be achieved with merely human effort, but depends upon the higher communication to man contained in the revealed scriptures, the Vedic revelation. These lead man finally to the salvation experience, which is the knowledge of Brahman. The ignorance caused by attributing eternal and absolute being to transitory things is healed only in this way. Finally, when man is turned completely toward Brahman he is led by the revelation to a higher experience in which he sees that all things in the phenomenal order are Maya, that is, ephemeral rather than true being.

The entire thought of Shankara is centered on Brahman, the realm of true reality, the other world, the world that is recognized with the intelligence but which is not seen with the eyes. This reality is veiled from man by the limitations of the finite mind, which must undergo a total transformation in order to attain the insight that leads to true knowledge. This concentration on Brahman leaves man without theology or ontology of the phenomenal world, or even an adequate spiritual discipline for attaining this vision. The radiance of the Absolute as it invades the world in some manner dissolves the world within an eternal brightness which contains its own truth, its own reality, its own bliss. The main theses of Shankara can be listed in the following manner:

1 Reality is non-dual. Thus the name of the world vision of Shankara is *Advaita Vedanta* (non-dual Vedanta). The Absolute is one and unalterable. There is no other. The absolute character of this final reality is such that it does not leave room for any opposition, for any addition or subtraction, any enlargement or diminution, for any change or alternation whatsoever.

2 Brahman, the Supreme Reality, must be considered under two basic designations, as *Nirguna Brahman* (Brahman without attributes or qualifications) and as *Saguna Brahman* (Brahman with attributes). The first, Brahman in his absolute being, is so beyond human powers of comprehension that no terms used by man can apply to Brahman in any literal sense. Brahman is absolute simplicity containing in itself all that can be, eternal silence containing in itself all speech. Men can speak of Brahman and designate the sublime attributes of Brahman so long as they realize that this is a human way of speaking. The reality designated is not Absolute Brahman, but Brahman as he is known within human limitations.

3 All that exists is produced by Maya, or mysterious power of Brahman. This doctrine involves one of the most difficult of all theological concepts—creation and the relation between the absolute creator and the transient creation. Sometimes Maya is translated as illusion; it designates the world

of unreality or points to a magic-produced world. All these concepts are to some extent present in this word, but essentially it indicates something that is too mysterious for man to fully comprehend. Nothing in the entire range of Shankara's composition is so difficult as this to manage in a satisfying way, although he has used this term with superb delicacy in expressing the relation between the eternal and the finite worlds and the power whereby this is produced. Related to Maya is Adhyasa (the imposition of the noneternal on the eternal, of the unreal on the real), which is derived from an innate tendency of the mind to impose the attributes of one thing on another. True wisdom consists in overcoming this tendency of the mind and appreciating the true nature of Brahman. Thus this world of phenomena cannot be said either to exist or to not exist in any absolute sense. In the final analysis there is something unreal, something illusory about the entire visible world.

4 The final subjective reality of all things is simply Brahman, designated also as Atman, the true Self, the final basis on which all things rest.

5 Salvation is achieved by a discriminating knowledge of the final unreality of the world and by a consequent absorption of the individual self into the universal Self, that is, in Brahman.

6 The source of all true knowledge concerning Brahman is the Vedic scriptures, especially the Upanishads. These constitute the infallible source of all saving knowledge.

While Shankara was an intellectualist of high achievement, he was also a man of intense devotion. His devotional life was centered on Shiva as the highest expression of the divine reality, as this had been communicated to man. But his devotion to Shiva was lacking in the sectarian quality that is found at times in such well-defined traditions. Sectarian allegiance did not enter at all into his theological thinking. Completely universal in his basic orientation, he had an appreciation of the larger range of the Hindu tradition. He wished in a special manner to bring forth and to strengthen the unity of the entire tradition.

As a spiritual teacher Shankara traveled throughout India instructing the people. Although he came from the Malabar region, he traveled throughout India both to the North and to the East. In at least four centers in different parts of India he established communities of spiritual personalities in Ashrams (small monastic establishments) that continued in existence long after him, even into the modern period. Shankara can be considered the supreme genius of later Hindu tradition. Perhaps no single personality has contributed so much to its establishment in the form in which Hinduism still survives. His thought has been the greatest single influence in the intellectual life of the country. He was largely responsible for restructuring the whole of Hinduism and providing a basic theology widely accepted by both Vaishnava and Shaivite. He sought to preserve in a single tradition the total Hindu heritage, to bring it to a full consciousness of its own principles.

Special note should be made of Shankara's relation to Buddhism, which he opposed. Along with the saintly poets of the period, he is largely responsible for the elimination of Buddhism from the country and for the revival of Hinduism. Yet he was capable of understanding and appropriating the highest intellectual achievement of Buddhism, the doctrine of *Sunyata* (emptiness). Earlier Guadapada, a central figure in the intellectual life of India, had recognized the need for integrating the Buddhist doctrine of Sunyata with the Hindu doctrine of Brahman and first understood how this could be done. Yet this assimilation of the two doctrines was not completed until the time of Shankara, who fully developed the distinction between *Saguna Brahman* and *Nirguna Brahman* (qualified and unqualified Brahman). While the implications of the Buddhist doctrine of Sunyata are quite different from that of Nirguna Brahman, they do have much in common. Both are reaching out for that doctrine of pure simplicity which is the primary and essential mark of the absolute and final reality.

Ramanuja. After Shankara, five major divisions developed within the Vedanta tradition: (1) the non-dualism of Shankara himself; (2) the qualified non-dualism of Ramanuja; (3) neither dualism nor non-dualism of Nimbarka; (4) the dualism of Madhva; (5) the pure non-dualism of Vallabha. In all of these the Vedanta thought tradition shows itself as one of the most subtle of traditions that have investigated the nature of absolute reality and its relation with the phenomenal world. Two of these are by far the most significant, the non-dualism of Shankara and the qualified non-dualism of Ramanuja.

Ramanuja (1050–1137) came from southern India, from the Tamil region. As successor to the Vaishnava tradition of the *Alvars* and of such earlier theologians of Vaishnavism as Acharya Yamuna (918–1038), he brought the entire range of thought to a new status. Well-grounded in Upanishadic studies, he knew the Vedanta Sutras, the Puranas, and the religious works of the saints. He was also a thorough student and vigorous opponent of Shankara's thought.

Ramanuja's theistic orientation is the most important aspect of his thought. In this manner he challenges Shankara for the dominant position in the religious thought of India. The thought of Shankara is theologically more impressive and has greater speculative thrust and consistency. If in some ways Ramanuja enters into the devotional tradition more effectively, Shankara is more universal, for he did not establish his thought within any of the sectarian traditions. Ramanuja was a devoted member of the community committed to the worship of Vishnu, whom Ramanuja identified with the ancient Brahman concept of the Upanishads, in much the same way that the Christian Fathers associated the Greek concept of Being with the God Yahweh of Biblical descent. This process involved the modification of both concepts, but the result was extremely significant in the history of these thought traditions. This was the first time in the Hindu tradition that the theistic development attained this height of expression. Ample basis for this development exists in the later Upanishads, in the *Bhagavad-Gita*, and in the Puranas, but this entire tradition attained scholastic expression and academic status through Ramanuja's work. Devotional enthusiasm was supported with a superior theology. Ramanuja was able to assert that the personal, theistic devotion of the *Alvars* was in accord with the Upanishadic tradition and the *Bhagavad-Gita* and was therefore within the range of traditional Hindu orthodoxy.

This synthesis of Ramanuja was also a comprehensive approach to the Hindu tradition as it existed. He emphasized more than Shankara the ritual obligations, the basic carrying out of external religious duties, of worship, of fasting, of recitation of the Vedas. Thus he was much more in accord with the religious and spiritual needs of the people, much more earthly, more human in his approach. While Shankara had refused to associate his theology with any definite Hindu sect, Ramanuja associated his theology directly with the Vaishnava tradition. This strengthening of the tradition in the twelfth century was one of the forces that led to the eventual ascendancy of Vishnu worship over Shiva worship in most of India.

The three major elements of the tradition came together in Ramanuja: the Puranas, the Hymns, and the scholastic tradition. In this general context the central scripture of the Vaishnava tradition, the *Bhagavata Purana*, had been composed, most likely in the tenth century. Both Ramanuja and the *Bhagavata Purana* assisted in bringing together into a powerful synthesis the major elements of the larger Vaishnava tradition. The greatest single contribution of the *Bhagavata Purana* was the story of Krishna and his devotion to the milkmaids, especially to Radha, contained in the tenth book of this work. Here the story of human love is used to express the intimacy and intensity of the divine-human love relation, with the divine person assuming the role of the supreme lover. From this time onward expression of the love of God in the most intimate terms of affection was unrestrained in the Vaishnava tradition. With the support of this Purana and the theology of Ramanuja, the permanent foundations of the Hindu tradition of mystical love were established.

Chapter Five

Decline and Revival

After the time of Ramanuja, India was gradually invaded by the Islamic peoples. This period of new developments is known as the medieval period of India. The new Hinduism of the Puranas and the theologians, sectarian Hinduism, had been established along with a new richness of Hindu mythology which had assimilated much from the local religious cults. A synthesis of all this has been constantly taking place in India—a vast interchange between the highest intellectual achievements and the most primitive thought and devotion of local cults. These had influenced each other from the beginning. But several changes were about to occur; for one thing, a period of political differentiation within India was to develop. Local kingdoms came into existence in these years and were established as political centers in much the same way that the various states of Europe were established as integral political units after the year A.D. 1000. This led to the prospering of local cults and to royal patronage of the various deities. Some of the finest temples of India were constructed during this period.

Of direct spiritual significance a number of extremely important things were happening after the year 1000. Buddhism had declined to such a degree that it was hardly an important element in the spiritual life of India any longer. Main cause of this decline was the restoration and revitalization of Hinduism, which absorbed many aspects of Buddhism into its own life. Some of the highest attainments of Buddhist thought were brought into the Vedanta tradition. Personal devotion to Buddha was replaced by the new devotion to Krishna as an incarnation of Vishnu. An even greater element is the fact that Hinduism had a complete life program, whereas Buddhism in India never did have one. Furthermore, it had no adequate social or sacramental forms. Hinduism provided the rituals according to which a person was initiated into the higher life of the society: the rituals for daily conduct were Hindu; the marriage ceremony and all the customs concerning the carrying out of married life were Hindu; burial ceremonies were Hindu. Indeed, the entire social structure of India remained dominated by Hinduism. To be Buddhist purely and simply was not possible except to those who led the homeless life of the mendicants or who joined a Buddhist monastic community. At this time also the scriptural writings of Buddhism were taken out of India to China and Tibet and to other parts of Asia, many into the region of Nepal. In these regions the manuscripts were preserved, translated, and studied, while Buddhist life was declining in India after the sixth century.

As Hinduism was advancing and Buddhism was declining Islam began to enter India. At first this was not a complete conquest; rather, it was a type of infiltration that went on for centuries with border incursions and gradual penetration into the northern part of India. By the sixteenth century, the great power of Islam over India was completed by the Mogul dynasty that came to rule over much of India both North and South. India under the Moguls was as unified as it had been at any time since the time of Asoka and his rule in the third century B.C. Hindu life continued, but the religious attitude of the invaders brought about much destruction of religious edifices. Buddhist centers underwent a destruction from which Buddhism never recovered. The destruction of Hindu temples in the North is beyond estimation, although there was never any systematic effort to demolish all temples. Yet the iconoclasm of the Islamic peoples and their effort to do away with idolatry ruined many noble temples and their sculptured images.

There was, however, one area in which the Hindu and the Muslim could meet: the plane of the mystical intuition of the Absolute. The Sufi in Islam, especially in the Persian world, had developed an extraordinary attraction toward the vision of God in his absolute simplicity, in the state of his complete ineffability to human understanding. This awareness of the divine world was accompanied with an intense devotion, all within a mono-theistic context. The Sufi orders came to India from Persia and from Iraq where they had flourished for several centuries. The high period for their arrival in India is in the thirteenth, fourteenth, and fifteenth centuries. As the saints of Islam and the saints of Hinduism came to appreciate and to influence each other, a new religious group was created which became known as the Sikhs, in which the finer aspects of each tradition came to expression in the beautiful language of Urdu, a Persianized form of Hindi. The highest product of this meeting of Hindu and Sufi mystics is found in Kabir (1440–1518), a saint of Hinduism strongly influenced by the mystical conceptions of the Sufi and by the Hindu saints Jnanadeva and Namadeva. A firm monotheism combined with an intensity of devotion is found in both the Sufi and the Hindu saints.

At the court of Akbar in the sixteenth century a serious effort was made toward a mutual understanding and appreciation of Hinduism, Zoroastrian-ism, Christianity, and Islam. Formal discussions concerning these religions and their differences and the problems of reconciliation were held under the royal auspices of Akbar. The Jesuits arrived in India from the West during this period and provided the Christian contribution to these discussions.

The Portuguese, who began to arrive in India during the sixteenth cen-tury, found Christian communities that had existed since the fourteenth century on the southwest coast. The Portuguese were followed by the French and the British. Throughout the seventeenth century the entire country of India was caught up in the European quest for empire. In 1758, the British defeated the French in the eastern part of the country. From that time the British were the most powerful political force within India.

Meanwhile a general decline had begun in the native life of India. By the end of the eighteenth century, India had reached a low point in its cul-tural and spiritual life. Changes had taken place too rapidly. There was too much to assimilate, too much in every aspect of life, but especially in the spiritual order. This led eventually to a general deterioration in the social and intellectual orders also. There was at this time an increased growth of undesirable religious practices. The Abbé J. A. Dubois (1765–1848), a French priest, lived in India from 1792 until 1823. He made systematic studies of the native life and customs during this period and wrote his ac-count in a book entitled, *Hindu Manners, Customs, and Ceremonies*. There can be seen the extent to which widow-burning and child-marriage were practiced, the evils that arose from the caste system, the aberrations associated with religious observances, the decline of learning, and the low status of women. While all this can be and often is exaggerated, the reality of the decline in India at this period is recognized by all acquainted with the history of India.

One of the principal causes was undoubtedly the long period of foreign rule of the country which had been occupied at least in part since the year A.D. 1000. Another cause was the rise of unforeseen and disastrous consequences from social customs that were originally of great social benefit and inspired often by the highest spiritual motives. But the deepest cause was undoubtedly the lack in India of sufficient concern for the material, social, historical, and rational elements in human life in favor of a "higher" religious-spiritual experience. It is regrettable that contact with the West was not as helpful as it could have been, at least not until the nineteenth century. The re-creation of India in the nineteenth and twentieth centuries is an amazing story of extreme benefits and of disruptive impositions from the West. But the marvel is that India was able to manage a new spiritual, intellectual, and social adjustment to life that set her on the path of a new creative era. The story of modern India is the story of how this was brought about.

TRANSFORMATION AND RENEWAL

The dynamic element that finally initiated an effective reform movement came from the Protestant missionaries. Neither the Catholic missions of the sixteenth and later centuries nor the British political occupation produced any decisive social changes within India. The British did establish certain economic reforms and new judicial procedures, but they made no effort to alter existing practices in the customary religious life of the country. The Catholic missions had settled into a fixed status and had nothing significant to offer in this regard. The Protestant missionaries, themselves influenced by the new social and humanitarian ideals of life as they were found in the movements of nineteenth-century Europe, were disturbed by the prevailing customs of India and set about religious and humanitarian reform movements. This they did by influences brought to bear on British administrators and by educational programs initiated for the Indian people.

The first of these men from the West to achieve much in this manner was William Carey (1761–1834), an English Baptist who established himself in the region near Calcutta. He was the first to cut type for the Devanagari script and to begin modern printing in India. He was also the first to begin new educational programs on a serious scale. Carey and the men associated with him had a special abhorrence for childhood marriage and for the practice of burning the widow on the funeral pyre of her husband, whether voluntary or involuntary. The missionaries also strongly advocated the remarriage of widows, for one of the great afflictions of Indian women was the prohibition against remarriage even when the husband had died while the wife was still very young. Through their efforts, laws were passed prohibiting childhood marriage, the burning of widows, and other of the unreasonable practices common at the time. Many of these customs derived from very noble religious intentions and were undoubtedly, from a religious point of view, extremely meritorious for those performing them. But India, with its tendency to press things to their extremes, whether speculative or practical, had entered into extremes that needed correction.

Soon Indian leaders appeared who themselves led the drive for reform, leaders with extraordinary ability to guide India in this time of difficulty. Ram Mohan Roy (1772–1833), father of modern India, led the renewal of Indian life by his rejection of all forms of idolatry, by his efforts at the reeducation of the people, by his opposition to the burning of widows and to child-marriage, and by his sponsoring of the English language as a necessary medium for India to become acquainted with the world at large. Although Ram Mohan Roy did not accept the divinity of Christ, he was strongly attracted to the personality of Christ and to his moral and spiritual teaching. The thinking of Ram Mohan Roy was profoundly transformed by his contact with the West both in its Christian aspect and by its more recent humanitarian developments—benefits he wished to bring to India. He had a profound sense of what was needed by India. In order to insure that his work be carried on during his own lifetime and after his death, he founded a society that became a powerful force of renewal in India, the Society of God (*Brahma Samaj*). A central force in the intellectual, spiritual, and social life of India throughout the nineteenth century, this society produced leaders with a broader spiritual vision and a more intense social concern than had hitherto existed in the country.

Ram Mohan Roy was the first Indian in modern times to leave India to visit the West with the expectation of returning to India. He went to England to inform the people and government there of the real needs of India. Although he died before he could return, he had already established in Bengal, in the northeastern section of India, the main center from which the modernization of India would spread throughout the country. The saying became popular that what Bengal does today, all India will do tomorrow. If this was to some extent true it is due above all to the work of Ram Mohan Roy.

One of the greatest successors to Roy was Keshub Chunder Sen (1838–1884), also from Bengal, a person of extraordinary ability who was particularly fortunate in learning English while still quite young. He read and spoke English with rare fluency and thus became one of the most capable Indians in understanding and appreciating the Western world and its literature, its thought, and its religious heritage. He understood Christianity better than any of his contemporaries. Severely critical of existing Hindu practices, Keshub pressed hard for such reforms as the remarriage of widows and the abolition of child-marriage. He was an eloquent speaker who carried his religious and social thought to the people in a most impressive way. He had all the religious fervor of the medieval saints along with a range of learning and social consciousness of exceptional depth. He was a flaming figure in the India of his day. Through the use of English, which was now becoming the national language of India, Keshub was able to bring the thought of the Brahma Samaj to other parts of India, especially to the distant regions of the western coast, and to its major city, Bombay.

Keshub achieved much in his life, but the supreme spiritual contribution was the vision he set forth of unity of the religions of the world. He recognized with the genius of spiritual insight that the religious life of mankind must come to an ultimate reconciliation in which all the religions of the world would contribute mutually to the development of each other and to the higher religious life of mankind on a universal scale. He saw particularly the universal aspect of the Christian revelation, the manner in which this could be communicated to the other cultures of the world, without extinguishing but developing these cultures in a new bond of intercommunion. This vision of the spiritual unification of mankind had many exponents in India but none so clearly presented or so fruitful in its prospects as that presented by Keshub. His vision has as yet not been fully appreciated, but in the larger history of the spiritual development of mankind in the modern world the contribution of Keshub will have its permanent place.

Because Ram Mohan Roy and Keshub Chunder Sen were so critical of Hinduism and so strongly influenced by Western religion a strong reaction occurred in favor of Hinduism and for the recovery of the authentic and undistorted tradition of Hinduism as this had existed at an earlier period. This came with Dyanand Sarasvati (1824–1883), a person of strong disposition who can be credited with reasserting the strength and effectiveness

of the Vedic revelation in the midst of the new social and spiritual adjustment taking place in Indian life. He saw that many of the abuses in the
human and religious order of India were later distortions not due to the
original foundations of religion in India but to deviations that came when
the original genius of Hinduism had been weakened. The great need then
was not the abandonment of the traditional religion but its renewal and
purification. This should be done by return to the Vedas rather than by
seeking solutions imported from other cultures. By the return to the Vedas,
Dyanand meant return to the Vedic Hymns, the very earliest expression
of Hinduism.

Dyanand established in India a religious nationalism. In this manner he
awakened India to its own special genius and threw the country back on its
own resources. This was of inestimable value in establishing the foundations
of the New India that was awaiting its moment of self-assertion. Dyanand
was especially successful in northern India. In the Punjab region he established a tradition that has been carried through until the present day in
the reeducation of the people. To carry on his work Dyanand established
a new society, *Arya Samaj* (the Society of Noble Persons). This title
could also be translated as the "Society of the True Indians," meaning the
Aryans. It is important to note that Dyanand was the first of the great
reformers of India to be born outside Bengal. He belonged to a Brahman
family from the region of Gujarat, on the opposite side of India, a region
of greater sternness of disposition than that generally found in Bengal,
which is known for the lyrical and soft disposition of its people. Dyanand
had a fierce type of asceticism that marked his movement and his work. He
awakened India to itself as Ram Mohan Roy and Keshub Chunder Sen
had awakened India to the world.

In the last half of the nineteenth century, India produced one of its most
outstanding saints, Sri Ramakrishna (1836–1886). A Bengalese with little
education, he showed from his earliest years an extremely sensitive religious
soul. At nineteen he became priest at a temple dedicated to Kali near
Calcutta. There he lived an ecstatic life, performing extraordinary penances
and in almost constant prayer to God. With extraordinary visionary capacity, he saw divine reality shining forth everywhere in great splendor. Any
beautiful sight was sufficient to evoke in him the overwhelming awareness
of the devine presence. During his later years he was a spiritual guide for
many people who came to consult him. The guidance that he offered was
noted down by one of his followers and later published as *The Gospel of
Sri Ramakrishna;* he, himself, could neither read nor write. His spiritual

teachings were simple, pure, and noble; and he was all his life a devout, ecstatic, yet simple, prayerful person. Although he founded no organization he became after his death the spiritual inspiration of a movement that has spread throughout India and through much of the West. One of his great concerns was for the religious unity of mankind. Toward this end he sought an experiential understanding of all the higher religions with which he was acquainted. He had a deep appreciation of both Islam and Christianity. He had difficulty, however, with the excessive consciousness of sin that he found in many Christians. Often he pointed to the need for a more confident relationship with God to the forgetfulness of a person's self. He taught especially that God dwells in all things and can be found everywhere if only one responds to the divine presence that is there. Vividly aware of the need for divine grace, he insisted that all one's strength is from God.

It was through his follower, Swami Vivekananda (1863–1902), that Ramakrishna became known to the West. A fervent disciple of Ramakrishna Vivekananda dedicated his entire life to spreading the simple teaching of his Master, much as Plato sought to spread the teachings of Socrates. Vivekananda was the first Indian to teach Hinduism in any extensive way outside of India. At the first Parliament of Religions that was held at the Columbian Exposition in Chicago in 1893, he made a sensational impact on his audience by the spiritual vision he presented. Since Western religious movements had turned toward humanitarian preoccupations, the pure spiritual vision of the divine offered by Vivekananda provided something that was otherwise missing at this meeting of representatives of the religions of mankind. Through Vivekananda, the world became aware that India was profoundly alive and spiritually creative and that its religious heritage was capable of meeting and dealing with the intellectual and social challenges of the modern world.

Swami Vivekananda was well educated, read much of the Western thinkers, and appreciated much of the Western achievement, especially in the social order, but he found the West grown too materialistic and in need of a spirituality which India could offer and was offering to the world. Vivekananda is largely responsible for the widely accepted view that the West is materialistic, and India spiritual, and that they need each other and complement each other precisely for this reason. He had much less appreciation than Keshub had for the high spiritual aspect of Western Christianity. The great work of Vivekananda in India was to establish the need for social reform on a spiritual basis. He was constantly teaching that true spirituality could not exist without concern for the basic problems of living and helping the indigent. In this way he was a great help in taking the mind of India away from its preoccupation with the absolute and giving to religion a function in the human social order. He founded the Rama-krishna movement which is responsible for setting up many monasteries throughout India.

In bringing India from the nineteenth into the twentieth century there are three men of outstanding significance: Tagore, Aurobindo, and Gandhi. Tagore belongs primarily to the world of literature and culture; Aurobindo, to the world of the spiritual and intellectual; Gandhi, to the world of the social and political. The life span of these three were very close. Tagore was born in 1861, Gandhi in 1869, Aurobindo in 1872. All three lived up to the mid-twentieth century. Tagore died in 1941, Gandhi in 1948, Aurobindo in 1950. All three were powerful personalities, all have gained world recognition, all were inspired in their work by the spiritual traditions of India, all were highly educated in Western intellectual and cultural traditions, and all have left a heritage that has increased and expanded since their deaths.

Rabindranath Tagore (1861–1941), winner of the Nobel prize in litera-ture in the year 1917, was a highly literate and cultured personality. He composed lyric poems that are still sung in Bengal; he also did a sizable amount of painting. Both have an intensive religious aspect, for the ancient vision and inner experience of Hinduism is found in all his work. Yet it has a modern ring that makes him one of the bridges from the ancient world of Hinduism to the modern world. If Ramakrishna is the saint of modern India, Tagore is the one who brought India and its spirituality into the realm of world literature, especially through the collection of his English poems entitled *Gitanjali* (1912), the collection that merited for him a Nobel award. Tagore had universal interests in the arts, in education, in religious thought, and especially in the international brotherhood of man. He traveled widely and became an apostle of peace among the nations, on which subject he wrote and lectured in both Europe and America, and also carried his concern for peace to China. An admirer of Gandhi, he bestowed upon him the title "Great Soul" (*Mahatma*), even though at a later period he disagreed sharply with some aspects of Gandhi's program.

The outstanding theological thinker of modern India might very well be Aurobindo Ghose (1872–1950), a person of exceptional spiritual and intellectual gifts. Born in Calcutta, he was given a completely Western education from his earliest school days. While quite young, only seven years of age, he was sent to England for his education. There he remained for fourteen years, when after studying Western classics and graduating from Cambridge with a brilliant record, he returned to India. For some years he was a political activist in Bengal, a leader of the extremist faction seeking immediate independence from England, until 1907, when he determined to give up all active political life and to devote his life to the quest for spiritual insight. He retired to a place near Pondicherry where he established an *Ashram* and remained there until his death in 1950. He undertook the traditional spiritual discipline of India, studied the scriptural and theological writings of Hinduism, especially the ancient Vedic Hymns and the Upanishads, and became fully transformed into a Hindu contemplative and an exponent of the spiritual vision of Hinduism. Of modern Yogins he is the most outstanding for his intellectual capacities to set forth the vision of reality that is attained by this experiential contact with the world of the transphenomenal. During his years at Pondicherry he wrote considerably, especially in his early years there, works that might be considered among the most significant theological writings to emerge from India in modern times. Foremost among these writings is his work, *The Life Divine*, which is the basic synthesis of his thought. There are also his writings on the practice of yoga and his commentary on the *Bhagavad-Gita*. The great achievement of Aurobindo was to establish from Hindu spiritual writings a basis for interpreting the world of matter, of time, of man. These areas were never properly developed in the Hindu tradition. Aurobindo has thus supplied out of an authentic Hindu experience a spiritual vision of life, of matter, of time, and of change. Of particular importance is his exposition of developmental time and the manner in which a spiritual transformation of matter and of man is taking place that is leading to an ultimate fulfillment in God.

There is, finally, Mahatma Gandhi (1869–1948), a unique personality in the modern world. He made a supreme effort to bring spiritual vision into the practical functioning of man's political and social life. The central object of his concern was the spiritual rectification of society and social order. He lived in a period when the two great revolutions of modern times were in full development: the nationalist revolution of colonial peoples against imperial Western dominance and the social revolution of the depressed peoples within society against the higher social and economic groups with almost exclusive enjoyment of the economic, cultural, and even spiritual benefits produced by the society. He saw the need of accomplishing revolutionary ends within a spiritual context, with spiritual motivations, and spiritual ends. Thus he evolved a program of passive, peaceful resistance based on inner spiritual strength, a way that would strengthen the human qualities of life rather than foster inhuman ways of revolt that would in the end lead toward a new stage of savage conflict between nations and within nations, rather than toward a human reconciliation of all nations and all sections of society.

He achieved a large amount of success in his work because of the essentially spiritual character of India's traditional way of life. In India religion and spirituality have never been separated from life. Alienation of the spiritual from the other aspects of life destroys the inner substance of man's existence. All phases of life in India are manifestations of the spiritual, not deviations from the spiritual. But while the work of Gandhi is the fulfillment of Indian spiritual traditions, it is also in many ways the fulfillment of Western spiritual traditions. Much of Gandhi's inspiration was derived from his contact with the West, from Christ and the Gospels, from the social and humanitarian movements of the nineteenth and twentieth centuries, and from the Western sense of the human person and the administration of justice. There is especially the example of Thoreau, whose passive resistance to political authority pointed the way for some of Gandhi's methods. The sources of his thought and his spiritual insight were the traditions of spiritual universalism set forth by Keshub Chunder Sen and by Ramakrishna, a tradition that is strong in India to this very day.

Part Two:

Yoga

Chapter Six

Origin and Orientation

Yoga is a spirituality rather than a religion. As a spirituality it has influenced the entire range of Indian religious and spiritual development. In the ninth century Vacaspatimishra, one of the outstanding writers of the Yoga tradition, noted: "Everyone recognizes from revelation and tradition, from the epics and puranas, that mental contemplation (Yoga) is the guide to perfect bliss" (*Commentary on Vyasa*, Yoga Sutra, I, 1). Yoga has become intimately associated with both Hinduism and Buddhism. In a specific and technical sense, Yoga is counted as one of the six thought systems of Hinduism. Yet before studying Yoga in this specific sense it is important to consider Yoga as an all-pervading element of Indian spirituality.

Although Yoga is considered an inner discipline associated with special techniques of spiritual development leading to man's release from the bonds of the phenomenal order, there is a great variety of Yogic practices in India. There are the practices associated especially with the classical Hindu quest for intuitive vision, with Buddhism and Jainism, and with the devotional cults. Yogic practices have been associated with the finest

75

heights of Indian spirituality and with its lowest, least attractive forms. The objective of all these, however, is clear; it is a conscious, studied, sustained effort at so disciplining man's body and mind that the inner self of man (Purusha) is released from time into eternity, from the conditioned world into the realm of the unconditioned, from multiplicity into unity. As with the other aspects of India's religious and spiritual development, one can say that Yoga seeks the transition from the unreal to the real, from darkness to light, from death to immortality. Yet Yoga does not ask, as does Hinduism, to be "led" to this. It assumes the capacity of man to attain this and merely illumines the principles and directs the techniques whereby this is attained with personal effort.

The Yogic practices originated in the primordial depths of India's past. From this early period the inner attitudes and disciplines which were later identified and given orderly expression by Patanjali in the second century B.C. were powerfully at work throughout Indian history. There is evidence that Yogic practices were already functioning in the Indus Valley civilizations prior to the arrival of the Aryan peoples who came into India some time after 2000 B.C. This can be seen in the statuettes that have been recovered from archaeological sites in this region. One of them is a figure seated in the Lotus Posture with legs folded over each other, just as the Yogins of India have sat for some four thousand years, a figure apparently of a deity shown in the fullness of his power and in his total absorption in the blissful state of his own self-luminous being.

As a spirituality, Yoga is intensely concerned with the human condition, how man is to manage the human condition, to sustain his spiritual reality in the midst of life's turmoil, and to discipline his inner awareness until he attains liberation. Judging from its spiritual efficacy Yoga can be considered among the most intensely felt and highly developed of those spiritual disciplines that enable man to cope with the tragic aspects of life. The native traditions of India are all highly sensitized to the sorrows inherent in the world of time and the need to pass beyond these sorrows. Hinduism sought relief in the experience of an absolute reality beyond the phenomenal order. Buddhism was drawn to the Nirvana experience which effected a total extinction of the forms of experience available to man in the empirical order, even by the extinction of his own self-structure, his own capacity to say as a particular individual, "I am." Yoga, sustaining the existence of the Purusha (the inner spiritual reality of man), sought a discipline by which this principle would be released from the confinements caused by its contact with the world of time. This world of phenomena includes the realm of both matter and mind. Mind is not identified with the spiritual principle, the Purusha, but with the opposed principle, Prakriti. The Purusha is not mind but pure consciousness.

There are a number of terms that need to be distinguished. *Manas*, which refers to the psychic coordinating faculty of the senses, may be translated as "lower mind," or as "central organ." The individual subjective awareness of phenomenal existence, the phenomenal "I am," is the *ahamkara*. Above this is the thought instrument, the *buddhi*, called most often in Yoga, *cittam* (thought faculty). The term "Purusha," the highest spiritual reality, is most often translated as "pure consciousness." This pure consciousness is the Self, the Seer, the one who beholds all that goes on but is beheld by none. He is the unexperienced experiencer. He is not an object of knowledge or of the action of anyone or anything. This is the ineffable, the self-luminous reality which radiates light into the world but which is illumined by nothing in the world. The thought instrument (*buddhi*), also termed the "higher mind," is used by the supreme self (Purusha) as the principal instrument of knowing. Within man this Self tends to be confused with the activity of its instrument (*buddhi*) and the other operative psychic faculties. This is the cause of the pain, confusion, the frustration of life. The whole purpose of Yoga is to provide the specific disciplines and techniques of inner control whereby liberation of this spiritual reality from its confinement is brought about. Therein lies its most distinctive contribution to Indian spirituality. It was with the aid of Yoga that Hinduism and Buddhism established their own spiritual techniques whereby salvation was achieved. Buddhism is particularly indebted to the Yoga tradition for providing its basic mental discipline. Even though the philosophical orientation of Buddhism is entirely different from the philosophical orientation of Yoga, the two traditions agree in their basic effort at inwardness, at mental purification that brings about a liberating experience. For Yoga, liberation is the disengagement of the Purusha, the inner spirit of man, from its seeming contact with the phenomenal order. For Buddhism, it is a pure experience of transcendence in which there is no subjective experiencer.

Although Yoga aims at a liberation of man into the realms of the infinite and unconditioned, it also enables man to function more efficaciously in the realms of the finite and the conditioned. Yoga strengthens both the mental and physical powers of man. It provides an endurance, a capacity for total allocation of energies. It gives to man extraordinary control over himself so that he is neither distracted nor enervated by what he does.

Because of this new mastery of life, pain and tension are easily endured. These are attainments that man is constantly seeking, and to this Yoga has made a sizable contribution. Yet this strengthening is achieved by a spiritual discipline that is thoroughly individualistic. The subjective personality receives exclusive attention. For this reason the Western man who is objectively, socially, and historically oriented often finds Yoga more difficult to understand than Hinduism or Buddhism.

The entire effort of Yoga can be described as an inward movement leading to enstasis, rather than an outward movement leading to ecstasis. Western religious tradition is committed basically to ecstatic termination of the salvation process. Yet in the final analysis it may be that the end attained in both Yoga and in the West is by an experience that is both enstatic and ecstatic and beyond both. It is certain that the traditional religious man in the West cannot live spiritually without God. Only in a divine-human confrontation and communion does he find his true self. His dominant quest for ecstatic rather than enstatic discovery of God is supported by the strong element of anthropomorphism in Western religious literature. This has conditioned his imaginative powers, his conceptual processes, and his emotional responses, which makes it difficult, even impossible, to undertake the severe inner discipline of concentration and the breathing techniques employed by Yoga to attain its ends. This is not to say that there is no inwardness in the Western tradition. Spiritual personalities in the West have been profoundly aware of the need to pass, in inner recollection, beyond imagination and all conceptual processes into the divine darkness if they would truly know God. The inner trials, the passing beyond mind and emotion require not only a rare type of spiritual courage but also a willingness to experience a certain alienation from life, from social communication, from the structure of one's own being. Thus, inward experience is known in the West as well as in India; but in the end, Western spiritual disciplines have a human moderation, a greater willingness to retain the emotional, the imaginative, the conceptual, the social, than is found in the Yoga-influenced traditions of India, which consider active involvement in these aspects of life as hindrances to the liberation process.

One must remember, however, that in the background of Yoga there is the larger tradition of India with its religious and spiritual mythology. This mythology is as anthropomorphic as that of any religious tradition. The emotional and imaginative expressions of religious experience are kept and highly developed in the theistic cults of both the Shaivite and Vaishnava.

The temple worship of these devotional traditions of Hinduism are even more anthropomorphic than the worship of the other higher religions of the Eurasian world. Along with this there is a general warmth of affection for life in its every form that can be seen in the literature and in the visual arts of India. But even though these depict the splendor of earth in all its delightful qualities, there is still in India a feeling of frustration with the visible world, a feeling that man must pass beyond it. Beauty itself, recognized as such, becomes painful in the world of time, which destroys all things.

This constitutes the ambivalence of the Indian experience, the tension in the Indian attitude toward the natural world. There is an appreciation, an attraction, a response to the natural world that surpasses at times the response of naturalism and romanticism in the West. But this is offset, and, to some extent even negated, by awareness of the inherent limitations, the thinness, the fragility, the evanescent quality of all things subject to time and change. Thus there is a constant movement in India toward withdrawal from all sense, imaginative, and mental experience into a state of pure inwardness, in which man is either identified with Brahman, lost in the Nirvana experience, or established in the Yogic state of perfect freedom known as *Kaivalya*. Only here, in his transearthly experience, does India find its true release from the agonies of time. Though fascinated with the splendor of the world, traditional India, with its special sensitivity, finds life on the human plane too restricted, too painful, too confused. The human condition, unacceptable, must be transcended. Yet this pain, this emptiness in man's experience of temporal existence, is its most valuable element. It teaches man to pass on to a higher experience. Relentlessly it drives man, forces him to seek a transearthly, transtemporal, transhuman salvation. This is the cause of the highest human and spiritual achievement of India. It is also the cause of the extravagance and inadequacies in India's life formation and life attitude. It gives great ability to cope with life spiritually, but it often results in an inability to manage the earthly aspects of life.

As a consequence of these opposed attractions, in India extreme sensuality and extreme asceticism exist together—pure sense delight on the one hand, puritanism on the other. These evoke and intensify each other to extreme and at times tragic dimensions. The constant preoccupation with morality is seen in the story tradition of India. This beautiful literature is often interrupted and frequently spoiled by insertion of moral lessons that are explicitly drawn for the reader. These opposed tendencies constitute one of the principal characteristics of Indian human and cultural development. Each tendency finds extreme expression, but each is somehow balanced by its opposite. Thus the need to see India as a whole. Were a person to consider merely the erotic approach to spirituality depicted in some of the temples of India, he would conclude that India was totally given to sensuality even at the heart of its entire religious and spiritual experience. Were he to take the severity of asceticism taught and practiced throughout Indian history, he might conclude that India has no sense of life or love or beauty. These opposites are found even within such particular traditions as Buddhism. In Buddhist literature there is an extreme effort at alienation from the natural world and man's sense awareness, yet in the art from Sanchi, Amaravati, and Ajanta there is extraordinary joy, freedom, appreciation, and immersion in the natural and the human in all their gorgeous aspects.

Yoga belongs basically to the ascetic, disciplined, solitary, meditative tradition of India. Yet a person studying Yoga must be aware that it is part of the larger whole of Indian life, learning, and spirituality. Yoga does not intend to supply for India what is supplied by Hinduism, which is simultaneously a religion, a spirituality, a humanistic culture, and a social structure. Yoga is purely and simply a spirituality. Taken in itself it has all the rigor of the ascetic practices of early Christian hermits and monks with little of the larger human attractions that are found in Buddhism and Hinduism. But when Yoga is considered as part of the larger complex of India's spiritual and human development it is appreciated more fully as part of a rich complex of human development. Its lack of social concerns is understandable, for Yoga supposes the social structure of life provided by Hinduism. Neither Yoga nor Buddhism could exist without the basic context for all Indian traditions. Thus Yoga should not be considered in isolation from its larger context. In the end it is seen to have considerably enriched the social and religious life of India even though it seems to have neglected both these aspects of life.

What Yoga proposed was a technique of spiritual development that would enable man to discover his true nature on a higher plane of existence wherein he would attain freedom from the restrictive forces that bound him to the world and to the psychosomatic structure of his own being. Yoga thus seeks to "decondition" man, to remove the limitations imposed upon him both from without and from within, both from the structure of the cosmos and from the structure of his own being. For India, disengagement from the surrounding external world was simple. The real problem was disengagement from the inner determinations of man's own reality. This required the restraint of the latent forces deep within the subconscious depths of man. It also required removal of the impression of past deeds *(vasanas)*, which bind the spiritual man to the phenomenal world in a profound manner. Dealing with these forces is especially difficult, for they lie so fixed within human nature that man has only a dim awareness of their existence even though they are exercising extensive control over his life. This deconditioning of man, this profound alteration of the terrestrial context of his existence, involves what might also be called a dehumanization of man, a dehumanization, however, viewed not as deterioration but as integration and elevation into a higher state of being, a state that is truly human, for the present "human" status of man is in reality not human. To become human in any adequate sense requires man's release from the tragic binding forces that make his present life so cruel and oppressive. As in the other Indian traditions, Yoga was aware that the total change required in the spiritualization of man must be taken seriously. It is not a slight modification or purification. It is radical renewal, even radical suppression of phenomenal life, in favor of a transphenomenal experience in which man finally comes to himself in his real human identity.

Chapter Seven

The Problem of Alienation

As with Buddhism and the other traditions of India, Yoga begins with the experience of sorrow (*dukkha*). This is the given, the point of departure, the basic, irrefutable fact of human existence, that which makes supposedly human life inhuman. In this elemental experience of sorrow, of pain and tensions of life, is the basis on which the higher religious traditions of Eurasia proceed in constructing their salvation programs. In western Eurasia, the opening passages of Genesis tell of the creation of things. Then, immediately afterward, there is an account of the way sorrow entered the world. This was a cataclysmic event which profoundly dehumanized man and disoriented the entire cosmic order. Ever since, the existing order has been "groaning for its deliverance." Man has the task of a radical readjustment of life. In some sense this task is that of a counterdestruction, the shattering or suppression of a distorted world and the reestablishment of an ordered normal world, the reconstitution of cosmos out of chaos. If the existing world is the ordered, normal, real world, then this effort at remedy must be considered supremely inhuman. But if this existing world is distorted and abnormal, then the effort at remedy must appear as supremely human.

Furthermore, in the West alienation is seen as an alienation from God through a moral misdeed on the part of man, an alienation that, in Christianity, is overcome by the incarnation and redemption accomplished by a divine person, entering into historical time, who also produces the new man. There are two distinctive aspects that might be noted here concerning the Christian problem of alienation and reunification. First the alienation is associated with a sense of moral guilt which is not found in India or in East Asia. Thus Western man is profoundly concerned with forgiveness, a forgiveness that brings about in man a restructuring and even a recreation of his inner being, a spiritual rebirth. But this very emphasis on man's becoming a new creature shows that Western man basically accepts a structured, limited, conditioned being even in his status of salvation. He does not, apparently, seek the experience of total deconditioning such as this is sought in India. The second distinctive aspect of the Western salvation problem is that the alienation is seen to have affected man as a community. Therefore the restoration of man must take place as a community of the redeemed. There is in the West no purely personal salvation, even though personal responsibility and personal effort are strongly emphasized. The interrelationships of the members of the community are a part of the redemptive program itself. This, too, is something different from the usual Indian way of salvation, which is severely individualistic.

In Hinduism the primary problem is seen in more ontological and gnoseological terms. It is seen to be the alienation of the phenomenal world of Samsara from the world of Atman, the true Self of all things. This alienation involves a disorientation and confusion of man's perception of the surrounding world and of his own being. In this state of misunderstanding and alienation nothing has true reality. All is illusory, all is the result of ignorance. This alienation is overcome by true knowledge in Upanishadic Hinduism, by a love relation in the *Bhagavad-Gita* and in the later theistic cults of India. In Upanishadic Hinduism the salvation is strictly individual even though the sacred scriptures are handed down through a community process and even though there is extensive dependence on the spiritual guidance of a teacher, a Guru. While a person must fulfill his Dharma (the duties of his state in life), this is merely a condition for his personal salvation; it does not enter into the salvation experience itself. The saving wisdom attained leads a person to break the bonds of ignorance holding him within the phenomenal order and to attain release into Brahman, in which reality he is immersed and even absorbed as a drop of water into the great ocean. Social and community bonds constitute a part of the alienation that must be overcome to attain this higher experience. The ideal solution of the devotional cults is expressed in terms of the Bhagavad-Gita: "Those who worship me with devotion; they are in me and I in them" (IX, 29). This expression is lived out by the saints of later Hinduism with an intensity, sensitivity, generosity, and mutual self-giving of such amazing proportions that it frequently evokes an attitude of surprise in Westerners who are unaware of the spiritual attainments of mankind in these other parts of the world. This devotional solution of the alienation problem in Hinduism has the beginnings of a community salvation although the bliss attained is strictly individual.

In the Yoga tradition the alienation is that of the absolute spiritual reality of each person, the Purusha, from itself by contact with the nonspiritual world, the material, the natural world, which originated in and is an expression of primal nature, Prakriti. The entire effort of Yoga is to overcome this alienation of spirit from itself and to reconstitute the spirit in its own proper identity. To accomplish this there is need of an intense prolonged discipline carried out by specific techniques of inner control whereby the bonds linking the spiritual to the natural are recognized and then removed in their deepest roots.

To understand in any adequate fashion the basic orientation of Yoga one must first understand the teaching of the Sankhya tradition. Yoga must not be limited to its expression within the Sankhya context, yet Yoga cannot be understood without a basic knowledge of Sankhya, which outlines the basic structure of reality as this is conceived within the Yoga tradition. Historically, Yoga has been so closely related to Sankhya that the two are generally considered together as parts of one whole, the Sankhya-Yoga. Sankhya has been an extensive influence on the thought development of India, just as Yoga has been an extensive influence on the spiritual disciplines of India. Sankhya has given to India much of its philosophical terminology.

For example, of supreme importance in early Indian thought is the Sankhya distinction between the spiritual and the nonspiritual, between Purusha and Prakriti. Purusha is eternal quiescence, absolutely undisturbed by contact with the world of matter, time, and change. In experiencing the reality of his own being, man experiences his spiritual nature, his Purusha. It is for this spiritual reality that all things exist. The Purusha is of the nature of pure consciousness which constitutes the essential nature of spirit. Spirit is uncaused; it cannot be the effect of anything; nor does it cause any effect in direct fashion. It remains absolutely in isolation, unchanged and unchangeable.

Prakriti, on the other hand, is the ultimate substrate of the world of objects. It is also the dynamic force within the entire cosmos. Prakriti is as eternal as Purusha. But whereas Purusha is uncaused and uncausing, Prakriti is a first, uncaused cause. Not the effect of anything, Prakriti is the origin of everything. Sometimes designated as "primal matter" or "primal nature," it is the origin of matter, mind, and thought. All of these belong, not to Purusha, but to Prakriti, which produces both the psychic and somatic aspects of reality. It is important to recognize that the Purusha-Prakriti difference is not that of a creator and the primordial matter out of which he creates. Above all Prakriti is not created by Purusha. Matter, form, and movement are all within the realm of Prakriti. Matter is a dynamic force; it is not the passive reality of the Aristotelian matter. Nor is this dualism of Purusha and Prakriti similar to the dualism of the Persian type with the opposed principles of Ahura Mazda and Ahriman, the first of which produces light and goodness and spirit, while the second produces darkness, evil, and matter. Sankhya-Yoga is instead a unique type of dualism which has as its dominant purpose the identification of Purusha in its true and pure spiritual reality and the restoration of Purusha completely within the realm of the transphenomenal, apart from the disturbing conditions of time, even though the disturbance producing the cosmic order is itself the result of the presence of Purusha to Prakriti; this upsets the equilibrium within Prakriti which in turn brings forth the cosmic order such as it is perceived. This, in the West, is the problem of preserving a creative deity from being himself effected by his own creation and thus in some manner destroyed by his own creation.

The teaching of the Sankhya-Yoga also differs from the basic teachings of China with its doctrine of Heaven and Earth as the two primordial principles that produce the cosmic order through mutual response. This cannot be considered an adequate parallel with the Yoga principles of Prakriti and Purusha since the two latter cannot enter into such a mutual relationship. Yet there is something in the relationship of Purusha and Prakriti which indicates that Purusha is an initiating if not a fertilizing principle. It is principally the presence of Purusha which evokes the original dynamic impulse within Prakriti.

Turning to Prakriti and the cosmic order, there are within Prakriti and in all of its productions three strands, or qualities *(gunas)*: goodness *(sattva)*, passion *(rajas)*, and darkness *(tamas)*. To goodness is attributed all that is bright and pleasing—the upward movement of things, the sense of joy, bliss, satisfaction. To passion is attributed the basic dynamic force in things—the restlessness within reality, the basic cause of the striving, the longing, dissatisfaction, the pain of things. To darkness is attributed the passive, the opaque aspect of reality, the downward movement. These three strands are found everywhere and in everything. The distinguishing quality of things is determined by the dominance of one or the other of these qualities. There is both tension and conflict as well as cooperation between these strands. The balance is always being altered. Indeed the constant alteration is what produces the changing aspect of reality. So long as the dynamic relationship among the strands is manifesting itself the cosmic order emerges into being. As soon as there is a relaxation of tension, a state of equilibrium, then the cosmic order ceases its evolution and experiences an involution. This occurs when the spirit attains its state of full independence from primal nature. The existing cosmic age is then ended. Quiescence ensues until another cosmic age is brought about by another upset in the equilibrium of Prakriti resulting from the presence of Purusha.

When the evolutionary process is begun by the disturbing influence of Purusha, the first production that emerges from Prakriti is the Great One, Mahat, also known as *buddhi*. As the Great One it is the first expression of the cosmic-physical order of things. As *buddhi* it is an instrument of thought, the first expression of the psychic order. The reality known as Mahat and as *buddhi* in the Sankhya is often designated as *cittam* (mind or mind-stuff) in the Yoga writings, especially in the work of Patanjali.

Once the Mahat, the Great One, emerges from Prakriti, then it brings forth the next principle, the "I" principle *(ahamkara)*. It is through the *ahamkara* that man experiences his own ego, asserts his subjective phenomenal existence, claims possession of things as "mine." Much of man's spiritual difficulty, according to Indian spirituality, is founded in this sense of the phenomenal "I" and "mine." The word itself is a combination of two words: *aham*, the first person singular of the personal pronoun, and *kara*, a word derived from the verb *kri* meaning "to make" or "to do." The composite word, *ahamkara*, is translated as "self-making" or as "self-doer." This principle causes man to appropriate to himself his own activity and the possession of the surrounding reality. This is a supreme alienation from his true Self. In virtue of this self-assertion man is blinded to the true reality of his own deeper self, the reality beyond all phenomenal being and activity. The ultimate "I," the ultimate "Self," does not act or possess in the earthly realm. This confusion of an absolute self with a phenomenal self causes an endless series of evils. The *ahamkara* and the entire inner structure of the individual belongs to the world of Prakriti. Thus to be united within its own being the true self must be abstracted from its confinement within the psychosomatic structure of the individual, especially from the thought instrument *(buddhi)*, the "I" principle *(ahamkara)*, and the lower mind *(manas)*.

The next stage in the evolution of reality from Prakriti, after the Mahat and the *ahamkara*, is the lower mind *(manas)*. Then come the five organs of sense perception (sight, hearing, touch, taste, and smell); the five organs of action (hands, feet, speech, the organs of excretion and generation); the five subtle elements (sound, color, tangibility, odor, and savor); and finally the five gross elements (ether, air, light, water, and earth). Thus are constituted the twenty-four elements of reality as these are expressions of the Prakriti principle. Purusha is the twenty-fifth element, the true, the "divine" reality which is to be rescued from its apparent contact with the world of affliction, which is coextensive with the world of Prakriti. Within this cosmic order the inner self of man, by a false impression, fails to understand the absolute difference between spirit (Purusha) and primal nature (Prakriti). The inner self sees all that is taking place in the *ahamkara* and in the *buddhi* and considers these activities as its own; and thus it becomes "involved" in the world of Prakriti, the world of matter, from which it must be released by an illumination of its own nature of eternal quiescence, bliss, and supreme consciousness. The Yoga discipline proposes to guide man out of this situation, to return spirit to its own self-identity.

Chapter Eight

The Scripture of Patanjali

The Yoga tradition has a vast and varied tradition with a long history that extends over some four thousand years, at least from the Indus Valley civilizations until the present. During this period Yoga has constantly differed in the modality of its presentation. There are as many forms of Yoga as there are varieties of spiritual traditions in India. Each has its own way of saying exactly what Yoga is and how it effects the liberation of man. Despite this obvious complexity and multiform aspect of Yoga, there is a tendency to isolate some segment of the tradition and to proclaim this as the authentic Yoga. It would be difficult, perhaps impossible, to isolate any essential core of content of Yoga found in all its manifestations other than by saying that Yoga is a spiritual discipline associated with special techniques of spiritual development leading to man's release from the bonds of the phenomenal order.

The most classical expression of the tradition and one that presents Yoga in its most genuine form is found in the Yoga of Patanjali (second century B.C.). But this Yoga of Patanjali, which is intimately associated with the Sankhya thought system, is only one of the forms of Yoga. Yet the work

88

of Patanjali deserves all the praise lavished upon it, for it is in truth one of the masterworks of the spiritual history of man. Impressively scientific in its precision of thought, it communicates much of the best that is contained in the Indian spiritual traditions. It is so universal in its basic outline that it has proved wonderfully adaptable to the various religious movements in India throughout the centuries that have found spiritual support in the Yoga tradition.

The basic work of Patanjali, the Yoga Sutras, comprises some 194 aphoristic statements arranged in an ordered series so that a complete program of individual salvation is presented to man. Each of these statements carries an extraordinarily condensed expression of some significant phase of man's spiritual life. This work has been the subject of commentaries in which the fuller, more complete expression of the tradition is brought out. Of most help is the early commentary by Vyasa in the eighth century, *the Yoga Commentary*, and a subcommentary on the work of Vyasa written by Vacaspatimishra in the ninth century, the *Tattvavaisaradi*.

The first statement of the Yoga Sutras of Patanjali is a simple introduction: "Now begins the explanation of Yoga." A more adequate translation of this very condensed expression would be: "Now begins our presentation of the discipline leading to the highest development of spiritual consciousness" (I, 1).

The second statement identifies the basic purpose of Yoga: "Yoga is the suppression of the modifications of the mind" (I, 2). The word used here for suppression, *nirodha*, is one of the most significant terms in the entire Yoga vocabulary. It indicates that there are spontaneous forces at work that must be prevented from producing their effect on the mind. These activities resulting in the modifications of the mind are both cause and result of the phenomenal world. Once these modifications in the particular consciousness of man are removed, he is cured of his confusion of the spiritual and non-spiritual and attains his true self-identity.

This final objective is indicated in the third of the Yoga aphorisms: "Then the seer exists in his own reality" (I, 3). This objective attained, the spirit discovers itself in a state of pure consciousness. Man attains a unity which removes him from the transient, sorrowful, unreal world, the world of appearance, to the world of absolute reality and total bliss.

The fourth of the Yoga propositions is "Elsewhere the seer accords with the modifications" (I, 4)). The "seer" in these statements is Purusha, the spiritual reality of man which, in its proper state, is pure consciousness.

When alienation from this pure state has taken place, there is confusion of this principle of pure quiescence with the active instrument of knowing and the things known. To consider that Purusha is the agent, the cause, the maker—this is the error, the alienation that must be overcome. This must be overcome in the mind of man, which is itself within the realm of Prakriti. That is what is so difficult. It requires that the knowing instrument of man, the *buddhi*, recognize that it is not the final self of man even though in some manner it mirrors the self. As a principle that emerges from primal nature it is destined to pass back into the realm of Prakriti, the realm of primal nature.

The scattered activities of the mind, ultimately derived from sense experience of the outer world, are the basic causes of all pain and sorrow. This is fully understood only by those who have attained a certain higher capacity for discernment: "To those with discriminating judgment, everything is in a manner painful since everything brings pain either as an actual effect, as anxiety over the future deprivation of joy, as desire newly arising from past impressions, or as the conflicting activity of the three qualities of things" (II, 15). Yet none of this would affect man except for "the union of the seer and the seen" (II, 17). This union of seer and seen brings about the immersion of man in the world of transient phenomena. A confusion is produced between the ultimate subjective spiritual reality of man and the natural world of which man is a part. In his ordinary state man carries both within himself. The confusion remains until by a profound interior reflection he realizes: "The seer is consciousness only; remaining itself pure, it sees through the activities of the mind" (II, 20). These activities in the particular understanding of man seem to be the activities of the true self, whereas in reality they are due only to the natural world. The great human task of man is to realize that he carries within himself this confusion of the eternal and the temporal, the unconditioned and the conditioned, that he will never be released until he discerns the difference between them. It is especially difficult for man to identify the proper qualities of Purusha. As a state of pure self-consciousness, it cannot be directly understood by the thought faculty (*buddhi*), which functions only within the realm of Prakriti and its productions.

The supreme difficulty of man lies in his lack of understanding: "Ignorance consists in considering the transient, the impure, the painful, and what is not the self, as the eternal, the pure, the pleasant, and the self" (II, 5). The remedy is through discriminating judgment. This, however, is a task of some magnitude, for it involves a reversal in the basic tendencies that man finds within himself. This reorientation is not some superficial recognition of this difference but a reorientation of the entire being of man. Otherwise there is no remedy and man is still in his misery. He is still victimized by appearances and his ill-understood sensations. The means of eliminating this inner defect is by an inner discipline: "The means of destruction of ignorance is by continued practice of discriminating judgment" (II, 28). The word for discriminating judgment is *viveka-khyati*, meaning to separate by the activity of the mind. What is needed then is to take apart, to divide. Man must clearly differentiate and spiritually isolate the two primordial principles, primal nature and spirit, from one another so that the spirit can exist in its own radiance, its own being, in the realm of infinite freedom.

A twofold process of separation and identification is at work. The false identification is that which brings together spirit and matter; the true identification is that which brings spirit together within itself in a perfect act of self-consciousness. In a corresponding way, the false differentiation is that which separates spirit from itself; the true differentiation is that which differentiates spirit from primal nature and from the cosmos derived from this source. In this true status of spiritual self-identity by an act of perfect self-awareness the primordial alienation is overcome, and the absolute simplicity of being is restored.

Chapter Nine

The Spiritual Discipline

Yoga teaching is not merely exhortation to virtue, nor is it simply advice concerning the path to liberation. Yoga is a step-by-step spiritual leading by the hand according to a detailed series of instructions which provide specific exercises through which the desired liberation can be attained. This spiritual program and its techniques fulfill in Yoga the function of both the moral teaching and the sacraments in the Christian way of salvation. The moral teaching of Yoga is contained in its first two stages; the ritual-sacramental equivalent would consist in the next three stages of Yoga discipline: posture, controlled breathing, and abstraction of the senses. Sacramental rituals in the Western sense would be considered a hindrance to this effort at higher experience of a transcendent nature.

The specific name of the Yoga technique is Sadhana, a word derived from the verb root *sadh*, which means to go straight to any goal or aim, to attain some objective, to correct, to control, to master. India is aware that spiritual faculties need specific and conscious training and development just as do the physical faculties of man. There is an art and style for everything. The craftsman, the musician, the scholar—all have their specific training programs which enable them to attain the skills needed in their work. Even more necessary, however, is training in those activities that lead to spiritual liberation. The difficult nature of this attainment was recognized and procedures established to carry man to the successful conclusion of this, his great human task. This procedure is Sadhana. It is taken for granted in traditional India that everyone with a serious approach to life is carrying out a Sadhana, a program of practical spiritual discipline.

Another word used to indicate the repeated, continued nature of Yogic exercise is abhyasa, a word indicating the consistent exercise of the inner spiritual faculties of man, the faithful fulfillment of a Sadhana. Abhyasa means especially to concentrate attention for a prolonged period, to practice or study by repeating a prescribed activity. This is the word used in the first section of the work of Patanjali, which deals with the modifications of the mind: "These are suppressed by practice (abhyasa) and by elimination of desire" (I, 12). "Of these two, practice is sustained effort to attain a calm, steady position" (I, 13). "This, if well cultivated over an extended period of time, sedulously, without disturbance, is firmly established" (I, 14). A little later there is advice to engage in "continued thought of the suppression of mental activities" (I, 8). From these directions it can be seen how much insistence is placed on inner spiritual discipline in the Yoga tradition. This leads eventually into the condition wherein a person attains the "subjective radiance" (I, 47).

This development in the spiritual order of man's life presupposes a virtuous life. Before steadiness of mind is attained there must be cultivation of the virtues. These ward off the great obstacles to the interior life. Among these obstacles are illness, laziness, doubt, carelessness, indecision, desire, mistaken view, mental distraction, and general instability (I, 30–31). These afflictions are prevented by cultivating friendship and compassion, by nonattachment to delight and sorrow, goodness and evil. By cultivating these virtues, the mind then becomes purified of its disturbing elements. A profound rectification of life achieved, a person becomes established in good conduct and is not bothered by the inner struggle of undisciplined emotions.

THE EIGHT STAGES OF SPIRITUAL ASCENT

The full exposition of the Yoga discipline and the stages whereby the disturbing activities of the mind are suppressed begins with the statement: "Restraint, spiritual discipline, posture, breath-regulation, abstraction of the senses, concentration, meditation, and full spiritual consciousness are the eight elements of Yoga" (II, 29). These lead a person to the final perfection of *Kaivalya*, a state of pure inwardness, a serene state of consciousness apart from all earthly affliction.

Yama: restraint. The first, most basic spiritual need of man is negative restraint, or discipline of his activities, the fixing of the path that he is to follow, the movement toward a goal that eliminates movements away from the goal. This is *yama*, which means a rein, a curb or a bridle, one of the most common ways of indicating the spiritual controls man needs to impose over himself in order to cure the aimless wandering about in the meaningless world of change. Man is drawn powerfully by a variety of stimuli in every direction. If he abandons inner control, if he cannot resist the variety of attractions and repulsions that he feels, he will be driven back and forth between the opposites, especially between pain and pleasure, in a maddening series of movements that leaves him ever more bewildered from moment to moment. Reference to a bridle indicates also that there is need of a driver or charioteer who is in charge of forces that are acting blindly in reference to the destination foreseen by the driver. The blind life forces are deep in the subconscious realms of the mind, frequently as the result of past actions binding man to the realm of time and change. The beginning of control can be made through the five basic imperatives of Indian moral discipline. They are fundamental in the Yoga tradition although they are found also in Hinduism, Buddhism, and Jainism and, indeed, can be considered pan-Indian in character.

The first of these principles of moral conduct is *Ahimsa* (non-injury). This most elementary of Indian moral precepts, which applies not only to conduct toward other men but toward all living creatures, is founded on a sense of the unity and sacred character of life. This is not simply a moral dictum, it is a religious virtue concerned with the realm of the sacred. Infringement of this precept has in it an element of the sacrilegious. This is felt particularly among the Jains who carry this doctrine of *ahimsa* to its extreme expression by straining drinking water lest they inadvertently destroy some living creature and by sweeping the path before them lest in walking they destroy some form of life. The Jain is further sensitized by belief in the presence of souls in everything. In the Yoga context this doctrine of *ahimsa* is stated simply as a basic precept but without excessive attention since the main concern of Yoga is the inner spiritual orientation of man rather than such directions of the moral order. Later Gandhi emphasized the positive meaning of the term *ahimsa,* that of love for all living creatures, especially for suffering mankind.

The second precept is that of veracity *(satya).* This term covers much more than simply truthfulness. It includes the commitment to what is genuine, to the pure and virtuous, to the honest. There is to be no distortion of reality, especially in the life and deeds of anyone dedicated to spiritual perfection. The entire effort of Yoga spirituality is to become the genuine personality that a person should be, to be removed from the realm of falsity in all its manifestations.

The third precept is that against stealing *(asteya).* After life itself, the social order is to be preserved by regard for the possessions of others. These may not be taken by anyone. This is generally phrased in Indian tradition as "not taking what is not given." This precept accords with the Western assertion of justice, the rendering to others of what is due to them. Corresponding to this precept of not taking what is not given is the high value Indian tradition sets on giving alms, especially to mendicants, but also to anyone in need.

The fourth precept is that of continence *(brahmacariya).* This requires purity of life in those things concerned with sex attractions. The ideal of the highest order was that of perfect continence, of perfect detachment from all enticements in this area of human experience. This virtue is especially significant for the student in the early period of his life, the period of study of the Vedas; it is often spoken of as the Great Way or the Supreme Path, the path of noble restraint.

The fifth of these virtues is non-covetousness *(aparigraha),* not grasping after things. Expressed in traditional Western terms, it is the virtue of detachment. This implies renunciation of possessions except for those things necessary for life. For those who lead the homeless life, who dedicated themselves to a complete and exclusive life of sanctity, the only needs are a robe, a begging bowl, a drinking cup, and a staff. Little is needed by those mendicants dedicated directly to spiritual liberation. To seek this spiritual freedom in the midst of possessions binding a person to earth is recognized as a basic contradiction. This doctrine of detachment finds its fulfillment in a life attitude similar to that expressed by the traditional vow of poverty as this is known in the West.

In this elementary outline of Yogic ascetic discipline it might be noted that there is no flagellation, no exaggerated asceticism. There are simply the basic virtues of the spiritual life. If little explanation is given to these precepts in the Yogic writings it is because they are universally supposed in any tradition of Indian spirituality. In the list given by the Yoga Sutras, overindulgence or the use of intoxicants is not mentioned, although the prohibition of intoxicants is given fifth place in the parallel list of basic virtues in the Buddhist tradition. Intoxicants were considered as proscribed also by the basic vow of continence.

Niyama: spiritual discipline. Niyama is a second group of five precepts that serves as a further and more positive guide to the spiritual life. "Spiritual discipline includes purity, contentment, asceticism, study, and dedication of all actions to the Lord" (II, 32).

Purity (*sauca*) is first and involves a "disdain for one's body and the elimination of contact with others" (II, 40). If a certain puritanism is suggested in the Yoga discipline it arose from an intense awareness of the burdensome aspect of physical existence, the uncleanness, the pain, the disease, the dissolution caused by age, and finally death and its repulsive disintegration. Aversion for the physical order was considered necessary to cure man of false attractions which arise from the beauty and delight associated with physical existence and bodily activities, both in a person himself and in his relations with others. There was obvious need of recognizing the disaster hidden within all physical life. Once this attraction was eliminated, then extensive benefits became immediately manifest. These were the very highest: a true and lasting cheerfulness of mind instead of a false and momentary succession of pleasures; a unified mind which cured the intelligence of its dispersion amid the transient phenomena with which it was surrounded: The senses became subject to the higher vision of man; above all there arose the capacity for reflexive vision of the spiritual principle itself in the state of bliss resulting from a higher consciousness. As stated in the Yoga Sutras: "The higher nature becoming pure, then comes cheerfulness, one-pointedness of mind, discipline of the senses, capacity for a deepened consciousness of the inner self" (II, 41). These consequences of the first of the positive disciplines indicate the high regard in which it was held and the lofty achievements that followed its practice.

An inner serenity of mind (*santosa*) is the second of the positive elements of the higher spiritual discipline: "From contentment comes the attainment of supreme joy" (II, 42). This experience of inner peace, this rich feeling of harmony and lack of antagonism, can be recognized in the spiritual personalities of India, although there is a seriousness, an abstraction which sets these men apart from the spiritual personalities of the Zen tradition in T'ang China, in whom laughter and fun and a human zest for play are found in more expressive forms.

A third element of spiritual practice is an inner ascetic discipline known as *tapas*, sometimes translated as "purifying action." Austerity or asceticism in India has a long history that goes back to the very beginnings of India's cultural development. This had a greater place in India than in other traditions of the Eurasian world. The word *tapas* itself means "warmth" or "heat." This inner spiritual intensity became the source of power. All great actions required a certain inner vigor derived from *tapas*; the act of primordial creation, especially, is considered in India to be associated with *tapas*. This designation may perhaps derive from the physical fact of heat produced by great physical effort. Then the idea was apparently transferred to the production of a spiritual heat by intensity of effort. This same efficacy in the Yogic tradition is associated with intensity of mental concentration, with discipline of rhythmic breathing and the power of breath retention. The consequence of this inner intensity is stated thus: "By ascetic discipline there is the elimination of impurity and the perfecting of the body and the senses" (II, 43). This effort pushes the purification process deeper into the psychosomatic structure of man. It brings about a higher degree of perfection in both the physical and psychic faculties.

The fourth activity of prescribed discipline is study (*svadhyasa*). This involves devotion to the sacred tradition, attaining of intellectual insight, profiting by the teaching of the masters, and meditation on the advice of spiritual guides; but in a special way it brings man into relation with the higher powers: "Study brings about union with the favored deity" (II, 44). The deities in the Yogic context of Patanjali are superior powers, or what the West might call the preternatural order. Contact and communion with these higher realities belong to the perfection of the communication between man and the surrounding world.

Fifth of the prescribed observances is complete devotion to the Lord (*pranidhana*). The Lord, here, is not a creative deity, although the Lord is of exceptional help in attaining supreme concentration of mind in preparation for liberation. The "Lord" in the Yoga Sutras is the perfect one, the omniscient one who guides, sustains, and strengthens human personalities striving for liberation. This introduction of the Lord, a personal higher being, into the scheme of Yoga distinguishes the Yoga from the Sankhya tradition, which, at least in an earlier phase of its development, denied the existence of such a Lord. The highest reward is promised for this devotion to the Lord: "By complete devotion to the Lord there is the attainment of *samadhi*, supreme consciousness" (II, 45).

Asana: posture. In the second stage of Yogic development a lofty spiritual achievement is already found. Yet the major advance remains, for only with the third stage, that of sitting in meditation, does the proper Yogic discipline begin. A completely new phase of Yogic training begins here. The first two stages have affirmed the common basis of Indian spirituality. They are similar to the basic life discipline of spiritual personalities the world over. But there is here a sudden break, a technique of inwardness developed to such a high point of perfection nowhere else in the other higher civilizations of man. The sitting in proper posture appears a simple thing, yet it is difficult to achieve with any perfection. Once this skill in sitting is attained, it proves to be one of the most fruitful of all methods of attaining inner recollection. When the body is seated firmly in a relaxed and serene mood, the mind can enter into the dispositions required for effective withdrawal from the distractions of the surrounding world.

There are a variety of sitting postures in the Yoga tradition. Some of these are so strained in their first practice that they cannot conduce immediately to inner quiet. They do, however, establish a spiritual control over bodily function and in this way are profitable as basic disciplines whereby a unity is attained within the complex structure of man's physical and mental being. There is one posture, however, which is of supreme importance, a posture grown famous in past centuries throughout India and the entire Oriental world east of Persia, and which is now rapidly becoming known over the entire earth; it is known as the Lotus Posture. In this posture a person sits on a small cushion on the floor, or on a slightly raised platform, with the legs folded over each other. The hands, turned downward, rest on the thighs near the knees. The head, neck, and back are kept in a straight line. To sit in this way over an extended period can be a strain for a person not accustomed to such a posture. Circulation of the blood is restricted in many cases. Yet, through practice, ease in this posture can generally be attained. Once learned and practiced, this method of sitting establishes a person in a firm yet relaxed position that is conducive to prolonged mental concentration. In the Yoga Sutra two statements set forth in direct manner the efficacy of posture: "Posture is firm and relaxed" (II, 46). "By easing of tension there is infinite attainment" (II, 47). This culminates in the elimination of all difficulties that arise from the pairs of opposites, that is, from heat and cold, from pleasure and pain, from acceptance and rejection. This sense of the opposites, or the dualities of things (*dvandva*), is very strong in Indian spiritual traditions. This extends also to the spiritual realm, to the dualities between good and evil, truth and falsehood, for it is part of the inherent turmoil of life that man should constantly be faced with opposed choices in the physical, emotional, mental, and volitional orders. Man is caught between time and eternity, the one and the many, the conditioned and the unconditioned. Eternal bliss is considered to be the status wherein man passes beyond all these things into that state of pure simplicity in which there are no *dvandva*, no opposites. Here, seated in deep quiet, one attains to the immobility that is proper to the world of eternity. This provides a first full experience of the total unity of man. This position is even physically set off against the world of change. The still mind can be found only in a still body. A mind in which the modifications are eliminated must be a mind in which the physical fluctuations of the human frame have been quieted in a profound and all-pervading manner.

Pranayama: controlled breathing. Breathing is one of the most fundamental of the physiological activities of a living being. It is also one of the activities partially under the control of man's conscious faculties and partially a spontaneous process that goes on whether or not man is aware of it. Respiration is also intimately associated with the functioning of the entire psychic structure of man. There is a profound mutual influence of respiration and emotional life. The emotions are directly affected by respiration and the rhythms it engenders in man. Thus this is one of the faculties with which a beginning can be made toward establishing a complete unity of the physical, emotional, and spiritual elements in man with a gradual pervading and controlling of the entire functioning of man by the higher faculties. The basic objective is bringing the life forces into subjection to the conscious faculties rather than allowing these higher faculties to be subject to the changes in the physical ones. For achieving this, a gradual dominion over breathing is effected; then there is a gradual quieting of the breathing process itself. The consequence of this regulation of breathing is stated: "Then the covering that veils the light is destroyed" (II, 52). "The mind is now ready for inner concentration" (II, 53). As the realm of space is in some manner conquered by posture, so by the gradual quieting of breathing, the time succession is brought under control. The scattered aspects of life come into a harmonious order. An elation is attained, a sense of a person's dwelling in his own being. Also there is an expansive feeling that encompasses and pervades the whole cosmic order. In this condition the mind attains a mirrorlike calm so that the *vritti* (mind activities) are stilled into a perfect quiescence; then the true self, the true spiritual reality of man can appear.

Pratyahara: abstraction of the senses. After posture and breathing comes the third and last of the specifically Yogic processes by which the entire man is prepared for the development of a higher mental consciousness leading to the liberation experience. The statements of Patanjali concerned with this moment of inner development indicate that it is the first moment of real disengagement from the ordinary mental processes: "Withdrawal is the alienation of the senses from their proper objects and their consequent functioning according to the activities of the mind" (II, 54). "Thereafter there is complete mastery over the senses" (II, 55). Here a new psychic process is initiated. The ordinary process of objective knowing is turned about. By intuitive vision the mind knows in a higher form although the senses participate in this higher way of knowing their objects. This begins the manifestation of the higher modalities of functioning that are proper to the Yogin as his command over the knowing processes is extended. The objective world remains; there is no effort to reduce the world to a subjective idealism. It is an effort to know multiplicity in a more unified and effective fashion. The distractions of the mind derived from the dispersion of the senses, from their responsiveness to the unpredictable going and coming of eternal stimuli, are cut off. So long as the normal sense contact is maintained with the world of changing realities, the mind will itself be disturbed and the spiritual faculty of man will identify itself with these disturbances and remain unable to achieve liberation.

Dharana: concentration. After the withdrawal of the senses there is an ingathering of the mind and a total fixation on a single object. In this phase of inner development the psychic activity of the person is brought to an absolute unity. The Yogin, seated with firmness and ease, breathing controlled, senses withdrawn from their objects, fixes his mind on some one point. Vacaspatimishra, in his commentary on this point, insists that there can be no fixed attention without some object upon which the attention is fixed. This focus of attention may be the space between the eyebrows, the tip of the nose, the tip of the tongue, the navel, the lotus of the heart, the Lord, or some other set object. This most important exercise is known as one-pointedness *(ekagrata)*. Just as the body must be fixed in the posture of immobility, so the mind *(buddhi)* must be fixed, seated as it were, in total stillness in order that the inner process of self-awareness takes place without any movement of the mind. When the mind becomes fixed in perfect stillness then the dialectic of spiritual disengagement enters its final phase.

Dhyana: sustained attention. The seventh stage is designated as *dhyana,* one of the most famous and significant words in the Asian thought world. Taken over by Buddhism as *jhana,* it was carried to China where it was pronounced as *ch'an,* then into Japan where it was pronounced as *zen.* In origin it is derived from this stage of the Indian meditation procedures especially as this took place in the Yoga discipline. In the Buddhist tradition *dhyana* is associated with the eighth and final stage of the eightfold path. In both traditions this most significant phase of spiritual development requires long and sustained effort. The amount of time spent in quiet concentration is extended until a person can remain for hours completely absorbed in the state of mental concentration. As expressed in the Yoga Sutras: "Continued application of mind to the chosen point of concentration is sustained attention [Dhyana]" (III, 2). The clear mind is progressively absorbed into the object so that it does not advert to its former modifications. The separating of the mind from its own modifications by fixing attention on a single object is a preparatory stage before releasing the mind from attachment to any object and enabling man to rest in his own deeper reality.

Samadhi: the superior state of consciousness. The final stage of spiritual development is exceedingly simple but also extremely important. After continued application of the mind to the object chosen, a moment is reached when the mind is taken out of its own limited, particular, subjective context and attains a higher type of identity both with the object and with itself. Thus in the words of Patanjali: "This mental effort of Dhyana, shining with the radiance of the object alone and devoid, as it were, of its own form, is the higher stage of mental awareness (Samadhi)" (III, 3). At this time the *vritti* (modifications of the mind) are stilled. The way of knowing is further altered. There is a new immediacy of the mind with its object. When the mind has attained this high form of expression there is a penetration of the object in such a way that the crude form of the object, its materiality, is in some manner overcome and the reality of the object appears in its pure form, radiant with light ultimately derived from the inner self of the knowing subject. The knowing faculty also has come forth from its own subjective limitations. At this moment an identity is attained between the knowing act, the knowing faculty, and the object known. The contact with the object is immediate on the part of both subject and object. The objective cosmic order does not disappear at this time. It is not annihilated; it is simply transformed in a higher experience.

The mind not only knows, it attains a dominance over reality. No longer subject to the external world as in the period when the senses dominated the mind, the mind controls the sense functions and knows in a manner beyond the senses. The world is no longer opaque. It comes together into an ordered cosmos. The dispersed elements of reality lose the nonintelligibility associated with their existence in temporal succession. The one point of meditation enables the light of the self to permeate the universe. The point on which the mind is fixed becomes simultaneously center and circumference of reality. The whole is known simultaneously as the notes of a melody, successive in execution, are heard simultaneously by the mind. This status of the mind is sometimes referred to as the "cosmic mind." A new awareness of the world floods the mind. It has such knowledge as to express itself in terms of omniscience, although this is attained only after a full awareness that the inner self of man is clearly distinct from the world, the mind, and all knowing activities: "Whoever attains a clear perception of the difference between pure subjective consciousness of the self and the multiple objects of existence attains mastery over all conditions of things and, in a manner, becomes omniscient" (III, 48). This power of knowing brings with it extensive control over the world. As viewed by Patanjali, a person with such attainments lives in new and more vast dimensions of experience than are generally available to men. There is insight into the minds of others (III, 19), comprehension of the starry heavens (III, 26), control over hunger and thirst (III, 29), capacity to eliminate contact with the earthly elements (III, 38), capacity to move through space (III, 41), and control over the elements (III, 43). In a special manner there comes about a splendor, grace, vigor, and endurance of the body (III, 45). Mentally the supreme attainment is a new subtlety of mind, an instantaneous quality of understanding, without reliance on the ordinary instruments and ways of knowing (III, 47).

This establishes a wonderful world for the Yogin, but one which is also dangerous. This is a period of high achievement, a marvelous reward for the spiritual effort put forth. A person knows the exaltation of exceptional experience, is able to accomplish what others do not accomplish, understands as others do not understand. He has a serenity that enables him to enjoy to its depths this new status in which the entire world has suddenly come into his possession. He lives in a cosmos completely responsive to his presence. Indeed there are some in the Yoga tradition who rise to this height, never to go further into the higher stages of development that are beyond this and which truly constitute the goal of the Yogin.

This is a moment similar to that of the temptation of the angels in the Western religious tradition. At this moment everything can be lost or everything gained; it is the moment when the superior powers are themselves to be rejected, even as the visions and ecstatic experiences of the saints are to be rejected since they are manifestations of the divine but do not themselves constitute the divine experience. To rest in these accomplishments and experiences is ultimately no better and possibly worse than to rest in the activities available to man in a lower realm. At this moment the inner spiritual reality of man, the Purusha, is to be experienced in a direct fashion. A dialectical process has been initiated. The mind has been quieted, its modifications removed, its full powers of· expansion outward have been achieved, the cosmic order has been brought into possession and control. The next phase of development is full entry of the Self (Purusha) into an act of perfect consciousness, of perfect spiritual "inseity." The mind *(buddhi)*, like a clear crystal, reflects whatever form is present to it. It reflects knower, known, and act of knowing. The original purpose of Yoga is fulfilled. Mind activities have been eliminated. The Self, the Purusha, the spiritual reality of man, is released from its dependence on its own knowing instrument, the mind.

The final phase of the Yoga process involves the relationship between the mind *(buddhi)* and the Self (Purusha). The mind is the thought instrument which functions at the service of the Self. As clear crystal, the mind reflects the Seer, the Self within: "When its modifications decline, the mind as a reflecting crystal attains the capacity to become whatever is presented to it, whether object to be known, the knowing subject, or the act of knowing" (I, 41). While there is great emphasis in the Yoga Sutras on the mind and its proper functioning, it must be remembered that "the mind is for the benefit of something beyond itself" (IV, 24), namely, the Self, or Purusha. This ultimate reality, the Self, is for the sake of nothing outside its own being. The Self is the Owner of all, the Experiencer in the final sense of the word. The Self does not undergo any change. It knows, but not through any activities of its own being. It exists in a pure state of consciousness totally undisturbed by processes of knowing. Nothing throws light on the Self; the Self illumines all else. It alone is self-enlightened. The mind does not illumine itself; it can only receive the illumination of the Self, the Purusha, the Absolute Spirit. The mind unites with objects; the Seer himself does not in any way unite with objects. He cannot be known as an object is known, but only in an act of self-awareness, of complete self-consciousness, of total inseity.

This distinction of the Self from the knowing faculty, the *buddhi*, is exceedingly difficult for man to understand. The difficulty lies in the fact that the mind, in its state of perfect quiet, reflects the Self with special clarity. Thus the Self seems to participate in the reality of the mind, just as formerly it seemed to participate in the actions and experiences of the mind. Yet the Self is recalled to itself in a full and complete disengagement even from the mind. In some manner the apparent association of the Self with the world of Prakriti and the activities of the mind has been necessary in order that the Purusha be finally revealed to itself as distinct from all these states of being. Yet before this disengagement takes place, the Self sees itself in the mind as the moon is reflected in the water. The moon in reality is not united with the water. It is only the reflection that appears and is subject to the ripple of the waves.

Within the most interior of all acts of the Self by which the final distinction is made between itself and the mind, there are two moments of self-awareness that must be distinguished: the supreme state of inwardness "with support" and the supreme state of inwardness "without support." The first of these, known as *samprajnata-samadhi*, is attained through the successive phases of Yogic discipline and has some reference to the external order of reality whence it has emerged by a process of progressive interiorization. In this stage of inwardness there is still a relation to the world of the non-self, although this does not essentially disturb the bliss that has been attained by this isolation from the affliction endured in the phenomenal world of time and space. This includes a remaining, if weakened, influence of the *samskaras*, which are the impressions of the past phenomenal existence as these remain within the being of man and provide a connection with the phenomenal order. This is still a period of purification in the deepest, most interior being of man. Yoga is vividly aware that past experiences have burned their impression into the psychic structure of man's being. While this stage of "inseity with support" is filled with joy and with a full sense of accomplishment there remain these impressions on the subconscious level. Only when these subliminal impressions are removed does the spiritual personality attain to the absolute state of absorption, known as seedless concentration.

This stage of Yogic discipline has been studied extensively by the commentators on the Yoga Sutras and forms one of the most subtle and penetrating expositions of the higher stages of spiritual consciousness that man possesses. This stage of "enstatic awareness with support" *(samprajnata-samadhi)* is considered the stage "with seed;" that is, it has inclinations that enable the mind to keep some contact with the world of phenomena. This stage is followed by a higher experience known as "seedless contemplation," in which the impressions of past deeds and associations with the extra-self are entirely eliminated. This stage of "enstatic awareness without support" has a depth purification of the inner principle of man that reaches to the least remaining impressions that bind man to the world of time and change, to the conditioned, limited, painful world. Transition from the seeded to the seedless self-indwelling, from contemplation with support to contemplation without support, is the single most decisive moment in the entire process. The entire understanding of Yoga depends on the capacity to understand the status finally arrived at through such an arduous spiritual discipline. This stage of Yoga, the most difficult to describe, is designated by three basic terms: enstasis without support, seedless enstasis, and the state of total self-identity *(Kaivalya)*. The latter term, one of the most significant in the tradition, indicates the stage attained when there is a complete enstasis, a perfect inner unification of the Self with its own reality, along with a perfect isolation from the world of the non-self. It is attained, of course, only by the final purification from all association with the former world of change. It can also be translated as total freedom from the limitations inherent in the ordinary human existence of man.

In an earlier section of the Yoga Sutras this state of *Kaivalya* was mentioned after the description of the great powers attained by the higher phases of Yogic discipline: "When even for these things there is no attachment, then the seeds of man's bondage are destroyed and man attains the state of pure inwardness [*Kaivalya*]" (III, 49). Slightly later, at the end of the third section, there is mention of the moment when both the mind and the Self exist each in a state of pure identity, fully distinct from each other but each perfectly itself: "When the purity of the Mind and of the Self both become equal, then arises for the Self the state of perfect freedom [*Kaivalya*]" (III, 54). After a certain amount of repetition concerned with this status of total independence, of perfect freedom, of isolation from all limitations, Patanjali concludes his presentation of

Yoga: "When the basic elements of the conditioned world, empty of the association with the Purusha, return to their primordial status, then there is perfect freedom (Kaivalya) or the vital reality of the self is established in its own being" (IV, 34). At this moment the mind (buddhi), along with the entire psychic structure and functioning of man, retires into Prakriti. In this transformed condition the mind has passed from its restlessness (ksipta) to stillness, from its dullness (mudha) to perfect clarity, from its dispersion (viksipta) to unity. Then finally the very mind itself enters into a state of equilibrium proper to Prakriti, and the Self, the Purusha, is revealed to itself in its ineffable peace.

Just prior to this moment of ultimate achievement there has descended upon the spiritual personality an experience of unique intensity. This is presented as the "cloud of truth," which might also be translated as the "cloud of spiritual experience": "When there is no longer any attraction even toward the highest processes of knowing, there arrives, from sustained discrimination of the spiritual self and the non-self, the intimate experience designated as the 'cloud of truth'" (IV, 29). The term dharma-megha is baffling to translate in this context. It is obviously an indication of some supreme spiritual experience related to the highest moment of spiritual realization. It could be considered as the manifestation at this moment of absolute truth or of supreme spiritual insight. This is the moment when something divine takes place within man. A new modality of existence is attained. The modality of being is transformed into a pure state of self-awareness that consists in the breaking of all barriers, the entry into perfect simplicity, the attaining of something that is totally other than what is the "normal" state of man in his earthly existence.

This final stage accords with the fourth stage of Hindu spiritual realization. The four stages are presented in the Mandukhya Upanishad as the waking state, the dream state, the state of dreamless sleep, and a final, fourth state, that designated simply as the fourth (turiya). These equate with the knowledge of the supreme reality attained by the external world, by inward thought, by a higher non-ideational awareness and finally by total immersion in the absolute unqualified Brahman. This final stage in Yoga also accords with the final stage of Buddhist contemplation which passes from reflection on the phenomenal world to that of unbounded space, then to the sphere of unbounded awareness, then to the sphere of nothingness at all, and finally to the sphere of neither perception nor non-perception. The latter is the condition of total simplicity. Thus in the Brahman state, in the Nirvana state, and in the Kaivalya state there exists in India a certain basic identity in reaching forward to an absolute experience that passes beyond the normal state of conscious experience into an experience that is both enstatic and ecstatic and beyond both. There are indeed serious differences in these experiences and the way thither. But it remains true that in all three there is a creative shattering of everything in order that the one unique reality be attained, as if a man were to sell not only all that he has but to deliver up all that he is to attain the single experience of incomparable bliss.

Chapter Ten

Religious Aspect

Historically Yoga has been associated with almost all phases of religious development in India from the earliest period until the present. It is true, however, that in its own structure Yoga represents a type of spiritual orientation that is barren in the ordinary terms of religion. There is no religious worship or prayer as such; there is no priesthood; there is nothing that can be identified as sacraments. There is simply the salvation discipline leading to an ineffable experience wherein the spiritual principle in man attains a blissful status beyond all affliction of the physical, emotional, and thought realms in which human life is lived within space and time.

Yoga is primarily, then, a spiritual discipline leading to a salvation experience. This salvation experience indicated in the highest state of seedless Samadhi should be interpreted as man's entry into the world of the sacred out of the profane world, entry into the unconditioned world out of the conditioned world, entry into the absolute, the blissful world of eternity beyond the world of changing phenomena. Thus, Yoga should be considered ultimately as a religious spirituality. It cannot be that this intense movement toward the absolute be considered merely a psychic process. Nor can a spiritual discipline so intimately associated with the religious traditions of India be itself purely a technique of acquiring extraordinary powers of the psychic and physical orders. One must recognize, however, that Patanjali, in the greatest of Yoga scriptures, does not explain the Yoga discipline in specifically religious terms. His insertion of a doctrine of Ishvara, the Lord, into his work is clearly an addition from outside the basic structure of his thought. Later writers saw better than Patanjali just where the doctrine of Ishvara should be placed—in the final experience of reality, in the appearance of Purusha in his own form (I, 3; IV, 34). Patanjali himself was working within a context that was itself too limited for an adequate development of Yoga teaching, a context that was overcome even in the time of Patanjali by the *Bhagavad-Gita* wherein Purusha and Prakriti, Pure Spirit and Primal Nature, become subject to Ishvara, a personal deity, the Supreme Purusha who manifests himself as Purusha in his higher nature and as Prakriti in his lower nature. Salvation in this context is attained by a religious devotion of man to a deity in whom he finds the origin and end of his own existence.

What can be said of the Yoga Sutras is that they contain simply the recognition that there must be a place for Ishvara, the Lord, in any adequate vision of reality. This established the principal point of difference between Yoga and the early period of the Sankhya tradition. The existence and place of Ishvara in the thought and spiritual traditions of India has been under continual discussion in the Indian tradition, especially the relation between the Lord and the absolute reality, generally designated in Hinduism as Atman or as Brahman. In the Upanishadic period Indian thinkers realized that the final ineffable reality could not rightly be spoken of in human language or even thought of according to man's modalities of conception. Especially it could not be spoken of according to analogy with such earthly realities as "person" or as "lord." Thus the tendency developed in large segments of Indian spiritual history to terminate religious thought and attainment in a transcendent absolute rather than in God, the Lord, or in some idea of heaven. These terms in traditional India designated something less than the absolute. It was only in the later period of Indian religious development, beginning with the *Svetasvatara Upanishad*, continuing through the *Bhagavad-Gita* and the sectarian cults of the Puranas, that God, Ishvara, the Lord, was identified with the impersonal absolute, Brahman, and even raised above this absolute. Two Hindu theologians who exemplify these different attitudes are Shankara and Ramanuja. Sankara continued in the earlier tradition of absolutism, while Ramanuja developed the theism of the *Bhagavad-Gita* and the *Puranas* with their identification of a personal deity with the absolute reality of Brahman. This theism of Ramanuja provided, of course, a magnificent vision of the Lord as creator, sustainer, and source of bliss in which terminate the spiritual aspirations of mankind. It also provided support for that extraordinary outpouring of devotion that came forth from Hinduism during the medieval and modern periods.

If the Yoga concept of deity is considered in this context one finds that God, or the Lord, as presented in the work of Patanjali did not function on the sublime scale of the Vedic deities, the *Bhagavad-Gita*, the Puranas, or the later devotional hymns. The basic difficulty can be found in the world outlook of the Sankhya tradition in which the Yoga of Patanjali developed. This Sankhya tradition represents another, a third position in the Indian tradition, the naturalist position. Strong atheistic movements have existed throughout Indian history. These movements, widely influential in the first millennium B.C., especially in the centuries just before the appearance of Patanjali, originated in the non-Aryan foundations of Indian development. The non-Aryan aspect of Indian thought was itself divided into a strong native, local theism in which the local village deities were worshipped with intense devotion, and into a more ascetical, more intellectual atheism as manifested in the Ajivika, Carvaka, Jain, Buddhist, and Sankhya traditions. Among the six thought traditions of India, Sankhya is most distinguished for its atheistic tradition, although the Mimamsa system is similarly oriented toward a liberation program not founded on any belief in God. Yoga developed during the period in the middle of the first millennium B.C. in close relationship with Sankhya. Thus Yoga has the same dualism of Purusha and Prakriti that is found in Sankhya. Yet despite this background, the followers of Yoga from the beginning were more responsive to religious developments than were the followers of Sankhya. Yoga recognized that the Lord must somehow be given a place within any acceptable vision of reality. In the vision of reality presented by Patanjali the Lord had his place, even though this notion entered the system from without, having been added to the basic pattern established by Sankhya. The Yoga vision of the order of things could stand as well with or without the presence of the Lord. Yet in the spiritual and religious functioning of Yoga, the Lord gradually found his position strengthened until finally, in the devotional cults of the later period, the Lord in Yoga is both a supreme deity and the absolute principle of reality. When this time arrived, however, Yoga was already functioning within a larger religious context, one considerably altered from the original thought of Sankhya.

In the writings of Patanjali the Lord is one of a multitude of spiritual beings known as Purushas. (As the supreme Purusha he is never involved in the world of Prakriti except to help others achieve the perfection toward which they are striving.) A profound relation between the Yogin and the Lord is advised. The first statement concerning the Lord reads: "The Lord is a special kind of spiritual being not affected by earthly sorrow, action, or pleasure" (I, 24). This indicates that the Lord is a being never involved in the life agonies of other spiritual beings. He has existed always in the state of perfect self-possession with no such dependence or limitation as are found within the world of time and change: "In him omniscience attains its highest expression" (I, 25). Here an effort is made to establish the Lord as supreme in the order of wisdom: "He was teacher and master even of the wise men of antiquity" (I, 26). There is even an effort to indicate that the Lord is the supreme reality generally designated as Brahman in Hinduism: "He is the one designated by the sacred word, Om" (I, 27). "Men should repeat and think upon this word" (I, 28). One can perceive in all this an effort to incorporate the Lord as a functional part of the Yoga spiritual program. But at no time is there an indication that religious devotion is strictly necessary to arrive at complete spiritual fulfillment. Nor is there any effort to establish the Lord himself as the origin, providential ruler, or ultimate destiny of the world. Thus the feeling of total religious dependence, the very basis of the devotional attitude, is not present. The Lord is an extrinsic aid to the salvation process rather than the inner dynamic and destiny of the process.

But if this figure of Ishvara, the Lord, is no adequate foundation for a religious attitude, there does exist in Yoga the supreme spiritual reality, Purusha, the highest reality known to Yoga, in which there is an adequate termination of the spiritual process. Enabling Purusha to attain a state of liberation from apparent involvement in Prakriti is the supreme religious duty of man. Purusha is referred to in the Sutras as the ruler to whom all activities of the mind are known because of his immutability" (IV, 18); as the one for whom the mind exists (IV, 24); and as the one absolute distinct from the mind even in its purest form (III, 34). From these and the entire pattern of reality in the Yoga system one can see that Purusha is the supreme reality, the unique existence which is somehow shared by the multiplicity of selves observable in the world but which is finally a single absolute reality in which a total fulfillment is sought. This corresponds with the realm of the "totally other," the realm of the sacred. Thus, awareness of identity with Purusha constitutes the final objective of all spiritual existence. All things find their rationale in this absolute spiritual experience which is liberation. He is the absolute One, the One who exists in his own right, whose vision is illumined from within, who uses all else as instruments without being himself an object of knowledge or of any action.

There is some difficulty in the Yoga system concerning the multiple purushas and the Absolute Purusha. This remains one of the most difficult of all the various aspects of the tradition. It can generally be considered that the multiplicity of Purushas are finally identical with the Absolute Purusha, although this question is never adequately dealt with in the doctrine of Patanjali. In the final resolution the deepest reality in each person, the Purusha, is itself the absolute reality in which all manifestations of the spiritual find their true identity.

In achieving this final experience man must undergo a process that must be described in the category of the death-rebirth initiation in religious ritual. In Yoga the death-rebirth process is of the psychical order; it is not imaged forth in ritual as is generally the case in religious traditions. In this sense Yoga constitutes a unique world of psychic experience. Everything is inwardly fulfilled in the silent, motionless ritual sitting discipline. This process is centered on the extinction (nirodha) of the mental activities, as these are described in the first effort to identify the very essence of the Yoga practice (I, 2). The Yoga Sutras describe an entry into death in the phenomenal order and a rebirth in the higher order, the resurrection of a spiritual reality alienated from itself in the emergence of the cosmos and reconstituted finally by the Yogic discipline when it again attains existence "in its own nature" (I, 3). A religious mysticism is at work in Yoga that was later appreciated by the Bhakti, or devotional, Yoga tradition. The entire cosmic experience of the meeting of Purusha and Prakriti can be interpreted as a mystical-religious drama in which the two absolute forces are implicated in an opposed but complementary pattern of reality. They assist yet eliminate one another. These are the great paradoxes that are found in the Yoga system. The cataclysmic disturbance of the equilibrium of Prakriti can be remedied only by a disciplined restoration in which the evolutionary process is countered by an involutionary process. Everything appears as its opposite: the transient appears eternal; the impure, pure; the delightful, painful; the non-self, the self (II, 5). In this state of misplaced values eternal life itself must appear as death. The supreme paradox, however, is that absolute bondage should be mistaken for absolute freedom. It is not a simple thing then to alter man's perspective so completely as to enable him to see the opposite of the way in which things appear. But this is precisely the drama, the work of every wisdom tradition. The wisdom traditions of mankind are all founded on this reversal of values, on this rectification of an original passage of man from wisdom to folly, from life to death, from freedom to bondage. Along with all these traditions Yoga seeks a rectification that will truly lead from the apparently real to the truly real, from apparent light to true light, from apparent freedom to true freedom. In this process man must attain cosmic realization by an outward movement and then suddenly, to achieve his own true being, he must withdraw into isolation from the entire order of Prakriti. In all of this there is a suppression of life for the purpose of expansion, a lowering of life vitality for the attaining of an extraordinary degree of life intensity.

Thus Yoga may be considered strictly soteriological in its concerns. If there is no religious worship as such, no anthropomorphic conceptions of deity, there is the quest for that higher order of reality in which the impurities and limitations of life are done away with. Investigation of the final stage of Yoga, that of "seedless indwelling of the Purusha in its own reality," the indwelling in which there is "no support," may very well reveal that there is in Yoga a mystical experience which equates with the experience of the divine as this is found in other world traditions. But even aside from this achievement within its own independent structure Yoga has contributed mightily to other higher religious traditions of the Asian world, especially to the devotional-religious traditions of India.

This leads to another presentation of Yoga, that given in the *Bhagavad-Gita*, a work composed in the same historical period as the Yoga Sutras of Patanjali. The *Bhagavad-Gita* is a vast, all-inclusive synthesis of the Hindu religious-spiritual tradition of the period prior to the Puranas, which were composed after the fifth century. Like the Yoga Sutras, the *Bhagavad-Gita* presents much of its teaching in terms of the Sankhya system. The *Bhagavad-Gita* also claims to present the true Yoga tradition. The Yogin is considered the supreme spiritual personality. Yet, both the Sankhya and the Yoga traditions are brought within the Upanishadic tradition of the Absolute

Brahman, which is the true reality of every being and the spiritual self of every man. Even beyond the Sankhya, Yoga, and Vedic elements, the *Bhagavad-Gita* adds a supreme personal reality, the Lord, Ishvara, in whom both religious devotion and spiritual discipline find their highest fulfillment. Yoga, within this context, is not an isolated, self-contained life program. It is rather a spiritual-religious discipline leading to divine union. This is seen in a more significant context than in the work of Patanjali. All the basic elements of the Yoga Sutras are preserved except the radical dualism of Spirit and Primal Nature. This dualism is overcome by a Supreme Reality which has Spirit as its higher manifestation and Primal Nature as its lower manifestation. Thus the lower order is also saved, validated, divinized.

This is the context within which Yoga has been lived and practiced most widely throughout the centuries. The commentators on Patanjali—Vacaspatimishra in the ninth century and Vijnanabhiksu in the sixteenth—turned their interpretation of the Yoga Sutras in this direction. The latter, in his work, is expecially committed to the personal deity who makes himself known with special clarity when discriminating judgment is finally able to realize the absolute disengagement of Purusha from Prakriti. This leads to a final ecstatic experience in which the fullness of bliss is attained. The part of Yoga in this personal mysticism that marks so much of Indian spiritual development is to ingather all the forces of the human reality so that the outgoing of the inner self of man can be complete. Without this inner discipline the dispersed activities of man lead to an alienation from himself. Thus even in the practical function of life he does not have the subjective capacity for life occupation, for intellectual or spiritual understanding, for devotional commitment or for ecstatic indwelling. The Yogic discipline enables a person to gather within himself the fullness of his own being; and thus, by a greater inward centering of himself, he is able to function effectively on all levels and in all directions, especially in the direction of higher spiritual attainments.

Later, as Yoga was adopted by the devotional traditions it became complementary to other traditions rather than an independent, self-contained tradition, although this independent Yoga tradition has survived in vital form throughout the centuries and is possibly stronger now than it has been in the recent past. Yet the major function of Yoga will probably be its association with the wider spiritual traditions with which it is in contact. Even within this wider context Yoga must keep its distinctive form if it is to be effective as a discipline and a technique of spirituality capable of leading man far on the way to spiritual liberation. While Patanjali did not give his followers a full religious program he did give them the quintessence of an inner life orientation that has since found its place within an increasingly wide variety of religious traditions.

Part Three:

Buddhism

Chapter Eleven

Historical Context

Buddhism, a spiritual movement founded by Siddhartha Gotama in India in the sixth century B.C., became the first multicultural spiritual tradition in the higher civilizations of the Eurasian world. Buddhism lasted in India for some fifteen hundred years, until the twelfth century A.D., when it disappeared from India as that country became progressively dominated by Islam. But already Buddhism had begun its movement southward to Ceylon (third century B.C.); northeastward across the Hindu Kush and Pamir mountains into China (first century A.D.), Korea (fourth century A.D.), and Japan (sixth century A.D.); eastward into Burma (first century A.D.), Thailand (third century A.D.), Cambodia (fourth century A.D.), Indonesia (third century A.D.), and the other countries of southeastern Asia except the Philippines. Later in a second northern development Buddhism became the dominant spiritual movement in Tibet (eighth century A.D.), and Mongolia (thirteenth century A.D.).

At the time of the rise of Buddhism, the entire Eurasian world was experiencing its most creative moment in its spiritual and cultural life. This was the period of Pythagoras and Parmenides, of Socrates and Plato in Greece; the period of Isaiah and Jeremiah in Israel; of Zoroaster in Persia; of Confucius and Mencius, Lao Tzu and Chuang Tzu in China. In India

119

this was the period of the Upanishads, of Mahavira, and of Buddha. The classical formulations of the spiritual and intellectual traditions of the higher civilizations of the Eurasian world were being established. Of the many common elements in these traditions the most significant was the discovery and elaboration of doctrines concerned with the transcendent world and the spiritual way to attain it. These centuries in the middle of the first millennium B.C. (from 800 to 300 B.C.), are the richest in the humanistic phase of man's entire cultural development. The intellectual insight, the spiritual orientation, the life disciplines, the social and political formations then established have been the principal guides of man in his higher civilizational phase until the present, when, for the first time, these earlier visions are being challenged both in their content and their ultimate meaning.

In India by the eighth century B.C. the Aryan peoples had moved eastward from the upper reaches of the Indus to the Middle Ganges region. Here a number of small kingdoms and republics had been founded. India was beginning to take shape as a people, a society, a culture. The fusion of Aryan and non-Aryan elements was well under way. The first vital centers of city life were coming into existence, although as yet there were no large structures in any enduring materials. Yet the courts of the various kingdoms had acquired a certain cultural and spiritual brilliance. Tribal life was giving way to larger and more complex social forms. A new class structure was asserted in the division of priests, warriors, farmer-merchants, and the lower working class. Conformity to social custom became more strict, although by no means so strict as it was to be in later times. The law codes establishing the proper order of human life were being composed: the laws of Manu, the Dharma Sutras, and the Grihya Sutras. The Hymn period was definitely over, the Upanishadic creations were still new. The great epics of the *Mahabharata* and the *Ramayana* existed in very primitive form.

Yet in the midst of all this vital activity India was having its most intense experience of the sorrow inherent in the human condition. If sorrow has also been experienced by other men and other societies, it has seldom been experienced with such depth of awareness and inner sensitivity. This was not the ordinary suffering implied by living in a physical world in which man is subject to the elements and to his own human limitations. This was something more than the experience of creaturehood mentioned by Rudolf Otto in *The Idea of the Holy* and even different from the *Angst* of Kierkegaard. This was a unique spiritual-metaphysical experience of the emptiness of all things, of the painful manner in which man is bound within his own being, his own thoughts, even his own virtues. It was an experience of the fact that the phenomenal world confines, alienates, and disintegrates man in his deepest spiritual reality. The expansion of life that others experienced as liberating man was seen in India as binding man. Thought and phenomenal consciousness themselves were oppressive rather than expressive. The entire world of change was experienced as an endless cycle of sorrow—birth, death, and rebirth.

The solution of the problem of suffering was, most generally, an inner withdrawal that would remove man from the dense and destructive world of change. By the infolding of man into his deepest self-identity the escape could be achieved. A man could remove himself from the world of nature, of matter, of mind, of thought, of consciousness, into an experience beyond all this. Alienated from himself, man must return to himself. Dispersed into a fragmented existence, man must restore the oneness of his being. Confined within a cyclic time process, man must recover his eternal status. Above all, movement must give way to quiescence. This is the mark of the eternal, the beginning of bliss.

Because of this painful experience of the world of change a palpable tension is found within all the Indian traditions, an inner pressure exerted against all structured forms of existence. This spiritual dynamic sent forth incalculable numbers of people in India into the homeless life. They could not endure confinement, whether this was domestic confinement of home and family, spiritual confinement of ritual, sacramental practices, forms of prayer, or the confinement of the mind within its own most sublime vision of reality. Man needed to go forth into the homeless state of the mind, the stage wherein the mind passes beyond itself, beyond its own thoughts, beyond its own conscious awareness. This is most effectively presented in Hindu tradition as attaining the stage of dreamless sleep. But how was man to slip out from this self-imprisonment of the world, out from the structure of his own being, his own mind?

India was not interested in some theoretical or schooled response. A life solution was needed, a solution that would be true liberation, or "Moksha," as this was expressed. This involved not merely a general direction in which a solution could be found, but a specific spiritual discipline by which men could be guided in their life activities within time toward an experience beyond time, an abiding transconscious experience in which alone were found the real, the true, the immortal. How within time to exist also beyond time? There were Hindu and non-Hindu solutions.

In its Upanishadic vision Hinduism had already gone far toward providing a solution. The escape must be found by subjective identity with an absolute reality beyond earthly experience. In identifying this reality beyond human conception men could say only, *Neti, neti* ("It is not this, it is not that"). Existing totally within itself, this ultimate being remained untouched by any event in the world of time. While so aloof, it was also the immanent force originating and sustaining all that exists in time. Hinduism, experiencing this reality as a presence abiding deep within man's own being, very quickly came to the view that salvation must be achieved by disengagement from phenomenal life and total identification with the reality beyond all thought, motion, and sorrow. Thus the Hindu prays that men be led "from the unreal to the real, from darkness to light, from death to immortality."

At this time, about the middle of the first millennium B.C., the higher spiritual life of Hinduism was institutionalized by addition of the fourth *asrama* (stage of life), the stage of the *Sannyasi* (the homeless wanderer). Even while living in time a person could also exist in that other world, the world beyond life and death, the abiding world beyond change, beyond multiplicity, beyond understanding. On entering this final stage there was in Hinduism an abandonment even of Hinduism. The sacred cord, the symbol of man's spiritual birth, was removed and a person entered into the higher life as someone freed from all establishments whether human or divine in origin. Then a person passed beyond the signs and symbols of salvation and experienced the supreme reality itself in a direct fashion. The person became a *jivan mukta*, that is, a person liberated while living within time. This was the highest stage of spirituality known to Hinduism at this period, the stage in which man attained the highest liberation from sorrow as this was experienced in the orthodox Hindu tradition.

But if the Hindu world experienced the sorrow of life with great sensitivity and sought by asceticism and meditation to pass beyond sorrow, the non-Hindu world of India experienced this sorrow of life even more profoundly and exerted even more strenuous efforts to attain an existence beyond sorrow. This higher sensitivity within the non-Hindu tradition derives from primordial non-Aryan sources. Followers of the original Yoga, Jain, Ajivika, and Buddhist traditions were non-absolutist and non-theist. Although some superior beings or deities were recognized, they were of a much diminished stature; they were not at all the equivalent of the Supreme Reality found in the Hindu world. Thus, followers of these non-Hindu traditions did not attain release from sorrow by union with some absolute principle or by devotional relation with a deity.

These non-Hindu traditions wished generally to face the problem of the human condition strictly from within the human resources of man. Release from sorrow was presented in terms of liberation, not in terms of union with an eternal principle. The idea of total freedom, of total release from the human condition, seemed incompatible with any quest for an absolute. All conceivable absolutes implied bondage. They could be thought of only as some other determination, even if it were the sublime determination of a deity or some absolute reality. The need of man was for release from all determination, from all limitation.

While there was a general tendency toward non-theistic attitudes in the non-Hindu traditions of India at this time, it is also true that these traditions at a later time introduced absolutist concepts and sometimes theistic concepts. This is particularly true of the Sankhya and Yoga traditions. Even the Jain tradition, so strictly atheistic, was later dominated by belief that Mahavira, the founder, was an *Avatar* (a human appearance of an absolute reality). Buddhism also was progressively transformed in the direction of a religious attitude toward Buddha. This culminated in establishing Buddha not only as a savior personality but as an ontological absolute. At this time, in the middle of the first millennium B.C., all of these were still in their early non-theistic stage and were striving for a salvation from evil by human effort within a pattern of spirituality based on a liberation ideal. There is, however, one non-Hindu tradition which stands apart as the one in which the possibility of liberation from the phenomenal world was denied in a total way. This is the Carvaka tradition, the most thoroughgoing materialism known to India at this time. Beginning with this one, several traditions will be considered to establish the context in which Buddhism arose and developed.

Carvaka. The Carvaka philosophy (seventh century B.C.) was committed to unmitigated materialism. It was thoroughly opposed to any religious or spiritual attitude, to any ascetic discipline. According to this doctrine, only the phenomenal world exists. There is no noumenal world, hence no liberation from the present life experience. Any bliss that man hopes for must be achieved within the context of life just as it is perceived. The idea of any true moral virtue is absent from this tradition. There is no satisfying basis for asceticism or any form of self-denial; there is only the emotional experience of the senses to be enjoyed while man is upon earth. Obviously the Carvaka is the most earthbound of the Indian traditions.

Madhva (fourteenth century A.D.), in his *Summary of All the Philosophies*, considered it extremely difficult to remove the attraction this philosophy had for the people generally. The Carvaka, as he describes them, are so attracted to possessions and satisfaction of desires that they deny the reality of anything else. Thus another name for this tradition is *lokayata*, or worldly tradition. The Carvaka consider that ritual, learning, and asceticism are all utilitarian ways of obtaining support from the society. One Carvaka writer, Brihaspati, considered that there is no heaven nor any final liberation and not even a soul in any other world than this one.

This position was considered so extreme that all schools that survived in India opposed the Carvaka. The system itself never attained the developed exposition found in the other systems. Thus knowledge of it depends almost entirely on the refutations given by opponents of the system. That it arose is significant; that it survived as an effective system for such a short time is also significant. India, in the final analysis, could not endure such teaching.

Yoga. Far more significant than the Carvaka, Yoga has been an abiding influence throughout the history not only of India but of much of Asia beyond India. Yoga supplied the psychological techniques whereby the inner spirit of man is liberated from all its confinement. Yoga has above all a conviction that a higher status is attainable by man in complete isolation of the spiritual element of man from the temporal changing element. What is needed is quieting of the mind, a psychic control over man's physical and emotional life, and finally a release of the deepest spiritual principle in man from all engagement with the phenomenal world in any form whatsoever.

Jainism. Another effort to bring about a liberation of man from his sorrowful condition was that of the Jains. This tradition also reached far into India's past. In the period under discussion the Jains found their great leader in Mahavira (died c. 470 B.C.), a man who brought together the basic elements of Jainism and coordinated the tradition into a spiritual system that has changed very little from that time until the present. Many systems have disappeared from India, such as the Carvaka, Ajivika, and Buddhist; others have beeen modified in time; others, such as the sectarian traditions of Hinduism, came into existence much later. But the Jain movement remains as it was, a kind of archaeological museum of the basic spiritual attitudes of large numbers of people in India's earliest period of development.

The Jains have a firm belief in the existence of souls, numberless souls, which inhabit every part of the universe. These souls, imprisoned in matter, are afflicted with the defilement of Karma, which binds the souls within the phenomenal world. By ascetic detachment the Karmic matter and the bonds that attach the soul to the non-living world are removed and man attains release from suffering. The supreme moral and spiritual law is that of *ahimsa* (non-injury). The final objective of life for the Jains is that of complete quietude of inward existence, the attainment of supreme wisdom, and a corresponding power over the entire order of reality.

Ajivika. Along with the Carvakas, the Yogic practitioners, and the Jains, with their intense asceticism, there were also the Ajivikas. These were completely atheistic and were identified mainly by their doctrine of fatalism. Man does not have control over his destiny. In the other Indian systems the present is determined by the Karma of the deeds of the past, yet there is a range of freedom for the moral act of the present that will determine the future. This basic moral freedom is rejected by the Ajivikas. The universe, to them, is wound up in a complex of cosmic tensions that must unwind themselves over some millions of years. Only then is release attained from Samsara, from transmigration, in which mankind is caught. Man's response must be that of acceptance. He must submit to the unfolding of the life process until the tensions have been released. This is a blind process. The impersonal determinant in the universe, designated as *niyati* (necessity), is not a reality separate from things, but a way of designating the unavoidable succession of events that we know as the earthly phenomena. Gosala, founder of Ajivika, lived at the same time as Buddha. The two were sharply opposed to each other during life, but both were effective spiritual leaders. Except for the Jains, the Yogins, and the Buddhists, the Ajivikas showed more enduring qualities than the other spiritual movements of the period. The Ajivika tradition lasted as a small group for some fifteen hundred years, until the fifteenth century A.D., when the tradition disappeared from the spiritual life of India. Strangely enough the Ajivikas were oriented toward a certain asceticism. Although this did not in reality improve their lot, it was a way of life toward which they considered they were impelled by inherent structure of the cosmos and the inner determinants of their own being. In this manner they were freed from the hedonism characteristic of the Carvakas.

These are some of the movements, persons, and forces that were at work in India during the sixth and fifth centuries B.C., at the time when Buddha was born in the foothills of the Himalaya Mountains in the northeastern portion of the Middle Ganges region, in the area presently occupied by southern Nepal. All were proclaiming a way to obtain release from sorrow. Some were proclaiming this release in subjective identification with an absolute reality, some with a supreme deity. Others found release through asceticism, others in hedonism, some in fatalism. Those that have been mentioned are still only a small number of those abroad in India at his time proclaiming a way of salvation. In the Buddhist writings of the period there is mention of "those who are guides in spiritual life, heads of companies, heads of groups, teachers of groups, widely known, famous, founders of sects, revered by the people. . . . Purana Kassapa, Makkhali Gosala, Ajitakesakambali, Pakuda Kaccayana" (*Majjhima Nikaya* II, 2). Obviously it was an age of intense spiritual inquiry centered on the problem of release from man's sorrowful condition. When Buddha was born in the year 561 B.C. no one had yet come forth with a spirituality developed on a sufficiently humanist pattern to attain a dominant position among these many movements. No one was sufficiently spiritual and yet sufficiently rational, sufficiently profound yet sufficiently simple to provide a universal message to the people of India.

Chapter Twelve

Buddha: His Life and Mission

Buddha (561–481 B.C.), born into the Gotama family of the Shakya tribe in Kapilavastu, was of the warrior class. The name bestowed on him was Siddhartha. After his spiritual illumination he was referred to as the enlightened one, the Buddha. His highest title was that of "Tathagata," a word designating a savior or prophetic personality, one with an extraordinary spiritual mission to mankind. He is also referred to as "Shakyamuni," the Sage of the Shakya.

Buddha was a historical person, but there is, however, little precise information on his life. Those who composed the stories of his life were so profoundly impressed with his spiritual mission that they speak of him in legendary language. Yet these writings are quite simple, direct, and believable in their basic message. The traits of Buddha's personality come through with surprising clarity: his experiential approach to life, his special concern for the inherent sorrow of human existence, his sympathy for the afflicted masses of the people, his capacity as a spiritual leader, his certitude concerning his mission, his sense of moderation, his modesty of bearing, his depth of insight into all aspects of human existence, his independence of judgment, his capacity to mark out a new spiritual path for mankind.

It is understandable that his followers should be overawed by such a person and that the accounts of his life should reflect some of this awe. It is also understandable that they should introduce the marvelous in the accounts they give of his life and conversation. Originally the story of his own conception and birth was told in very simple terms. Later marvelous incidents are introduced, incidents that emphasize the spiritual grandeur of the person being spoken about and the significance for all mankind of his entry into the world. The account of Ashvaghosa (first century A.D.) reads: "Like the sun bursting from a cloud in the morning—so he too, when he was born from his mother's womb, made the world bright like gold, bursting forth with his rays which dispelled the darkness. . . . When he was born, the earth, though fastened down by the monarch of mountains [Himalayas], shook like a ship tossed by the wind; and from a cloudless sky there fell a shower full of lotuses and water-lilies, and perfumed with sandal-wood. Pleasant breezes blew soft to the touch, dropping down heavenly garments; the very sun, though still the same, shone with augmented light, and fire gleamed, unstirred, with a gentle lustre." In the entire region life was changed. "The people, delivered from famine, fear and sickness, dwelt happily as in heaven; and in mutual contentment husband trangressed not against wife, nor wife against husband. None pursued love for mere sensual pleasure; none hoarded wealth for the sake of desires; none practised religious duties for the sake of gaining wealth; none injured living beings for the sake of religious duty" (*Buddhacarita*, IV, 26, 40–41; II, 12–14).

This, however, is a later account wherein the Indian feeling for extravagant rhetoric has given to the original accounts a context and influence which befits the extraordinary nature of the event which brought a spiritual way of salvation to so many persons. The account of his early concern for sorrow and the liberation from sorrow is told in more prosaic language in one of the finest of the early Sutras entitled, *The Noble Quest* (*Majjhima Nikaya* I, 160–175): "While I was still a bodhisattva and not fully illumined spiritually, because I was myself subject to birth, I inquired into the nature of birth; because I was myself subject to old age, I inquired concerning the nature of old age, illness and death, of sorrow and impurity. I pondered: 'Suppose I were to seek out the nature of birth and having seen the miserable nature of birth were to seek that which is unborn, the serene peace of nirvana' " (*Majjhima Nikaya*, I, 163).

This passage reveals that from the early part of his life Buddha was concerned with the general problem of suffering, of old age and death, and the need to discover a way leading to the supreme peace of Nirvana. Another story tells in dramatic fashion of the most basic experience of his life, the experience of sorrow. Anyone learning about Buddha must give special attention to this story of the four signs. It is obviously heightened in the telling to indicate the significance of the occasion when Buddha first became aware of the real depth of human sorrow. This was to be thereafter the center and focus of all his teaching. The story describes how Buddha lived sheltered from pain during his younger years. Later, as a young man, while driving through the park with his charioteer, he came upon a man bent with age, haggard, skin shriveled, tottering along supported by a stick. When he asked what this might be, he was told: "This is an aged man, my Lord." To the question whether this is the lot of all men, the answer given was that all men would surely see their beauty, health, and possessions fall away into the decline of age and the dissolution of death. This so affected the young Siddhártha that he was plunged into an awful depression. Of what use were health, beauty, or joy in possessions if they were already caught within a process of disintegration? His father, seeing him so depressed, commanded that he not be permitted ever again to behold suffering of any kind.

It happened, however, that the next time Buddha went for a ride in the park he came upon a man burning with fever, lying in a ditch, soiled, helpless. Again he asked what this might be and the reply was: "This is an ill person, my Lord." Then he asked: "Are we all subject to such illness?" to which was answered: "Yes, my Lord." Again he was depressed and he thought even more deeply on the tragic character of the human condition. The third time Buddha came upon a dead man being carried out to the funeral pyre. This so overwhelmed Buddha that he resolved to seek a more profound understanding of this tragic situation that he had yet attained. On a fourth ride in the park he came upon a mendicant, his face full of peace and joy. On inquiring, Buddha was told that this was one who, conscious of the human condition, had gone forth into the homeless life in order to triumph over his condition. Buddha resolved that he too would undertake this supreme quest.

At the age of twenty-nine he left home and gave himself up to meditation under the direction of two teachers, Alara Kalama and Uddaka Ramaputta. With their guidance he was led to the extreme limits of inward illumination as had been attained at their time. Even at this level of highest insight,

Buddha still did not feel that he had attained the liberation he was seeking. This seemed to require something much more severe, a transforming dis-cipline that would liberate him entirely from the limitations of the human condition. Thus he entered upon his great fast. He did this with such severity that he was soon emaciated and near death. His skin darkened, his flesh withered, his bones stood out from his body, and his countenance shrank so that his eyes appeared as flickering water in a deep well. With all this effort he still did not attain release. He resolved, finally: "There must be some other, some better way" (*Majjhima Nikaya*, 1, 246).

He then lived as a wandering mendicant for some six years. During this time he pondered on the sorrow inherent in the human condition and sought for an effective way of release. Finally one night at Gaya he had the experience he was seeking. Accounts of this night ring forth in Buddhist scriptures as a triumphant moment that has permanently altered the course of human life on a universal scale. As he entered into deep recollection he was assaulted by all the seductive forces of the world: "Beholding in the first half of the night that Battle of Mara and the bull of the Shakya race, the heavens did not shine and the earth shook and the regions of space flashed flames and roared. A wind of intense violence blew in all directions, the stars did not shine, the moon gave no light, and a deeper darkness of night spread around, and all the oceans were agitated. . . . But the great sage having beheld that army of Mara thus engaged in an attack on the knower of the Law, remained untroubled and suffered no perturbation, like a lion seated in the midst of oxen" (*Buddhacarita*, XIII, 28–29, 33). Over-coming these temptations, he continued with his inner meditation rising from one place of inner consciousness to another. "Then bursting the shell of ignorance, having gained all the various kinds of perfect intuition, he attained all the partial knowledge of alternatives which is included in perfect knowledge. He became the perfectly wise, the Bhagavat, the Arhat, the King of the Law, the Tathagata, He who has attained the knowledge of all forms, the Lord of all science. . . . When the Bodhisattva had thus attained perfect knowledge, all beings became full of great happiness; and all the different universes were illumined by a great light. The happy earth shook in six different ways like an overjoyed woman, and the Bodhisattvas, each dwelling in his own special abode, assembled and praised him. . . . A sun that destroys the darkness of delusion, a moon that takes away the scorching heat of the inherent sins of existence—glory to thee, glory to thee, glory to thee, O Tathagata (*Buddhacarita*, XIV, 67–68, 80–81, 85). Another description reads: "The system of ten thousand worlds was like a bouquet of flowers sent whirling through the air, or like a thick carpet of flowers; in the intermundane spaces the eight-thousand-league-long hells, which not even the light of seven suns had formerly been able to illumine, were now flooded with radiance; the eighty-four-thousand-league-deep ocean became sweet to the taste; the rivers checked their flowing; the blind from birth received their sight; the deaf from birth their hearing; the cripples from birth the use of their limbs; and the bonds and fetters of captives broke and fell off" (*Introduction to Jataka*, I, 68/5; Warren, *Buddhism in Translation*, p. 82).

Buddha remained in the area for some weeks, overcome with elation but also troubled as to the future course of his life. He was tempted to become a *Muni*, that is, a silent one who has gone apart from the world, who no longer has any converse with mankind except through his silent presence. He knew the difficulties of a ministry to the people. Yet he had a compassion for all those suffering the agony of the human condition, men with no adequate guidance, even though many spiritual leaders were wandering over the countryside at this time. The legends concerned with this period tell of the struggle that went through his mind. Finally the highest deity, Brahma, came to invite him to bestow this guidance on the people. From motives of compassion Siddhartha then went forth on his mission.

First he went to Banaras, already the holy city of India. There in Deer Park he preached his first sermon, speaking of the fourfold truth and the eightfold path. The fourfold truth declares the universality of sorrow, the origin of sorrow in desire, the need to eliminate desire to attain release from sorrow, and the eightfold path whereby desire is extinguished. The eightfold path consists of right view, intention, speech, action, livelihood, effort, mindfulness, inner concentration. The spiritual life begins with awareness of sorrow and ends with release from sorrow by a spiritual experience that carries man beyond the phenomenal order into the unutterable experience of Nirvana, the experience of serenity, of boundless peace. With this first sermon Buddhism was born as an integral spiritual movement.

All of this took place in the year 536 B.C., when Buddha was thirty-five years old. During the next forty-five years Buddha traveled back and forth through the region of the Middle Ganges preaching his message in the sixteen kingdoms and republics that existed in his time. He not only established a substantial body of teaching, he also gathered about him a mendicant community that would eventually send forth its members over most of South, East, and Southeast Asia carrying the message of Buddha to all the people of this region. Then arrived the moment of death. Buddha declined the petition to appoint a successor. He would leave only his teaching and the community of those who believed in his message and lived a life in accord with it. Details of his last days were recorded in the *Discourse on the Supreme Nirvana*. (*Digha Nikaya*, Sutta 16). This was the passing of Buddha into the experience of Nirvana in an absolute sense. When he died Buddha left the community without any institutional authority to direct its destinies and without any organizational structure. Yet the spiritual dynamic of the doctrine and the community brought about an expansion that continued its development for over twenty-five hundred years.

Chapter Thirteen

The Savior Personality

The teaching of Buddha was handed down to succeeding generations in the form of the threefold refuge: the Buddha, the teaching, and the community. These were the three treasures of Buddhism. Admission into the ranks of the chosen was by the threefold repetition of each phrase: "I go for refuge to the Buddha, I go for refuge to the Doctrine, I go for refuge to the Community." These can be considered the three aspects of the one Buddha reality. The teaching was itself a form of Buddha presence. The community also was a corporate expression of the Buddha experience. In various ways each of these has a priority. The teaching is supreme insofar as it is in virtue of the teaching that a person is guided to experience the saving illumination concerning the nature of sorrow and the way of release from sorrow. The community has a certain priority since it carries and sustains the entire Buddhist tradition. The doctrine would have had no inner development or preservation or propagation except through the community. This is the instrument that carried Buddhism across the Asian world. The community provided the centers in which Buddhist thought was

133

done, in which the vital elements of the illumination process were lived out in their fullest expression.

Yet supreme over everything is the Buddha reality. Both community and doctrine had a prior dependence on Buddha himself. He is the source of the teaching, the guarantee of its truth. Acceptance of Buddha soon became the central element of the tradition. The teaching was put in his name under the phrase: "Thus have I heard." This is the Buddhist equivalent for the biblical: "Thus says the Lord." The meditation doctrine was developed with a certain independence of the Buddha personality in the tradition that found its highest expression in Buddhaghosa's (fifth century A.D.) *Path of Purity*. This element in the Buddhist tradition was concerned primarily with development of the inner life and with the progressive stages of advance in the ways of mental concentration. Yet along with this the elaboration of a Buddhology gradually became the main preoccupation of the Buddhist tradition. In time this became as central to Buddhism as Christology is to Christianity. Buddha is much more important for Buddhism than Mohammed is for Islam, than Zoroaster is for Zoroastrianism, than Confucius is for Confucianism. In the extent of his influence, the intensity of devotion to his person, in the exaltation given him, the attitude of Buddhists toward Buddha is the nearest thing in the religious life of the higher civilizations of the Eurasian world to the Christian attitude toward Christ. Buddha became a savior personality, the supreme center of thought and affection. Reverence turned to religious devotion. To many in Asia Buddha was the supreme reality, the source whence the highest blessings came to earth.

Later Buddhism held such an exalted conception of Buddha that a problem similar to the Docetist problem of Christianity arose. Was Buddha really a human being or did he have only an illusory human form? Was he not a transcendent reality that only appeared to have bodily existence within the world of time and space? In the earlier Buddhism this problem did not arise. Buddha was seen as a truly human person who had attained supreme illumination in virtue of his own effort within the human context. This solidarity with mankind provided the basis for the intimate understanding that developed between Buddha and his followers. Men easily understood and identified with a savior personality who had lived within the human condition, who had suffered the universal sorrow of life, who had attained liberation in a manner in which all men must seek this.

In Buddha mankind had found itself in a liberated state. The first man to tread the way, he had removed all obstacles. The rest of mankind need only follow him. Every Buddhist repeats in depth the experience of Buddha himself. This gives to Buddhism something personally satisfying, something much more intimate than was found in Hinduism at this time. Indeed it prepared the way for more extensive development of the Hindu doctrine of *Avatar* (the appearance of the divine in human form). Prior to this time the Atman-Brahman absolute could not speak adequately in human language. This ultimate reality had personal embodiment in Rama and in Krishna. Yet it was some centuries after the time of Buddha that the full Hindu expression of the divine in human form came with Krishna in the *Bhagavad-Gita*. Only then did it become clear within Hinduism that an absolute being could speak with true compassion in a human voice, a voice that all men could understand and to which they could respond.

Although fully human, Buddha was from the beginning something more than human. He was the unique, the supreme revelation of truth, the center of the cosmic and human orders, the point of meeting of the phenomenal and the transphenomenal. He it was "whose name is truth" (*Anguttara Nikaya*, IV, 284). He radiated a saving illumination over the darkness of the world. He had an insight into the sorrow of life and its remedy such as was previously had by no one. If he had been thought of as only a human being, Buddhism would never have become the massive spritual tradition that it has become. Buddha would never have become the heroic spiritual figure that has so profoundly influenced the Asian world. He would have been only another of the wandering spiritual personalities who lived in India at the time. This was not the case, however; from an early period Buddha was seen as an absolutely unique being. Gifted with omniscience, with unique capacity for understanding the human condition and its remedy, Buddha alone could rescue mankind from its present sorrow and lead men to the saving experience of Nirvana. This commitment to Buddha as a savior personality was magnified through the years as the message of Buddha spread from person to person, from century to century, from place to place over the entire earth. There has been no diminution of his glory but rather a constant elevation of his unique status within the larger range of human history.

One of the earliest and finest works in which to study the Buddha personality as it appeared to his early followers is the *Sutta Nipata*, the "Lukean" account of Buddha. With exquisite charm the story of Buddha is told. It presents a world transformed by the Buddha personality. One charmingly human description of Buddha comes from the mouth of Bimbisara, ruler of one of the largest kingdoms of the period. "Behold, gentlemen, the man there, of noble stature, tall, composed, of stately bearing; his disciplined gaze is cast a mere plow's length ahead. He is not assuredly of any low family. Send servants to follow and see whither goes this monk" (*Sutta Nipata*, 410–411). In another passage a goddess is presented as informing the world of the birth of a savior bearing illumination for all mankind. "There came recently out of Kapilavatthu a leader bearing light to all mankind. Born of King Okkaka, son of the Shakya, the enlightened one, he as Brahman has gone beyond all things, has attained supreme knowledge and power, has eyes that perceive all things, has attained the final goal. Free from all binding affections, he teaches the true doctrine to all mankind" (*Sutta Nipata*, 991–993).

The unique quality of Buddha, the refusal to be identified with any of the three higher castes of Hinduism is seen in the statement: "I am neither priest, warrior or merchant, nor do I belong in any classification whatsoever; I walk through the world as a sage of nothingness, without home, my own self extinguished. It is improper to inquire concerning my descent" (*Sutta Nipata*, 455–456). He is the one gone forth into the nameless world wherein all earthly terms become irrelevant. This gives some indication of the absolutely new status sought in Buddhism. Eradication of sorrow required this extreme transmutation of the human condition, first in Buddha, then in his followers.

The greatest single title of Buddha is that which designates him as the "Tathagata." The word is frequently explained etymologically as "He who is thus gone" or "He who is thus come." But these are not the traditional explanations given to this title, which refers to Buddha and his high status beyond comprehension of the human mind. "Released from identification according to considerations of form, feeling, perception, aggregates, or understanding is the Tathagata; he is deep, inscrutable, unmeasurable as is the vast ocean" (*Majjhima Nikaya*, I, 487). This is further emphasized by the description of the Buddha in the *Dhammapada*. "His attainment is never again reached; into his conquest no one of this world enters. By what path then can you lead him, the awakened, the all-knowing, the trackless?" (*Dhammapada* V, 179). One of the most important characteristics attributed to the Tathagata is the absolute validity of his knowledge: "A Tathagata understands the world as it really is, in all its many and diverse aspects. . . . A Tathagata understands the diverse character of things as they are in reality" (*Majjhima Nikaya*, I, 70).

This leads to a further consideration concerning Buddha, one that is of the highest importance, the cosmic dimension of the Buddha reality. In the *Questions of King Milinda* (*Milinda Panha*), Buddha is considered to be like the broad earth: "Just as the earth, O king, is a support to the beings in the world, and an asylum to them, and they depend upon it, but as the broad earth has no longing after them in the idea that 'These belong to me'—just so is the Tathagata a support and an asylum to all beings, but has no longing after them in the idea that 'These belong to me.' And just as a mighty rain cloud pours out its rain, and gives nourishment to grass and trees, to cattle and to men, and maintains the lineage thereof, and all these creatures depend for their livelihood upon its rain, but the cloud has no feeling of longing in the idea, 'These are mine.' Just so does the Tathagata give all beings to know what are good qualities and maintains them in goodness, and all beings have their life in him, but the Tathagata has no feelings of longing in the idea that 'These are mine.' And why is this so? Because of his having abandoned all self-regard" (*Milinda Panha*, 160). Here is evidence of the effort of Buddhist writers to maintain in Buddha the bond of sympathy and benevolence with mankind proper to a savior personality and yet to keep him clear of any pain-producing involvement. His state of absolute bliss is not to be affected even in his bestowal of blessings upon creatures. This is a problem similar to that of the creative act on the part of a creative deity. How can an absolute, changeless deity bring about creation without involvement in the changing process?

The massive import of the Buddha presence on earth can be seen in the declaration: "This world system is a one-Buddha supporting world: That is, it can bear the virtue of only a single Tathagata. If a second Tathagata were to arise the world could not bear him. It would shake and tremble, it would bend this way and that, it would disperse, scatter into pieces, dissolve, be utterly destroyed" (*Milinda Panha*, 237). The reason for this is simple: "Whatever is mighty in the world is singular. The broad earth is great and it is only one. The ocean is mighty, and it is but one. Sineru, the king of the mountains, is great; and it is only one. Space is mighty, and it is only one. . . . A Tathagata, a supremely perfect Buddha, is great, hence he is unique in the world. Wherever one of these arises there is no room for a second. So it is, O king, that only one Tathagata, one supreme and perfect Buddha can appear in the world at one time" (*Milinda Panha*, 239).

These brief references to the implications of the title "Tathagata" show that it designates a unique savior personality, someone with a universal spiritual message to mankind, someone who sets aright all that is wrong, who guides man to peace, serenity, and joy in an absolute fashion. There is not as yet adequate exposition of the derivation of this term; nothing is known of its use prior to the time of Buddha. In the opinion of some it is a Sanskrit translation of an early Indian term which designated a person of messianic or at least savior qualities.

As to the fulfillment of his mission in bringing a saving wisdom to mankind, it is written that after his illumination Buddha considered the alternatives open to him in the future conduct of his life: to remain a *Muni*, a silent one, or to become a spiritual guide of the people. He thought: "If I were to proclaim this spiritual vision and the people did not understand, that would be a burden and an anxiety for me" (*Majjhima Nikaya*, I, 168). He had no illusions concerning the difficulty of providing such spiritual guidance for mankind: "That his heart inclined not to the preaching of the truth, but to inaction, was because he saw, on the one hand, how profound and abstruse was the doctrine, how hard to grasp and understand, how subtle, how difficult to penetrate into; and, on the other, how devoted beings are to the satisfaction of their lusts, how firmly possessed by false notions of individualism. So he wavered at the thought, whom shall I teach?" (*Milinda Panha*, 233).

Mankind was generally seen at this time as analogous to someone led blindfolded into a distant and terrifying region who does not know his way home except through a spiritual guide, a parallel drawn in the *Chandogya Upanishad*: "As a person might lead someone with his eyes covered away from Gandhara, and leave him somewhere apart from human habitation and as that person might call out to the east, north, south, or west, 'I was brought here blindfolded and left here in this condition; and as thereupon someone might loose his blindfold and say to him, 'Go that way and you will find Gandhara;' and so informed and now able to judge for himself, he would go along the road and inquire his way from village to village until at last he arrives at Gandhara; just so does a person with a teacher to inform him, obtain the true knowledge" (IV, 14/1–2). The legends of Buddhism dramatize the moment of decision concerning the salvation of mankind and present the picture of the high god, Brahma, coming to Buddha and imploring him to guide the lost and suffering world to a condition of relief: "As someone standing atop a mountain might behold the people in the surrounding countryside, just so, do you, illumined one, aware of all, look down from the sublime heights of truth; yourself freed from all sorrow, look down upon the people immersed in suffering, afflicted with birth and decrepitude. Then go, noble one, victorious in battle, leader of mankind, go throughout the world. Blessed One, teach the everlasting, saving truth. Those who listen will be healed" (*Majjhima Nikaya*, I, 168–169). It was important that Buddha teach, for he had discovered something never discovered before: "The Blessed One produced a path not produced before, made known a path not known before, manifested a path not manifested before; he himself was one who knew the way; who understood the way, who was skillful in what pertains to the way. His followers are those who come after him" (*Majjhima Nikaya*, III, 8).

Responding to this great need Buddha determined on a life of spiritual leadership among men. He took the road to Banaras, "beating the drum of immortality in the world of the blind" (*Majjhima Nikaya*, I, 171). Henceforth the general address given Buddha was: "The Blessed One is an Arhat, fully awakened, rich in wisdom and virtue, with understanding of the worlds, an incomparable guide for men ready to follow, a teacher of gods and men, a blessed Buddha" (*Dhammapada*, I, 49). Another phrase constantly in use in reference to Buddha was: "One not a prey to delusion has arisen in the world for the benefit of the people, for the joy of the people, with sympathy for the people, for the advantage, the welfare, and the joy of gods and men" (*Majjhima Nikaya*, I, 83).

The most direct and impressive statement about the saving aspect of Buddha's work is that which forms the conclusion of many discourses of Buddha. The person listening to the discourse responds: "Just as if someone were to set upright what has been toppled over, or were to make known what is hidden, or were to point out the right way to someone lost, or were to bring a light into the darkness so that those with eyes could see the shape of things, even so has the truth been revealed to me in many ways by the Blessed One" (*Dhammapada*, II, 132). References to Buddha's lifting up the fallen, revealing what is hidden, directing those gone astray, and illumining the darkness could be multiplied. But one which has been repeated very often by the writers of the Buddhist scriptures in the function of Buddha in lifting the veil that obscures the reality of things. Buddha was considered the first person who saw reality as it truly is. At the time of his birth there was a choice to be made; to become a great world monarch with infinite power and wealth, or to become a mendicant. "But if he leaves home and enters upon the homeless state he becomes perfect, fully illumined, one who lifts the world's veil" (*Majjhima Nikaya*, II, 134). The person who lifts the world's veil is the one who removes the darkness caused in man by attachment, hatred, confusion, pride, false views, ignorance, and wrongdoing.

Chapter Fourteen

Teachings

THE TRANSIENT WORLD

The primary teaching of Buddhism is that the world is impermanent, sorrowful, insubstantial. Man's salvation requires that he recognize this and by following a spiritual discipline attain release into the transcendent experience of Nirvana. When Buddha saw the aged man and beheld the ravages wrought by time on this bent, shriveled, feeble person, he became aware of the destructive aspect of time, the inherent tragedy of life, the insubstantiality of all things of earth. These three are the primordial foundations of all Buddhist thought. "Whether or not a perfect one appears in the world, the inherent condition of things remains as it is, the causal sequence and the interrelation of things" (*Samyutta Nikaya*, II, 26). The causal sequence indicates that all things are impermanent, conditioned, caused. Thus they are by their very nature "withering away, passing away, fading away, coming to an end" (*Samyutta Nikaya*, II, 26). The interrelation of these three qualities can be seen in the passage: "The Blessed One said, 'Body, brethren, is impermanent. Whatever is impermanent is

141

sorrowful. Whatever is sorrowful, that is without a self. What is without self is not mine; I am not that, there is no self that belongs to me in any way.' Thus should a man behold it by clear insight as it really is. Whoever sees the world in its reality by full insight, his heart is converted, he is freed from it by not seizing upon the Asavas" (*Samyutta Nikaya*, III, 44–45). The *asavas* mentioned here are the corrupt inclinations that attach a person to the phenomenal world. It is this penetrating realism, this insistence that life be faced in its true reality, that gave to Buddhism its overwhelming power, attraction, and influence. Of the Tathagata it is said: "By comprehending everything in the world just as it is, he is released from it all. In the entire world he clings to nothing" (*Anguttara Nikaya*, II, 23).

It is clear from the story of the four signs, from these quotations, and from innumerable passages in Buddhist literature that the basic experience of Buddha was the experience of the passing nature of things. The tragic sorrow of life was rooted in this temporal character of human existence. This very sensitivity to what is not eternal indicates the overwhelming attraction of Buddha toward the eternal. He could not endure the world of change. The word used to designate things in this world of change is *anicca*, a Pali word associated with the Sanskrit word *a-nitya*, which means "not lasting, irregular, unstable." Thus the constant refrain of Buddha: "Look, Ananda, how everything is gone, has passed away, has disappeared. Transient, Ananda, are all composite things. It is proper to be weary of them, apart from them, to be completely free from attachment to the world of phenomena. . . . Transient indeed the phenomenal world, its very nature is to rise and decline. Things come forth, they pass away. Their complete cessation, that is bliss" (*Dingha Nikaya*, II, 199).

The word used for component things is *sankhara*, the Pali equivalent of *samskara*, one of the most important and difficult words in the entire Buddhist vocabulary. Literally this is a compound expression with the prefix meaning "together" and the root verb meaning "to make." Thus it refers to a made-together or put-together thing and is quite precisely translated as "composite reality." These composite foundations of reality in Buddhism are quite different from anything we are acquainted with in the Western thought tradition. Yet the basic idea is quite simple; it deals with the composite world over against the world of the noncomposite, which is designated as the world of *Sunyata* (emptiness). The realm of the phenomenal, the world of *samskara*, the put-together world, has in it nothing that is true or lasting. Nor is there any noumenon underneath the phenomenon. There is only the shifting world of unstable elements. The word *samskara* must often be translated as "mental-formation." Yet here and in other places it indicates the entire composite order of things, including both the physical and psychic realms in a unity, inasmuch as this exists only in an imperfect fashion, as transient and insubstantial precisely because it is put together. This impermanence of the *samskaras* is described by Buddhaghosa: "The five sankharas are transient. Why? Because their very being is the rise and fall and change in those same sankharas, or it is their non-existence after having been. This means that impermanence is the disintegration of produced sankharas through their instantaneous dissolution since they do not survive in any abiding form" (*Visuddhimagga*, VIII, 234). With a rather colorful example this is explained further: "In an absolute sense the life course of living things is extremely brief since it is constituted of only a single conscious moment. As the wheel of a carriage, when it is rolling, rolls only on a single point of wheel, and when it is stopped, it rests only on a single point, just so the life span of living things endures only for a single conscious moment. When that awareness has passed the thing is said to have ceased to be" (*Visuddhimagga*, VIII, 39).

In the larger sphere this same principle is applied to the birth-death-rebirth process. As things that are born die, so things that die are born. Birth and death are inseparable from each other. Death is no release. It is but another phase of the tragic ephemeral experience within which man is caught. This has neither historical development nor eschatological fulfillment in the Western sense of these words. Nor is there a single life cycle. The process continues on and on from birth to death and from death to birth without cessation or interruption in a kind of eternal agony. The salvation problem is more immediate and more urgent although more caught up in an eternal process than is the case in the West. Within the Indian and Buddhist context the only relief is the attainment of Moksha, the supreme liberation from all this, which is also designated by the term "Nirvana."

THE SORROWFUL WORLD

The tragedy inherent in the impermanent world was perceived in its full depth by Buddha as soon as he saw what change had done to the aged man. From that moment Buddha's entire effort was to release man from sorrow. He often said that he taught only two things: sorrow and release from sorrow. "Monks, if anyone asks, 'Why listen to such instructions that are of noble derivation and guide men to spiritual illumination,' you should answer them: 'We listen to learn the basic twofold truth. This is sorrow, this the origin of sorrow—such is the first truth. This is the end of sorrow, this the way thereto—such is the second truth'" (*Sutta Nipata*, II, 12). But even this twofold designation of the Buddha's teaching was reduced to a single statement: "Just as, brethren, the mighty ocean has but one savor, the savor of salt, even so brethren, has my teaching but one savor, the savor of spiritual liberation" (*Udana*, 56). The full pain of this human condition of earth is expressed by Buddhaghosa: "All health ends in illness, youth in decrepitude, life in death; earthly existence is originated by birth, afflicted by age, upset by illness, and destroyed by death. Thus it is said:

> 'As though great mountains composed of rock
> So vast they soared into the heavens
> Were to advance from all four directions
> Crushing beneath them all living beings;
> So age and death oppress every thing that lives,
> Warriors, priests, merchants, and shudras,
> Outcastes and gatherers of refuse,
> Passing by no one, overwhelming all;
> Nor do armies of elephants, nor men in war chariots,
> Nor soldiers, nor any form of magic spell, nor earthly treasure
> Avail to hold them off.'"
>
> —Visuddhimagga, VIII, 15

THE INSUBSTANTIAL WORLD

No-substance, no-soul, no-self, no-person, no abiding reality whatsoever— these are the basic expressions needed to describe the third of the basic characteristics of reality, after speaking of the transient and the sorrowful nature of things. In the realm of metaphysics this doctrine of the insubstantial nature of things is the most distinctive doctrine of Buddhism. It is the foundation of the other two characteristics of things, their transient and sorrowful nature. Also this is the most difficult for us to appreciate. The other things that we have mentioned, the transient and sorrowful aspects of reality, are common to other Indian traditions and to many traditions of mankind. But unique to Buddhism is its spirituality based on its denial of any underlying subject, any abiding nature. This doctrine is especially difficult for Westerners because Western religion, spirituality, thought, and literature have generally been committed to acceptance of both the objective and the subjective orders as real. We are committed to the reality of the soul, the inner principle that gives to man the distinctive qualities of his being. This has been further developed in the acceptance of the human personality as an abiding and indestructible principle that even survives physical death in a transtemporal order of reality. We have also a positive conception of divine reality that provides the basis on which all created reality rests as its support. Both the Hellenic philosophical tradition and the Christian religious tradition have insisted firmly on the substantial aspect of things, however this was explained.

None of this is found in Buddhism. All that Buddhism asserts is Nirvana, which is the extinction of all infratemporal experience. When inquiry is made as to the reality of Nirvana the answer is found in the mysterious fourfold denial of Buddhism concerning the existence of Buddha after death. "He cannot be said to exist, he cannot be said not to exist, he cannot be said both to exist and not exist, he cannot be said neither to exist nor not exist" (*Samyutta Nikaya*, IV, 376). Thus there does remain an opening into a further mystery which is presented most often as the experience "beyond perception and non-perception." This may very well be a negative manner of indicating the infinite and eternal, the transcendence of what is beyond the composite and the momentary, beyond thought and imagination. There is a particular aversion from assertion of the individual self. Of all divisions of reality, form, feeling, perception, habitual tendencies, consciousness, it must be said that none of these is the self. Of everything it must be said *n'eso 'ham asmi* ("This am I not"). Thus the *aham* (the "I") is beyond designation within the particular, the phenomenal order. Also it is forbidden to use the first-person singular of the verb "to be," forbidden to say *asmi* ("I am") (*Sutta Nipata*, 916). *Asmita* (I-am-ness) is the supremely vicious act, that which more than anything else excludes from salvation.

What is experienced as a soul, a subject, a person, or a nature is only an unstable composite. These composite structures do not inhere in any stable subject. The clustering and the association are all momentary. Everything is, from moment to moment, put together and taken apart. Reality is

changing from moment to moment just as the flickering light of the candle
is not the same from one moment to the next. "Just as a puppet is empty,
without life, without activity even though it walks and stands through the
manipulation of strings and pieces of wood and seems as if it had initiative
and activity, just so this realm of names and forms, the physical-psychic
world is empty, without a soul, without activity even though the composite walks and stands through its physical and psychic components, and
seems to have initiative and activity. This is how it should be looked upon.
The ancients tell us:

'The psychic and the physical elements are really present
But no human being can be identified
There is only emptiness fixed up like a mechanical doll
Only a heap of sorrow, piled up like straw and sticks."
—*Visuddhimagga*, XVIII, 31

The reality of the world is analogous to the bubbles on the surface of a
stream: "It is as though the Ganges should carry down on its surface a
frothy mass of bubbles and a person with good eyesight should observe
and examine its composition. So viewing it, he would find it empty, insubstantial, unreal. What reality could there be in such bubbles? So it is
with any physical being whatsoever in past, present, or future, which a
person sees, observes, and examines; he would find it empty, insubstantial,
unreal. What reality could there be in any bodily being?" *(Samyutta Nikaya,*
III, 140–141). What is said of the bodily reality or form of things could also
be said of feelings, perception, and all the other *skandhas*. All these are empty
of reality, as so much airy foam or bubbles that burst and nothing remains.
Perhaps the most precise expression of this doctrine of Buddhism is that
given by Buddhaghosa:

Suffering exists, but there is no one who suffers;
Deeds are, but there is no doer of deeds.
Nirvana is, but no one is blissful;
The path is, but there is no traveller on it.
—*Visuddhimagga*, XVI, 90

This leads to the supreme and last difficulty encountered in the rise to
spiritual perfection according to Buddhist doctrine: abandonment of the
conviction "I exist." "Let a person by correct understanding destroy the
deepest root of that which is such a hindrance, every conviction of 'I am'"
(Sutta Nipata, 916). This is the final abandonment, the breaking of the

last ties to the phenomenal order. Then comes the experience of Nirvana—total liberation. This is generally attained in the height of the fourth realm of mental concentration: "A monk who gets beyond the realm of infinite consciousness, considering that there is nothing at all, enters into and dwells in the realm of nothingness" (*Majjhima Nikaya*, I, 297).

Chapter Fifteen

Spiritual Discipline

The spirituality associated with the Buddhist evaluation of the world and of man is characterized by the quest for a wisdom that will liberate man from his mental illusions concerning the world and by a discipline that will release him from his emotional attachment to the world. Man must attain an experience that is totally "other." The solution for life's sorrow must provide an absolute transformation of life, a total release from the transient, sorrowful, insubstantial world. Both in its analysis of the world and in its salvation discipline Buddhism is marked by the feeling of certitude. There was no doubt in the mind of Buddha and his followers that they possessed a spiritual treasure of the highest value, something that had never yet existed in such a pure state. In the analysis of the situation, in its transforming spiritual discipline, in the goal established, there is the certitude that marks all the higher spiritual traditions of mankind. The analysis and the solution were as big as the human situation. The vision was presented, the path outlined, the goal assured. Man had only to respond with appropriate vigor.

The response of the people was worthy of both the program and its author. The simple grandeur of the spiritual advice of Buddha supplied the expectancy of all Asia. It illumined a darkness that had hitherto existed. "As in the last month of the rainy season at the harvest period, when there is a clear and cloudless sky, and the sun, rising in the heavens and dispelling the darkness, shines forth in its resplendent glory, even so this teaching of Dhamma which is happiness both in the present and in the future, driving away the contrary doctrines of other mendicants and brahmans, shines forth resplendent over the earth" (*Majjhima Nikaya*, I, 317). This radiance also marks those who follow the prescribed path. "The mendicant, however youthful, who responds to the teaching of the Enlightened One, illumines the world as the moon, coming forth from behind a cloud, lights up the night" (*Dhammapada*, 381). This illumination is also vivifying power. "As in the forest the trees blossom forth anew in the first month of summer's heat, so did the Blessed One set forth for the profit of the world his teachings that lead to Nirvana" (*Khuddhakapatha*, "The Gem," 12).

The Middle Path was such a human way—not the path of resignation or of violent effort, not the way of indulgence or of ascetic rigor. Disengagement from the phenomenal world was not to be attained by a wrenching apart or by a sudden twisting of human life out of its customary orbit. What was offered was a program carefully adjusted to what was humanly possible. Considering the severity of asceticism practiced in India, one can say that Buddha did not propose an ascetic path, but a path immediately recognized as the Middle Path, the way between severity and indulgence. Considering its combination of calm and effort, of the affective and the intellectual, the social and the individual, the mystical and the moral, the human and the transhuman, Buddhism can be said to have developed the highest norms and most thorough spiritual discipline of the Asian world. Everything is founded on the simple yet profound proposition: "Keep yourself from every evil deed, do that which is good, purify your thoughts within. This is the teaching of the saints" (*Dhammapada*, 183). This was early recognized as the most basic of norms for the guidance of human actions. It soon became the most famous verse in the Buddhist canon. For the monks the most general rule of life was stated with equal simplicity:

> *Do not revile, do not injure, live disciplined by the rule;*
> *Eat with moderation, dwell in solitude,*
> *Meditate with earnest concentration.*
> *This is the teaching of the enlightened ones.*
> —*Dhammapada*, 185

In accord with this fundamental moderation and simplicity, the famous
first sermon of Buddha in Deer Park at Banaras begins with the proposition
that there are two extremes to be avoided by those who have given up the
world. The first is a life given over to pleasure, one immersed in delights of
the senses and desires, which is ignoble and profitless. The other is a life of
excessive austerity, which is not only painful, but ignoble and humanly
stifling. Avoiding these two extremes the Buddha presented his Middle
Path, "which leads to understanding, to wisdom, which brings about serenity, knowledge, enlightenment, Nirvana." With even more directness the
same basic principle is stated in the *Dhammapada*:

> *Not nakedness, nor tangled hair, nor uncleanness,*
> *Nor prolonged fasting, nor resting on the earth,*
> *Nor dust or dirt, nor sitting on one's heels,*
> *Can sanctify a person disturbed by doubt.*
> *Whoever lives a peaceful quiet life,*
> *Even if brightly clothed*
> *So long as he live a disciplined ordered life,*
> *Following the way of truth*
> *Avoiding injury to any living being,*
> *He is the true mendicant, the true ascetic, the true Brahman.*
> —*Dhammapada*, 141–142

The Dhammapada (Way of Perfection), the scriptural text from which
these quotations are drawn, constitutes one of the spiritual treasures of all
mankind. It has a splendor found only in the works of the highest spiritual
insight. Here and elsewhere in Buddhist writings we find another quality
that characterizes Buddhist spirituality along with its sureness, its moderation, its attractiveness. This is the insistence on spiritual effort. Many words
are used to indicate the personal drive that should mark the spiritual
personality: exertion, striving, concentration of mind, getting up, rousing
a person's self, the use of energy, zeal, manly vigor, industry. The word
viriya (energy) is frequently used. "Rouse yourselves, O Monks, to a still
greater effort to what is as yet not reached, to conquer what has not yet been
conquered, to realize what is yet to be realized" (*Majjhima Nikaya*, III, 79).
No one else can supply for personal effort. The *Dhammapada* opens with a
forceful expression of this: "What we are is the consequence of what we
have thought, it is based on our thought, it is constituted of our thoughts.
If anyone speaks or acts with a wicked thought, pain follows him as the
wheel follows the foot of the ox drawing the cart. What we are is the
consequence of what we have thought, it is based on our thoughts, it is

constituted of our thoughts. If anyone speaks or acts with a virtuous thought, joy follows him as a shadow that never leaves him" (*Dhammapada*, I, 2). In much of this insistence on personal responsibility Buddhism is seeking to offset the influence of the Ajivika doctrine of fatalism. "If from negligence, sir, you avoided doing good in deed and word they will certainly do unto you in accordance with that negligence. For this wrong deed of yours was not done by your mother or father, it was done neither by brother or sister, by friends or acquaintances: it was not done by any relatives, by any monk or Brahman, nor by any deity. This evil deed was done by you. Within yourself you will experience its consequences" (*Majjhima Nikaya*, III, 179–180).

The detailed program of perfection provided by the Buddhist life discipline is marked with the same basic wisdom which characterizes many of the higher spiritual and mystical disciplines of mankind. There are three stages of perfection, designated as virtue (*Sila*), a deepened inner awareness (*Samadhi*), and saving wisdom (*Panna*). The famous eightfold path is itself divided according to these stages of spiritual development. "The three divisions are not arranged in accord with the eightfold path, but the eightfold path is arranged according to the threefold division. Right speech, right action, and right livelihood are in the class of virtue. Right effort, right mindfulness, and right concentration are in the class of concentration. Right view and right purpose are in the class of wisdom" (*Majjhima Nikaya*, I, 301).

VIRTUE

This is of course the foundation of everything in man's spiritual formation. Nothing can be done unless there is a basic order in man's discipline over himself and in his relation to others. "Virtue is the ground on which the wise person establishes himself and develops wisdom. Thus the ardent monk, undeceived, disengages himself from needless involvement of life. This is the foundation, like the solid earth to men. It is also the root of all growth in goodness, the starting-point of all the Buddha's instruction. Virtue, on this depends true bliss" (*Milinda Panha*, 34).

The guidance offered by Buddhism is not limited to generalizations concerning virtue; it is quite specific in establishing the basic norms of human conduct. Regarding the monks there were specific rules, some two hundred twenty-seven, which governed their conduct, but many of them were simply rules for the orderly living of community life. The most basic of the moral teachings were contained in a list of ten prohibitions, according to which a monk must refrain from:

1 killing living things
2 taking what is not given
3 unchastity
4 falsehood
5 intoxicants
6 eating at unseasonable times
7 seeing displays, dancing, singing, and music
8 use of garlands, scents, and unguents
9 use of a high or a big bed
10 receiving gold or silver

—*Kuddhakapatha, II*

The first five constitute the basic moral precepts for all Buddhists, laymen as well as monks. To these first five, laymen added the next three during the special periods of fasting. An even more detailed listing of norms of conduct for the people is given in many of the other scriptures. Of special significance is the discourse entitled the *Sigalovada Suttanta* (*Digha Nikaya*, Sutta 31). Here, in what is known as the religious rule for the layman or the householder, a deeply human approach to life can be found along with a sincere affection for others. The virtues recommended to all range over the whole list of possible virtues, but some seem to dominate. Faith is especially prominent, along with spiritual energy, mindfulness, and wisdom. In one instance seven good qualities are mentioned: "Faith, uprightness, conscientiousness, learning, spiritual vigor, mindfulness, and wisdom" (*Anguttara Nikaya*, IV, 145). Sometimes four are listed. To a householder is said: "By these four conditions a man attains to benefit and bliss in the future world; advance in faith, virtue, generosity, wisdom" (*Anguttara Nikaya*, IV, 283).

MENTAL CONCENTRATION

The next stage of development after these basic virtues is the stage of mental concentration. Buddhism is above all the practice of detachment from frivolous external things along with a serene indwelling of a person within his own being. It is in this phase of the eightfold path that the full brilliance of the Buddhist way is seen. This development of inwardness includes right effort, right mindfulness, right concentration. Effort has already been mentioned in outlining the general qualities of Buddhist spirituality. This effort is expected to be shown especially in attachment to the inward recollection of mind. Since this required long training it could be carried out fully only by the monk who lived apart from the cares of home and family. It was for this that the monk went forth into the homeless life. Once there the training in interior recollection could be carried out in full earnestness. Final purification of virtue took place only in the stage of mindfulness. "Just as water fallen on a lotus leaf drips off from it and disappears, not adhering to the leaf, just so when a monk is adorned with the jewel of meditation, then thoughts of lust, of anger, cruelty and all other evil thoughts founded in pride, self-righteousness, obstinacy and doubt, these coming into contact with such recollection, flow off, dissolve and do not adhere to him because of the great purity in the discipline of meditation. This is what is designated as the Blessed One's 'Jewel of Meditation' and such are the meditation jewels displayed in the bazaar of gems of the Blessed One.

> 'Evil thoughts cannot arise beneath the forehead
> Adorned by this circlet of jewels.
> It removes all confused and distracting thoughts.
> Take it for your own, wear it as a crown.' "
> —Milinda Panha, 337

This stage of mindfulness, the seventh stage of the eightfold path, is one of the most typical aspects of Buddhism. In its full development a person becomes conscious at every moment of precisely what he is doing both in the bodily order and in the functioning of his own mind: "A monk on going forth or coming back, acts with a clear awareness of what he is doing, when carrying his outer cloak, his bowl and robe; when eating, drinking, chewing, tasting; . . . when he is walking, standing, sitting, asleep, awake, talking or silent, he acts in a clear and conscious manner" (*Majjhima Nikaya,* I, 57). This involves constant reflection on the full implications of what it is to be a physical being, to have a body subject to dissolution. While we in the West may recognize this theoretically but remain unimpressed, the Buddhist wishes to be thoroughly and absolutely aware of the inevitable corruption to which the body is subject. Thus the famous cemetery meditations of Buddhism were instituted, as described in the sixth chapter of the greatest of all Buddhist guides to meditation, the *Path of Purity* of Buddhaghosa.

Among the most difficult of all realities for man to face is death and the bodily corruption consequent on death. Yet life must be lived aware of this end of man's physical being. In spiritual traditions generally, meditation on this subject is strongly recommended in order to release a person from excessive attachment and emotional involvement with bodily health and beauty. Buddhism feels the need for something more than abstract consideration of the subject. Buddhism advises the viewing of and meditation on a dead and disintegrating body. This may be a shocking confrontation, but such effort at total realism is part of the Buddhist spirituality itself. If anything successful is to be done about the full depth of human sorrow and affliction then man must not flinch before the extreme afflictions to which he is subject. If death and disintegration are inevitable, then man must never forget this for an instant in the conduct of his life. Everything must be done with this awareness present to him; thus follows the Buddhist need for actual viewing of the body of the dead to understand and remember that this is the lot of everyone.

That this might be done without upset and with most benefit the guidance of a teacher must be sought: "When setting forth the meditation subject to him, the teacher should explain it in every detail. He should give directions for going for the purpose of recognizing the manifestation of the repulsive, the relation with associated manifestations, the eleven ways of looking at the manifestation, the reviewing of the way to go and to return by, concluding with guidance about understanding the manifestation" (*Visuddhimagga*, VI, 12). One significant aspect of this meditation is that the person must go alone to the charnel ground to view a dead body. "He should go alone without a companion. He should not give up his fundamental meditation subject but keep it clearly in mind. Let him take along a stick to ward off attacks by dogs and other animals. Let him remain in constant mindfulness, establishing it well, not turning his mind outwards, determined that all his faculties, including his mind, should be directed inwards" (*Visuddhimagga*, VI, 23). Buddhaghosa is fully aware of the terrifying nature as well as the inestimable value of this meditation. "If anyone goes at the wrong time to the place of the distended corpse and there opens his eyes to view it just as it is, then as soon as he looks at it, the dead body appears as if it were standing up, terrifying and pursuing him. When he beholds such an awful and fearsome object, his mind grows dizzy.

He is as someone crazed, held in an extreme fear and fright with his hair standing on end. Indeed among the thirty-eight meditation subjects presented in the scriptures there is none so terrifying as this" (*Visuddhimagga*, VI, 56). Afterwards, however, a person has an experiential awareness of just what old age, illness, and death are. By becoming totally aware of these things man is finally relieved from them and is spiritually able to surmount them, and this is the great gain, the treasure finally won: "Certainly by this means I will be freed from age and death" (*Visuddhimagga*, VI, 87). Then "Just as a poor man who received a great treasure of gems would protect it, appreciate and be attached to it, 'I have got what is hard indeed to get!' so too this monk should hold on to this new awareness, be attached to it and experience a reverence for it as one who knows its value, 'I have obtained this meditation subject, which is truly as difficult to obtain as a rich treasure is difficult for a poor man to get.'" (*Visuddhimagga*, VI, 64–65).

Many other subjects of mindfulness are proposed for the person seeking the full spiritual development of life. In exacting detail the monk is expected to pursue these meditations on life in all its phases until he is totally confirmed in virtue and is spiritually relieved from excessive attachment to anything in the phenomenal order. Then he is ready for the next stage of spiritual development, that of full mental concentration and elevation of mind. This is the stage of the spiritual life prior to the attainment of the saving wisdom.

FULL CONCENTRATION OF MIND

Next comes the stage of mental ascent beyond mindfulness. The benefits of this higher stage of meditation are indicated in the *Questions of King Milinda*: "There are, O king, these twenty-eight excellent qualities of meditation in the perception of which the Tathagatas devoted themselves to it. And what are they? Meditation preserves him who meditates, it gives him long life, and endows him with power, it cleanses him from faults, it removes from him any bad reputation giving him a good name, it destroys discontent in him filling him with content, it releases him from all fear endowing him with confidence, it removes sloth far from him filling him with zeal, it takes away any ill-will and dullness, it puts an end to pride, it breaks down all doubt, it makes his heart to be at peace, it softens his mind, it makes him glad, it makes him grave, it gains him much advantage, it makes him worthy of reverence, it fills him with joy, it fills him with delight, it shows him the transitory nature of all compounded things, it puts an end to rebirth, it obtains for him all the benefits of renunciation. These, O king, are the twenty-eight virtues of meditation on the perception of which the Tathagatas devote themselves to it. But it is because the Tathagatas, O king, long for the enjoyment of the bliss of attainment, of the joy of the tranquil state of nirvana that they devote themselves to meditation, with their minds fixed on the end they aim at" (*Milinda Panha*, 139–140).

Consequent upon the full knowledge of things meditated upon in the stage of mindfulness a person is established in virtue and has destroyed in its very roots the attraction of the phenomenal world. Here the ascent of the mind begins in earnest. It is difficult to find a word to translate the term *jhana* of the early Buddhists, a word which is related to the *dhyana* of the Sanskrit, which means "inner recollection." It is sometimes translated into English as "trance," sometimes as "absorption," as "concentration," or as "meditation." None of these is fully satisfactory; all have at least partially false connotations. But whatever word is used one must realize that the end result is not some state of self-hypnosis, as has sometimes been suggested. It is something entirely different. Nor is it a state of unconsciousness. It is rather a state of superconsciousness. Again it is not the self-indwelling as in the case of the Yogic Kaivalya, or isolation status of the Purusha, the spiritual element of man. In this latter case the word entasis can be used to describe the final status achieved. But this is exactly what Buddhism does not possess since there is no Purusha, just as there is no Atman or Self as this is presented in Hinduism. Buddhism is more an ecstasis than an enstasis, or rather it is an ecstasis after an enstasis.

This final phase of Buddhist achievement must be dealt with as the Buddhists themselves dealt with it, as something which cannot be properly designated but which can be indicated in negative terms as being beyond the realm of perception and non-perception. Yet there are moments when the Buddhist scriptures do indicate that the final status is a type of self-awareness: "Suppose there were a pail of water, unclouded by coloring, unheated, not agitated, free from algae and water plants, without the least ripple, clear, limpid, transparent; suppose this pail of water were placed there in the open and a man were to gaze into it to see his own countenance. He would of course recognize his own features as they really are. Just so when a person lives with his heart neither bound nor oppressed by desire, passion, antagonism, laziness, worry or indecision, and knows how to free himself from these, then he recognizes, he sees his own goal, another's goal, the goal of both, as it is in reality. Then even the teachings he has not studied are clear, how much more those studied" (*Anguttara Nikaya*, III, 235).

But this serene state of higher consciousness undisturbed by the turmoil of time or its fluctuations is reached only by stages. These stages are worked out with utmost detail by Buddhist spiritual writers. Again Buddhaghosa is the master expositor. He outlines eight stages of inner absorption through which the mind passes. In these stages there is a progressive removal of rational thought, of feeling experiences, to the stage of consciousness beyond the perception of any form. Then there is the awareness of limitless space which is the preparation for the stage wherein the mind is aware of nothing whatsoever. This leads to the final stage wherein the mind dwells beyond perception and non-perception. This is the highest point in the recollections. This final stage of inwardness enables the person to attain the final purification of life. "By rising entirely beyond the plane of neither perception nor non-perception, a monk enters on and dwells in the cessation of perception and feeling; and having such insight his cankers are totally eliminated. This monk is referred to as one who has thrown a darkness around Mara. Having obstructed Mara's vision so that it cannot see, he goes invisible beyond this Evil One. He crosses beyond involvement in the world. He walks and sleeps with assurance. The reason for this? He has passed beyond the influence of Mara" (*Majjhima Nikaya*, I, 175).

Chapter Sixteen

Supreme Bliss: Nirvana

After discussing Buddha, his experience of reality, and the spiritual discipline he proposed for leading man beyond the phenomenal world, we come now to that experience itself. Everything in Buddhism leads to this moment; everything must be judged by this moment. Man is destined for ineffable peace, a higher vision, a bliss beyond this world in the realm of the unconditioned. This experience, presented with utmost delicacy in the early Buddhist compositions, required a corresponding delicacy of understanding in the reader. In this realm human language comes to its termination. Man must suggest what he cannot clearly present. Above all, he must keep his awareness of complete "otherness." Beyond the world of composition there is the world of simplicity. Man speaks only in the world of time and in human language, the world of complexity. Yet in this world of complexity he can at least indicate that there is a world of simplicity. He can indicate what he cannot directly express.

For the most part this must be by way of negation, by way of otherness. If this is the realm of sorrow, that is the realm of no sorrow; if this is the world of fullness, that is the world of emptiness; if this is the realm of de-

158

sire, that is the realm of no-desire; if this is the realm of the composite, that is the realm of the non-composite; if this is the realm of the conditioned, that is the realm of the unconditioned; if this is the realm of time, that is the world of eternity; if this is the realm of life, that is the realm beyond life; if this is the world of limitation, that is the world of liberation; if this is the world of perception, that is the world of non-perception; if this is the world of imagination, that is the realm without figure or image. This is not an easy process for the human mind, which desires positive if limited assertion. A slight bit of this negative process it can take, but a full carrying out of this process leaves the mind starved and destitute. This is the great transition to be made, to the world of no-mind, no-thought, of emptiness or Sunyata. It has never been easy for man to talk about this final experience. The Hindu would only say, "He who understands does not understand, he who does not understand, he understands" (*Kena Upanishad*, II, 3). Plotinus in the West develops the negative way of expression and is followed by Dionysius in the Christian tradition: "We earnestly beseech that we may enter that darkness which is beyond every light, and by losing all seeing and understanding may we thereby come to experience that which is beyond all vision and comprehension" (*Mystical Theology*, chap. II).

Outside of this mystical tradition influenced by Neoplatonism, Christian thought has been strongly centered on the positive aspect of that supreme reality. Buddhism was more consistently aware of its negative aspects. Buddhism could not give a name to this other world, but could only designate the experience of this otherness as Nirvana (extinction) or as Sunyata (emptiness). Buddhism was more concentrated on what it was moving away from than what it was moving toward. It spoke of this otherness as the further side of the stream of *Samsara* (the phenomenal world). There is a reticence even in speaking of this experience. This other state did have its real aspect, but this was not something that lay within the realm of intelligible description. The genius of Buddhism lay in its caution even in affirming the existence of this other realm. Buddhism denied both the affirmation and the denial of this other world. It denied the affirmation lest this be understood falsely in terms of some existence similar to earthly existence. It denied the denial lest men consider this other world to have no manner of existence.

It is obvious that the Buddhist way of speaking of Nirvana, this final spiritual experience of mankind, is not the manner in which we of the West present our ideas of heavenly bliss, of final salvation. It does not include positive ideas of union with a divine person. It dislikes picturing this final state as a place of heavenly bliss. It does not talk about the union of a blessed community in this final state of man. It speaks in its own way, or rather is reticent in its own way. To understand this reticence is the challenge.

Again it must be noted that all Buddhist ideas were in a state of constant change. There is no fixed explanation of Nirvana that is adequate for all periods of Buddhist development. Those moments in which Buddhists explained Nirvana in a nihilistic sense are extremely rare. Nirvana is consistently explained in terms that indicate an experience of ineffable bliss. Later there developed a master concept in terms of Sunyata, which is translated as "void" or "emptiness." This is the master concept of Buddhism, as Being is the master concept of Western thought. It is the keystone in the arch of Buddhist thought, the supreme way of indicating the experience beyond all that is discovered within the composite world. If the full exposition of Sunyata came at a later date, it had its foundations in the earliest period of Buddhism and is only a further explication of the experience itself. Buddhism does not explain the experience so much as describe the context in which man attains the experience. The experience itself cannot be expressed, described, or even discussed in any direct fashion. What can be done is to present the conditions in which the experience takes place. This is the purpose of the entire Buddhist spiritual discipline. If there is some way of indicating the qualities found in the experience it is by way of the concept of Sunyata. An explanation of this term must be saved for the discussion of the later Mahayana Buddhism, for only then was this teaching fully stated. This full statement is found in the works of Nagarjuna (second century A.D.), the supreme thinker of the Buddhist world.

Despite the consistent use of negatives in speaking of Nirvana there are some instances in which more positive expressions are used. The most significant passage indicating the positive qualities of the Nirvana experience is that contained in the Udana: "There is, brethren, an unborn, a not-become, a not-made, a not-compounded. If, brethren, there were no unborn, not-become, not-made, not-compounded, there could be no liberation from what is born, become, made and compounded" (Udana, 80). Although all the terms used are negative, there is at least the positive assertion that what is so indicated does exist. The important thing is that it cannot be placed in any category of earthly reality whether of the physical or psychic orders. It is not among the nama-rupa, that is, "the realm of names and forms," although this is better translated as "the mental and material order," as these are known to us in the West. Nirvana is consistently associated with removal from the world of changing realities. "The cessation of becoming is Nirvana" (*Samyutta Nikaya*, II, 116).

Buddhaghosa argues the reality of Nirvana with some thoroughness. "Does Nirvana not exist simply because it cannot be intellectually grasped, as the horns of a rabbit? Not so, for Nirvana can be attained in the proper way, that is by the proper means. . . . Thus we should not say that Nirvana does not exist because it is not grasped, just as we should not say that what the simple uneducated man does not understand is beyond understanding. If Nirvana does not exist, then we must conclude that the true way, including the three phases of development beginning with virtue and completed with wisdom, would be in vain. But this is not in vain since it does attain Nirvana" (*Visuddhimagga*, XVI, 67–68). Then Buddhaghosa passes on to discuss the modality of the argumentation process. The objection is brought: "But is not Nirvana really destruction, since the scriptures describe Nirvana as the destruction of greed, of hatred, etc.?" To which the answer is given: "This does not follow, for then it would indicate that perfection itself were mere destruction for that too is described in negative terms as the destruction of the vices of greed etc." Why, then is Nirvana described in negative terms? "Because it is so very subtle. This indeed is the very reason why the Blessed One considered not becoming a teacher after his illumination but to commit himself to a program of inaction" (*Visuddhimagga*, XVI, 69–70).

Since Buddhism is so consistently concerned with relief from the suffering inherent in human existence it is quite natural that Buddhism should on occasion be identified simply as the place "where there is no suffering" (*Sutta Nipata*, 79). This was the fulfillment of the original quest of Buddha. From the moment when he became aware of suffering he sought for the unborn, unageing, immortal, undecaying, unsorrowing, unstained, the absolute release from the bonds, Nirvana (*Majjhima Nikaya*, I, 163). Yet this place "where there is no suffering" is not any identifiable place in the physical order. It is a place of the spiritual and moral order. To the question of the king: "Is there any place on which a man may stand and, ordering his life aright, realise Nirvana?" the answer given is: "Virtue, O king is the place. For if grounded in virtue, and careful in attention— whether in the land of the Scythians or the Greeks, whether in China or Tartary, whether in Alexandria or in Nikumba, whether in Benares or in Kosala . . . wheresoever he may be, the man who orders his life aright will realise Nirvana" (*Milinda Panha*, 327).

This experience takes place in a timeless state, yet Nirvana is attained in this present life. "There time is not because of their having been set entirely free" (*Milinda Panha*, 50). Thus there is a simultaneous dwelling within time and outside time. But time in its ordinary sense is eliminated as an obstacle, as a source of sorrow. In the *Udana* there is a remarkable description of this experience.

> *Where water, earth, fire, air have no place,*
> *No stars shine there, no sun beams down.*
> *No moon gleams over the earth, nor is there any darkness.*
> *Thus when the illumined one, the brahman, by insight*
> *Has of his own self arrived at truth*
> *He is freed from form and no-form, from pleasure and pain.*
> —*Udana*, 9

This sense of freedom is one of the triumphal aspects of Buddhism. "This noble discipline is not for attainment of possession, honor, or renown. It is not for increase in moral goodness, for concentration or even for attainment of knowledge and insight. Indestructible freedom of mind! Such is the purpose, the end of this exalted discipline, its essence, its fulfillment" (*Majjhima Nikaya*, I, 197).

Of special importance is the bliss that goes with this experience. "Nirvana, O king, has no pain in it. It is bliss unalloyed. When you maintain that Nirvana is painful, that which you call 'painful' is not Nirvana. It is the preliminary stage of the realization of Nirvana, it is the process of seeking after Nirvana. Nirvana itself is bliss pure and simple, there is no pain mixed with it" (*Milinda Panha*, 314). The joy of Nirvana is available even here on earth, for it has nothing to do with time or with the life in this body. Indeed those that have not yet entered into this experience can know how joyful it is "by hearing the glad words of those who have seen Nirvana" (*Milinda Panha*, 70).

Chapter Seventeen

Tradition Transformed: Mahayana Buddhism

Thus far this study of Buddhism has been concerned with the early form of the tradition, characterized by awareness of the historical Buddha, by the spiritual ideal of the Arhat and disciplined living in a monastic community, by a program of perfection based on individual spiritual and moral efforts, and by the goal of Nirvana to be attained by the eightfold path. This Buddhism, after some five hundred years of development, around the beginning of the Christian era, underwent a transformation which considerably enriched and expanded the early tradition. A new Buddhism appeared that was characterized by the elevation of Buddha to divine status and to an ontological absolute, by the ideal of Buddhahood for all rather than Nirvana, by new intellectual insights, by a spiritual ideal of vicarious suffering for the salvation of others, and by a salvation bestowed through a heavenly grace in response to faith and devotion to Amida, the new Savior Buddha.

The transition period to the Mahayana is a fascinating phase of

163

Buddhism. The inner dynamic of Buddhism manifested itself to an extraordinary degree. This unfolding of its inner life brought about a restatement of Buddhist teaching in new and more expansive terms. The new Buddhism adopted for itself the name of *Mahayana* (the Great Way) and designated the prior tradition of Buddhism as *Hinayana* (the Little Way). Ever since, they have been among the most basic terms of the entire Buddhist tradition. This terminology is not known or used within the earlier tradition, but only in the later Mahayana tradition. The Hinayana tradition designates itself simply as the community following the Buddhist Dharma. When the Mahayana arose, the earlier Buddhism had already divided into various sectarian traditions, some eighteen in all, each of which had its own identity. Of these many expressions of Hinayana Buddhism only one survives as a living tradition of the present, the *Theravada* (the Doctrine of the Elders).

The Theravada form of Buddhism is found in the southern regions of Asia, in Ceylon, Burma, Thailand, Cambodia, Laos, and to some extent in Vietnam and Malaya, thus it is called Southern Buddhism. The Mahayana came to be called Northern Buddhism since it is found in central Asia, China, Korea, and Japan as the dominant form of Buddhism. The Theravada tradition has preserved, in the Pali language, the basic scriptural collection of the earlier Buddhism. This collection is known as the Pali canon. The only complete canon of the early Buddhism that remains, it is accepted by all traditions. In English translation this collection is contained in some thirty ordinary volumes, some quite brief, others more extended. Mahayana Buddhism has a large collection of scriptures of its own, in addition to the earlier scriptures. But whereas there is a clear distinction in the earlier Buddhism between the canonical books of scripture and the non-canonical expositions of Buddhist teachings, this is not entirely true of the Mahayana Buddhist scriptures. The Mahayana Buddhist writings in their entirety include a vast collection written in some fifteen languages throughout the Asian world. Four of these must be considered the major languages of Mahayana Buddhism: Sanskrit, Tibetan, Chinese, and Japanese. Among the early Mahayana scriptures generally listed as of special importance are the Wisdom Sutras, the *Lotus, Vimalakirti, Lankavatara, Avatamsaka, Surangama, Samdhinirmocana,* and *Sukhivativyuha Sutras.* This is only a partial list of the best known of the Mahayana scriptures.

The Mahayana called itself the Great Way because it had a more exalted concept of Buddha, a more impressive ideal of salvation in the attainment of Buddhahood rather than Nirvana, and because it provided a more abundant salvation program for all mankind. It fulfilled the spiritual needs of a larger number of people and provided a sublime ideal of vicarious suffering whereby a person might bring about the salvation of others. Also the Mahayana inspired a more lofty intellectual expression of Buddhist teaching than anything found in the Hinayana tradition. The magnitude and complexity of this accomplishment is matched by its historical extension and cultural influence throughout the East-Asian world, as well as in Tibet and in central Asia. It was also from this tradition that Tantric Buddhism developed, which became prominent especially in the Indian region of Bengal and in Tibet.

Buddhism in the Mahayana tradition became definitely a religion, with Buddha as a supreme being worshipped as such with ritual, festival, and prayer. To him were attributed the origin, inner sustaining presence, and final goal of the entire order of things. Even since the second century A.D., the savior aspect of the Buddha has been especially exalted. Because of this religious development Mahayana Buddhism seems to bring about a clear break with the earlier Buddhist tradition, yet it is more proper to say that a basic continuity remained. Everything found in the later period is contained in seminal form in the earlier traditions, although a vast expansion of the tradition did take place. Yet in this process Mahayana Buddhism remained absolutely faithful to the original genius of the tradition. Buddhism had a religious aspect in its development from the beginning. Buddha was never considered simply another human personality; his earliest followers had a fundamentally religious attitude toward him as a savior figure. The successive developments of devotionalism within the tradition can hardly outdo the devotion expressed in such early compositions as the *Sutta Nipata*. Even the supreme intellectual concept of Mahayana Buddhism, the doctrine of Sunyata, was in the tradition from the beginning.

What we observe in the Mahayana is a radical dissatisfaction with the mere negative critique of the phenomenal order. The Mahayana sought for contact with an absolute realm of being. During the period when Buddhism was concerned with the world as transient, sorrowful, and insubstantial, there was immediate satisfaction in sounding the depths of nothingness in the phenomenal order. But this had no satisfactory meaning unless there were some other order standing over against this realm of transient phenomena. There was an increasing concern for the true, the real nature of the Buddha, for the positive aspect of perfection attained by the new wisdom, and above all for the true relationship between the absolute and the phenomenal realms of reality. There was also an effort to understand the stages of the revelation process, for it became gradually clear to the most penetrating minds of the tradition that a developmental process was taking place in the Buddhist tradition itself. The doctrine of Buddhism as a developing process or as a progressive revelation provided the basis for an orthodox interpretation of the changes introduced in the later period.

BUDDHA AS AN ONTOLOGICAL ABSOLUTE

Docetism. In the last two centuries of the pre-Christian era and the early centuries of the Christian era there were several points of controversy within Buddhism. The first and most significant concerned the nature of Buddha. The extraordinary attributes associated with Gotama Buddha gradually brought about a deepened reverence. This led to an ever-higher conception of the Buddha personality and the mission he accomplished on earth. All of this found expression in the later lives of Buddha, the *Lalitavistara* and the *Buddhacarita.* In these Buddha is presented as a unique being, illuminating the entire world and fulfilling wondrous deeds on a cosmic scale. The entire universe responded to his birth, the various phases of his life, and to his death. The impact of these stories was felt throughout the Buddhist world. In other compositions, in works such as the *Points of Controversy* and in the *Questions of King Milinda,* the problem was discussed as to whether or not the Buddha had truly lived upon the earth. Already the tradition was being strongly influenced by those convinced that Buddha belonged strictly to the world of absolute reality. Any contact he had with this phenomenal world was only apparent. In the *Points of Controversy* (Kathavatthu) the challenge is stated: "It is not correct to say, 'The Blessed One lived here in this world of mankind.'" The Theravada answered by pointing out the phenomenal aspect of Buddha's existence. "But are there not specific shrines, parks, villages, towns, kingdoms and countries all mentioned by Buddha? Was he not born at Lumbini, did he not attain enlightenment under the Bodhi tree? Was not the dharma-wheel set rolling by him at Banaras? Did he not abandon his will to live at the Chapala shrine? Did he not terminate his existence at Kusinara?" (*Kathavatthu,* XVIII, 1). Thus the effort to control the exaltation of Buddha and to keep at least some reality to his earthly existence. If this was successful with those who remained faithful to the Theravada tradition, within other schools of the Hinayana and in the entire range of the Mahayana tradition this deeper experience of the Buddha reality could not be so restricted in its expression. The tendency to exalt Buddha to absolute status beyond the empirical world was due mainly to the identification of Buddha with absolute truth. This truth was expressed in the Dharma, the teachings of Buddhism. The word "Dharma" refers to "law, truth, order, reality," as well as to Buddhist teaching, and it had gradually come to have a meaning somewhat close to the term "Logos" in the West. Thus the identification of Buddha with Dharma results in giving Buddha a Logos status. At an early period the expression had been put forth: "He who sees Dharma, sees me" (*Itivuttaka,* 91). Originally this referred simply to the spiritual teachings of Buddha, but later it took on more extensive ontological implications. This expression could then be translated as "He who sees Truth, sees me." On another occasion Buddha was referred to as "He whose name is Truth" (*Anguttara Nikaya,* IV, 284). Gradually this sense of an absolute truth identified with Buddha took precedence in thoughts concerning Buddha. Henceforth Buddhist doctrine takes on the aspect of revelation in time of eternal truth by someone who was himself identical with this ultimate order of things. Buddha becomes himself the essential constituent of things, the Tathata. This final status reached its full expression in the work attributed to Ashvaghosa, *The Awakening of Faith in the Mahayana.* Here Buddhism is committed to an absolute reality which expresses itself within the phenomenal world.

At this stage, or even in the earlier stages, the problem of Docetism had arisen. For once the identification of Buddha with an absolute reality had taken place, then the problem of Buddha was reversed. At an earlier period his human aspect was evident, his divine aspect hidden. Now his divine aspect was evident, his human aspect in question. The historical Buddha had now been dissolved into the world of the eternal outside of time completely. He had disappeared as a real being from the phenomenal world. How were these two opposites to be held together—the eternal and the temporal, the absolute and the phenomenal? One of the most decisive and influential solutions was that offered in the *Mahavastu,* a work fully committed to the Docetist position.

The *Mahavastu* was composed within one of the Hinayana sects known as the Mahasanghika, the sect which followed the Teaching of the Great Council rather than the Teaching of the Elders. Since each eon of time has its own Buddha, this work speaks of the characteristics of the "Buddha," in the plural. It further states that even the physical qualities of a Buddha can be understood. Nothing of the Buddhas can be measured or designated according to the norms or categories of this world, for every aspect of these great Seers is "transearthly." There is constant objection in this work to those who do not understand these higher qualities of the Buddhas, who do not teach that "Buddhas transcend the world." In reality all the apparent actions of the Buddha are done simply to conform to the ways of men and to establish a needed converse with men, thereby to bring about their salvation. Even the body of the Blessed One is not derived from the sexual union of his parents, although he seems to have father and mother. Again this is because the Buddha adopts the ordinary ways of mankind. The Buddha does not have the passions of ordinary men, yet he has a son. Although he has attained perfect wisdom, he seems to be ignorant. While Buddha condemns those with erroneous belief, the Buddha associates with such men. Even though enlightened to the supreme degree, he seems to be without zeal. To these extremes is the Buddha adapted to the ways of man.

Here is presented the doctrine of the *kenosis* of the Buddha, his emptying of himself in order to live among men and bring them to salvation. It is done only in appearance, by way of conformity; yet in this context it indicates the manner in which the exalted type of savior personality in Buddhism deals with mankind. He takes upon himself the form of man. Not only that, he also assumes the limitations and afflictions of man in order not to overwhelm mankind with the extent of his perfection. This principle of conformity goes even to the extent of accounting for the physical activity of the Buddha. Even though he goes through the physical activities of men moving about in the world, yet all these activities are something different from what they are in the ordinary course of human affairs. If the Buddha washes his feet, this is only to conform to the ordinary ways of mankind, for in reality no dirt from the street ever soils his pure feet. He remains ever as pure as the leaf of the lotus.

When one passes from this Hinayana work to the first great Mahayana work treating of this subject one comes to the *Lotus Sutra*. It is difficult to indicate the great importance of the *Lotus Sutra* among the Buddhist scriptures. The best known and the most influential single work among the writings of Mahayana Buddhism, it is sometimes called the Johannine Gospel of the Buddhist tradition. It is at least that central in its basic teaching and in its influence. This work, Docetist in its basic doctrine as is the *Mahavastu*, presents the first direct assertions in the Mahayana tradition of the eternal existence of the Buddha. "The Tathagata who so long ago was perfectly enlightened is unlimited in the duration of his life, he is everlasting. Without being extinct, the Tathagata makes a show of extinction, on behalf of those who have to be educated" (*Lotus Sutra*, 302). In the apocalyptic context of the opening passages of the *Lotus Sutra*, Buddha appears in his glorious body in the midst of the heavens surrounded by numberless celestial beings and casting his light over an infinite expanse which encompasses all space and time. This theophany is of a significance matched in India only by the theophany of the eleventh book of the *Bhaga-vad-Gita*. All living creatures gaze on the Lord Buddha in astonishment and in ecstatic delight. His knowledge encompasses all that can be known. The supreme revelation he makes at this time is the revelation of his own eternity and the call to Buddhahood extended to all mankind. In the *Lotus Sutra* the term "Swayambhu" is applied to Buddha, a term meaning "self-existent." This is the same term applied to the Atman-Brahman reality of Hinduism. Also applied to him are the terms *Purusottama* (Supreme Spirit), *Lokapita* (Father of the World), and *Dharmaraja* (King of the Law). These terms indicate that Buddha is the supreme being of the universe, for these are terms also used in the Hindu tradition to indicate the absolute reality beyond the phenomenal world. Clearly a being designated in this fashion is not a being subject to the world of time and change, to the limitations and afflictions to which men are subject in the ordinary context of human life. This is a being whose appearance within time is that of someone beyond time, whose eternal existence is in no manner affected by his entry into time.

Tathata. In designating this eternal, this transearthly status of the Buddha, a number of words are used: *Bhutakoti* is a word which means the highest or culminating point of all reality; *Paramartha* means the highest truth or the highest reality; *Dharmadhatu* means essential being; *Animitta* means without cause. These are all used to indicate the Buddha as the final reality of things. But the most frequent words indicating Buddha as an ontological absolute are *Tathata* and *Sunyata*; *Tathata* (thusness or suchness) has positive connotations; *Sunyata* (void or emptiness) has negative connotations. Both Tathata and Sunyata are extremely important in the thought tradition of Mahayana Buddhism. No real depth of understanding can be obtained of this tradition apart from these two words.

"Tathata" is a word with exceptional effectiveness in designating the undetermined final reality. Using the most indefinite expression, it indicates without determining. The basic exposition of this term is found in the Mahayana scripture entitled, *The Awakening of Faith in the Mahayana*, a work of unknown origin that appears in Chinese in the fifth century A.D. as the translation of an original by the Indian Buddhist writer, Ashvaghosa. In reality this cannot be a work by the illustrious Ashvaghosa of the second century A.D., who wrote the life story of Buddha known as the *Buddhacarita*. Whether *The Awakening of Faith* is in truth a translation from an Indian work or an original Chinese composition cannot presently be determined. In any case this work had a great history and influence in East Asia and deserves attention as a most important influence in establishing the concept of suchness as the essential nature of the Buddha and as one of the most significant words in the Mahayana vocabulary. According to this scripture the word "Tathata" is used to terminate the use of words. Termination of the definable aspect of things is emergence of the undefinable and unlimited. Where the nameable world ends, the real world begins, for the real world is finally unnameable. "In its very origin suchness is of itself endowed with sublime attributes. It manifests the highest wisdom which shines throughout the world, it has true knowledge and a mind resting simply in its own being. It is eternal, blissful, its own self-being and the purest simplicity; it is envigorating, immutable, free. . . . Because it possesses all these attributes and is deprived of nothing, it is designated both as the Womb of the Tathagata and the Dharma Body of the Tathagata" (*The Awakening of Faith*, section III).

Sunyata. Penetrating still further into the nature of the Buddha as suchness, as Tathata, we come to an expression which is the ultimate in the Buddhist use of language, *Sunyata* (emptiness). The concept of Tathata needs to be further refined to indicate that simplicity which is the primary attribute of absolute reality. This is achieved in Buddhism through the concept of Sunyata. There can be no adequate understanding of the Buddha nature as suchness, except through the experience of emptiness. These two, suchness and emptiness, are the positive and negative designations of the one experience. Both have implications of simplicity over against complexity, of oneness over multiplicity, of the unconditioned over the conditioned, of the eternal over the temporal, of the unchanging over the changing. The doctrine of Sunyata was elaborated earlier and more completely and had a more universal understanding and acceptance than any of the other terms used in the metaphysics of Mahayana Buddhism. Found in Buddhism from the earliest period, it cannot be considered purely a Mahayana development, even though the full exposition of this doctrine did take place within a Mahayana context.

In the *Middle Length Discourses (Majjhima Nikaya)* of the Hinayana scriptures there is an entire division of ten Sutras presented under the title of the "Division of Emptiness." Two of these are entitled "The Lesser Discourse on Emptiness" and the "Greater Discourse on Emptiness." The Buddha announces. "Dwelling in emptiness, I now dwell in its full perfection" *(Majjhima Nikaya,* III, 104). In attaining an awareness of Sunyata a person must begin by considering the surrounding external things and people and the need for purification of the mind from attention to any of the particular, changing aspects of reality. Eliminating the perception of the surroundings in which he is located, the person meditating is then to make a transition to the infinite realms of the mind through the meditation on space. His mind is satisfied with, pleased with, and finally freed in "awareness of the plane of infinite space" *(Majjhima Nikaya,* III, 105). A transition is then made to the plane of infinite consciousness, then to the perception of nothingness, then to the plane of neither perception nor non-perception, and finally to the solitude founded on the concentration of mind that is without reference to anything whatsoever, exterior or interior. "Thus he attains the true, unmistaken, completely clarified and highest realization of emptiness" *(Majjhima Nikaya,* III, 109).

This is the entry into a high state of interior experience in which the mind is purified from its dispersion throughout the various entities and activities of the phenomenal and mental orders. But the experience of emptiness does not at this earlier period have adequate reference to the ontological order. Development of this state of consciousness and its application to the ontological order came when this inner condition of the mind was associated with the transient, insubstantial aspect of things, which had been the basic Buddhist experience of reality from the beginning. This new development came in the earliest of the Mahayana Sutras, the group of scriptures known as the Wisdom Sutras, some forty of which appeared in India, written in the Sanskrit language, at the beginning of the Christian era. The central feature of these writings is to assert that the *skandhas* (the basic components of reality) were empty in their very being, *sva-bhava-sunya* (own-being-empty). The general view of the Hinayana schools had been that the five components of reality (form, feeling, perception, mental-formations, and consciousness) did have some existence, although this was only a momentary aggregation and dissolution. The innovation of the Wisdom Sutras was to assert that these composite structures were completely empty in their very being. This came as a significant discovery. The earlier commitment to a transient if not a substantial existence was found to be unsatisfactory. The true word henceforth was *Sunyata* (emptiness), emptiness in the very being of all things of the phenomenal world. In the final analysis this did not take away entirely the phenomenal existence of things as this was asserted by the prior traditions, but it did modify this considerably by saying that there was an all-pervading emptiness present so intimately as to be identified with things. All of this is enunciated with clarity, precision, and brevity in the *Heart Sutra*, one of the shortest of the Wisdom Sutras.

The *Heart Sutra* states that from the standpoint of the higher order of things, of absolute wisdom, all things are empty in their very being. Then beginning with form its states: "Form is emptiness, emptiness is form. Form does not differ from emptiness, emptiness does not differ from form. That which is form, that is emptiness, that which is emptiness, that is form." Thus by assertion of simple identity, by denial of difference, then by demonstrative identification, the basic principle is set forth. There is no possibility of misunderstanding. This identification with Sunyata is then applied to the other four composite structures of reality: feeling, perception, mental-formations, and consciousness. Then, with surprising and devastating consistency, this assertion of the emptiness of things and their consequent non-being is applied to the entire range of sense faculties and their objects. "There is no eye, ear, nose, tongue, body, mind. No form, sound, smell, taste, touch, or objects. There is no sight faculty and so on until we arrive at the negation of both knowledge and ignorance." The final extreme is reached when this most important scripture denies the very foundations of Buddhism itself, the fourfold truth and the eightfold path: "There is no suffering, no origin of suffering, no cessation of suffering and no path thereto." The conclusion then is that there is "no attainment and no non-attainment," for the mind in this new status is without thought limitation. A person without thought limitation has reached the final vision; he attains the realm beyond all change; he is finally and absolutely released from the bonds of the phenomenal order.

The tradition of thought first initiated in the Wisdom Sutras was taken by the supreme Buddhist thinker and possibly the most influential thinker in the Asian world, Nagarjuna (second century A.D.). He evolved the full implications of this type of thinking in a tradition known as the *Madhyamika* (the Doctrine of the Middle Way), the middle way between nihilism and positivism, the middle way between the assertion that things have absolute existence and the assertion that they do not exist at all, between the cosmic and acosmic view of things. Among the remarkable teachings of Nagarjuna is his doctrine that the phenomenal and the absolute are identical. "There is no difference whatsoever between Nirvana and Samsara, no difference whatsoever between Samsara and Nirvana" (*Madhyamika Karika*, XXV, 19). Samsara is the word for the phenomenal world; Nirvana, the word for the absolute world.

In understanding this way of thinking one must be aware that the Wisdom Sutras and Nagarjuna were not concerned with metaphysics in the Western pattern as a quest for knowledge to satisfy man's curiosity. They were seeking salvation from the human condition. So long as the human condition was fundamentally accepted they saw no way of ever obtaining release from this condition. So with the thought processes. Once man enters into the rational order there is no escape for it; he is caught in the perceptual processes of the mind from which there can never be any escape except by a sharp break in the plane of inner awareness. Once man admits even the Buddhist teachings of the fourfold truth and the eightfold path, then there can be no escape from these very means of his salvation. Thus everything must be denied; man must refuse to be involved in a life process or a mental process or a salvation process. Once involved there is no escape; the refusal of involvement is his only hope. As Nagarjuna stated: "True bliss consists in the elimination and in the calming of all activity. Nowhere did Buddha teach anything whatsoever" (*Madhyamika Karika*, XXV, 24).

The way to the ultimate reality is through the involution of the mind rather than its evolution. It is the way of negation rather than assertion, the way of simplicity rather than complexity, the way of no-way. It is the way of no-way, for man has never been alienated from the absolute. Since there is nowhere to go, there is no path to follow. Nor is there need for Buddhist teaching except that, in the end, the Buddhist teaching is the teaching of no-teaching. Every path is a false path, every thought a false thought. There "nothing arises, nothing declines; nothing ends, nothing abides; nothing is the same, nothing is different; there nothing moves, nothing does not move" (*Madhyamika Karika*, prologue). This is the manner in which the Mahayana Buddhism finds its way to that which can only be described as totally other than what man knows. Yet even while it is totally other, it is totally and absolutely the same as what is observed and experienced. Here is the coincidence of opposites such as this was taught in the West by Nicholas von Cusa in his work *On Learned Igno-*

rance; other Western authors who have expressed themselves in this way are Dionysius and Eckhart.

THE THREEFOLD BODY OF BUDDHA

The full teaching concerning the ontological status of Buddha is expressed in the doctrine of the Threefold Body of Buddha: the Truth Body, the Bliss Body, the Transformation Body. The Truth Body, also known as the Dharma Body, is the absolute reality of Buddha. The supreme foundation of all things, it is the everlasting, unchanging Buddha, the self-existing support on which all else depends. The Bliss Body is the spiritual and glorious manifestation that Buddha makes of himself to the blessed, to the Bodhisattvas and the perfect ones. The Transformation Body is the body with which he appears upon earth and walks among men to guide them to their salvation. This doctrine of the Threefold Body of Buddha is the masterpiece of synthesis in Mahayana Buddhism. More than any other single doctrine it enables the later Buddhism to establish continuity and consistency throughout the entire range of Buddhist teaching.

The origins of the doctrine go back to Hinayana Buddhism where there is mention of several bodies of Buddha. There is first the body of Buddha formed by the four elements—earth, water, fire, wind—which is corruptible. This is the body of Siddhartha as it emerged from the womb of his mother. There is also the mind-formed body which is mentioned in the Hinayana writings. The mind-formed body can be produced by all those who have entered the higher stages of inner recollection. Buddha possessed this mind-formed body in a special way. With it he was able to appear in the realm of the spirits. There is finally the body of Buddha's teaching, the Dharma Body of Buddha, which is the Truth Body but with less ontological significance than it came to have in the later period. Nevertheless the existence in the early period of multiple presentations of the Buddha reality formed the beginnings of the Threefold Body of Buddha, as this was later expressed in more developed fashion.

It was in the Yogacara, the idealist school of Mahayana Buddhism, especially in the teaching of Asanga (fifth century A.D.), that the doctrine of the Threefold Body of Buddha came to its full expression, although many of its basic elements had been set forth in earlier Mahayana Sutras, especially in the *Lankavatara Sutra*. Later the doctrine was elaborated by Asanga, and brought to the Chinese world in a full and final expression by

Hsuan Tsang. But there are also three other scriptures in which this doctrine is taught with clarity: the *Splendor of Gold Sutra*, the *Flower Garland Sutra*, and *The Awakening of Faith of the Mahayana*. The Tathata of *The Awakening of Faith* and the Sunyata of the Wisdom Sutras are both identical with the *Dharmakaya* (the Truth Body of Buddha). *The Awakening of Faith* concerns itself in some detail with the manner in which this Buddha reality is able to enter into the world of time and change although it is itself beyond time and change. Buddha can accomplish this without stain or affliction because of his awareness that things of the world have only apparent existence.

The Dharma Body is the most significant of the three bodies, the one that stands without the others, the one on which the others depend. It is in the final analysis the only real body of Buddha. The others are manifestations whereby the eternal Truth functions in the world of time for the salvation of those existing in time. The other manifestations of Buddha are destined to lead men to experience the eternal Buddha. This is itself the moment of salvation. From all of this it can be seen that the doctrine of the Dharma Body, the Truth Body of Buddha, carries in it something of the Logos doctrine of the Western religious and philosophical traditions. It serves to express the absolute in itself and in relation to the phenomenal order. It is the most positive of the three great terms used to indicate the final reality: *Tathata* (suchness), *Sunyata* (emptiness), *Dharmakaya* (Truth Body of Buddha). Tathata and Sunyata are more ontological, more metaphysical. The Dharmakaya, the Truth Body of Buddha, is more religious, more spiritual, more personal, although at the same time it is more anthropomorphic. Yet it enables the Buddhist tradition to obtain a full ontological expression of the grandeur of its savior-founder and his teaching. The teaching, the founder, the ultimate truth of things—all come together in this one expression, the Truth Body of Buddha, as they come together in the Logos doctrine of the Christian tradition.

Speaking of the Dharma Body of Buddha, Vasubandhu (420–500 A.D.) writes: "This is the unstained, the unthinkable, the beautiful, immutable, blissful, liberated body, the Dharma Body of Buddha." These attributes also bring the doctrine of the Dharma Body of Buddha into the realm of the Upanishadic teaching concerning the ultimate reality of Brahman, for these attributes are those predicated of Brahman. From these references we can see that the Buddhist thought tradition was establishing Buddha in a status equivalent to that of Brahman in the Hindu tradition. The Buddhist teaching is much more complex but possibly richer in its spiritual and metaphysical doctrines. If one wished to pursue the parallels in Hinduism for the Threefold Body of Buddha, we would find them set forth most clearly in the *Bhagavad-Gita*. There we would find the Lord, the Supreme Spirit, the Purusottama, the equivalent of the Dharma Body of Buddha. Krishna, the Charioteer of Arjuna, would equate with the Transformation Body of Buddha. This equation deserves attention both regarding the similarities and the differences involved. The manifestation of the Lord of Lords made in the body of Krishna in the eleventh chapter of the *Bhagavad-Gita* would equate with the Bliss Body of Buddha as this is portrayed in the introductory section of the *Lotus Sutra*. Some attention to these parallels and the corresponding parallels and differences in the Christian tradition would be most instructive in appreciating the deepest mysteries of these three traditions. All three have an ontological absolute, a glorious manifestation, and a manifestation in the strictly human order. The purpose of the manifestation in the human order is to bring about a healing of the evils to which man is subject in his earthly existence.

DEVOTIONAL BUDDHISM

While there was a movement within the Mahayana tradition toward an intellectualism leading to the salvation experience, there was also a movement within the Mahayana tradition toward a devotionalism which sought salvation through the mercy and grace of the savior Buddha. Both movements attained extreme expression. The intellectual movement went into the ultra-refined type of thought that we have presented. This produced some of the highest intellectual insights ever attained by the human mind, insights that rival the best that have been produced in any of the greater world traditions. The devotional tradition manifested extreme sensitivity to the need of mankind for salvation through the aid of a savior personality. Through these two trends, the intellectual and the devotional, the diverse needs of the people were supplied. Not all could follow the same path. But salvation was for all, not for some segment of humanity. This universality of salvation was emphasized strongly in the Mahayana tradition, which asserted the overarching providence of Buddha as savior of mankind. Thus the individualism that marked some phases of India's spiritual development was overcome.

The earlier Buddhist development had required extensive moral effort in the individual follower of Buddha. The last words of Buddha directed mankind to intensive personal effort: "Those who now and after my death live as their own light, as their own refuge and without any other refuge, who have the truth as their light and their refuge and no other, they are the ones who go beyond the darkness, they who love to learn" (*Dhamma-pada*, II, 101). The emphasis on self-effort was strengthened by the sixth stage of the eightfold path which insists on constant personal exertion toward the goal of Nirvana. This emphasis on independent attainment of perfection must not be taken too literally, however, for a spiritual guide was always considered essential for attaining perfection at all times. Such a guide was designated as the *kalyana mitta* (the beautiful friend), the one who encourages and instructs as a spiritual adviser. A person is always advised to seek such a spiritual guide and to follow his directions. Even beyond this there was the concern felt in the Buddhist community for all mankind. One of the loveliest sections in the early scriptures tells us that we should have a concern for every living being: "Just as a mother with her own life protects her only child from harm, so within yourself foster a boundless concern for every thing living" (*Khuddakapatha*, "The Gem," XII).

These were some of the forces working in Buddhism toward modification of the strict injunction to individual effort given by Buddha at the time of his death. But even more important than the assistance that men render to each other is the heavenly assistance rendered by Buddha. The need of help from a higher source received increasing emphasis through the years. The reasons for this might be listed as follows: 1 realization of the inherent limitations of the masses of mankind; 2 conviction that the world had deteriorated considerably since the time of Buddha and that in this new age of depravity men generally could of themselves do very little for their salvation; 3 awareness that Buddha had infinite compassion and infinite ability to aid others and that one of the greatest ways of honoring and glorifying the Buddha was by casting a person's self in total dependence on his aid. Impelled by these forces, Buddhism at this time reached out to encompass the multitudes of mankind—the poor, the ignorant, the helpless, the suffering, the unwanted. This tide of compassion that reached forth to the people was something unique in the Asian world. While Hinduism did not have this sense of compassion for human suffering found in Buddhism, it did manifest a similar movement away from salvation for an elite through sophisticated ritual and intellectual processes toward a salvation bestowed from above in response to faith and devotion. This rise of Hindu devotionalism took place at the same time as these developments were taking place in Buddhism. It is difficult to know which influenced the other most. It is likely that both were responding to common primordial forces within India and also to influences toward devotional worship of personal deities that came into India from the Hellenic world after the invasion of India by Alexander in the late fourth century B.C. Buddhism, which might easily have turned in the direction of an exclusive concern for a spiritually gifted elite, turned rather in the direction of a total concern for all mankind.

This concern is expressed with power, majesty, and tenderness in the *Lotus Sutra*, which establishes a kind of supreme covenant between Buddha and all mankind. It is a pledge of the capacity and the desire of Buddha to bring all creatures not merely to Nirvana but to Buddhahood, to a participation in his own modality of existence beyond the turmoil of earthly life. This was to be done with only the slightest requirement on the part of mankind. Buddha was conscious of how little man can do. Salvation is granted by grace in response to the simplest prayer, the simplest manifestation of devotion to Buddha. Here is the bending down of the great to the small, the effort of the transcendent and eternal world to enter into and to transform the world of time and change. In one of the most beautiful presentations of heavenly compassion in the *Lotus Sutra*, Buddha's saving grace is depicted as a raincloud that gathers massively above the earth: "That great raincloud, big with water, is wreathed with flashes of lightning and rouses with its thundering call all creatures. By warding off the sunbeams, it cools the region: and gradually lowering so as to come in reach of hands, it begins pouring down its water all around. And so, flashing on every side, it pours out an abundant mass of water equally, and refreshes this earth." In this manner Buddha pours down his salvation upon the earth, heals the entire world and brings all mankind to spiritual enlightenment. "I recreate the whole world like a cloud shedding its water without distinction: I have the same feelings for respectable people as for the low; for moral persons as for the immoral. . . . I preach the law to the mentally inferior as well as to persons of superior understanding and exceptional faculties." By this deluge of heavenly grace the world is transformed, all beings are refreshed, especially "all those beings whose bodies are withered and who are bound to the phenomenal world." Bliss is brought to those wasting away in their toil. Then after the deluge the wisdom of the Buddha "shines like the sun and moon, leading all beings without partiality" (*Lotus Sutra*, V, 7–8, 18, 24, 26, 46).

The response required of men only the simplest expression of devotion to the Blessed One. The *Lotus Sutra* glories in describing how the highest blessings are conferred in response to the simplest devotion. Those who offer a single flower, who bring a bit of perfume or incense to a Buddha image, those who sing a song of praise, those who make a melody of praise on a musical instrument, those who draw a picture on a wall, even little children who build a Buddhist *stupa* in the sand—all these attain a saving grace. A person need only join his hands in reverential greeting to Buddha or bow his head for an instant or speak the salutation, "Praise to Buddha!" Even though these things are done with distracted mind they all merit the grace of Buddha which descends as a torrent of healing for the sorrows of life (*Lotus Sutra*, II).

By the time of the *Lotus Sutra* other savior personalities had been associated with Buddha. These are designated as *Bodhisattvas* (Buddha-beings or enlightenment-beings), who are not yet but who are one day to become Buddhas, who wish to remain in association with the suffering world until all mankind is brought to its complete release from earthly affliction. They establish the foundations of a new mythology in the Mahayana tradition. Among these mythological savior-beings one of the most prominent is *Avalokitesvara* (the Lord who Beholds the Earth). Avalokitesvara is associated both with wisdom and with mercy. In the *Lotus Sutra* this Bodhisattva is presented in the twenty-fourth chapter as one who responds immediately to all cries for help from mankind. "If anyone is thrown into a pit of fire by a wicked enemy with the object of killing him, he has but to think of Avalokitesvara and the fire shall be quenched as if sprinkled with water. . . . If a man be surrounded by a host of enemies armed with swords having the intention of killing him, he has but to think of Avalokitesvara and they shall instantly become kind-hearted. . . . If a person, delivered to the powers of the executioners, is already standing in the place of execution, he has but to think of Avalokitesvara, and they shall instantly become kind-hearted. . . . If a heavy thunderbolt shoots from a cloud pregnant with lightning and thunder, one has but to think of Avalokitesvara, and the fire of heaven shall quickly, instantaneously be quenched" (*Lotus Sutra*, XXIV, 5, 9–10, 16). Such are the promises made by the majestic, all-powerful Bodhisattva. This savior personality, originally a masculine figure, was gradually changed by the Chinese into a feminine figure because the tenderness of the protection offered seemed more appropriate to a spiritual figure depicted with feminine compassion than to one with masculine strength. Eventually Avalokitesvara, as Kuan-Yin, became the goddess of mercy of the East-Asian world.

After the *Lotus Sutra* the historical Gotama Buddha took a lesser place in the devotional life of the East-Asian peoples of China and Japan. There was increasing emphasis on the Buddha to come, Amitabha Buddha, also known as *Amida Buddha* (the Buddha of Boundless Light), the personification of compassion. It is this Buddha that figures in the *Pure Land*, or devotional, scriptures in which promises of rebirth in the Land of Bliss are made to all who invoke the name of Amida Buddha. The simple invocation, "Praise to Amida Buddha," then became the most often-repeated prayer of the East-Asian world for hundreds of millions of people. In virtue of this simple invocation security and salvation were promised to all mankind. The doctrine of Amida Buddha is contained especially in the *Land of Bliss Sutra.* There all blessings are offered to one who believes in Amida Buddha and invokes his name.

Another figure that became important at this time is the future Buddha Savior, Maitreya Buddha, presently the supreme Bodhisattva. This deity also is depicted as a savior personality with inflnite concern for mankind. So important did Maitreya become that it was this figure more than any other that became the primary interest of Buddhist art in East Asia.

From the worship of Amida Buddha, Avalokitesvara, Maitreya, and several other Bodhisattvas, a new splendor was achieved in the construction of Buddhist shrines, temples, images, and pagodas over much of Asia. The devotion which began in the Buddhist art of Ajanta and Bharhut was carried to many sites in central and eastern Asia. Allied to the profound metaphysical insight of Buddhism, this devotion changed the mind and emotions of many and provided the greatest single dynamic of East-Asian art and literature.

The full story of this devotional tradition, as presently known, belongs to the story of Buddhism in the East-Asian world, but it must be remembered that the original impetus for this devotional development came from India. The earliest scriptures in the devotional tradition were written in Sanskrit, namely, the *Lotus* and the *Land of Bliss Sutras.* The tradition attained high expression and extensive influence in India as well as in central and eastern Asia.

While the intellectual and the devotional development of Mahayana Buddhism have been treated separately, it must not be thought that they were entirely separated from each other. While many men were capable of profound devotion but of little understanding, those who were capable of understanding were not alienated from devotional tradition. Images of the Buddhas and Bodhisattvas were found everywhere, even in Zen monasteries where a most iconoclastic type of Buddhist meditation was established and where the intellectual life of Buddhism flourished. Thus there was a unity of the devotional and the intellectual aspects of Mahayana development. Those who understood best knew that the highest intellectual attainments did not of themselves break out of the realm of the phenomenal any more than deeds of devotion. If sometimes the monks threw the images of Buddha into the fire, they also threw their own writings and even the Buddhist scriptures into the fire, knowing that neither images nor words nor any thoughts of the mind nor any infratemporal experience is adequate to the salvation experience which releases man from the sorrows and limitations of time. The objective was eventually to pass beyond both the intellectual and devotional activity to total quiescence of human effort, for only then was there a full and final entry into the realm of Sunyata, of emptiness; only in this way does man reach the Other Shore.

Chapter Eighteen

The Great Surprise

Among the most extraordinary achievements of Buddhism was the development of an explicit self-awareness of the Buddhist developmental process. This is not found in Hinduism, nor is it found in Confucianism, nor indeed in any of the other major traditions of the Eurasian world except Christianity. This is not to say that these other traditions did not experience a developmental process; it is to say that they do not have a full understanding or explicated doctrine of development. There was in these other traditions a commitment to the earlier phase of the tradition, the original scriptures, as the basic norm for the later development. In few cases have earlier scriptures been subordinated to the later as in the Christian tradition, where the earlier revelation and the earlier covenant were made subordinate to a later revelation and a later covenant. The earlier period of Israel was considered a pedagogical stage of preparation, a period when man was conditioned for a later superior event of such import that man could not receive the full teaching until he had undergone a long period of preparatory instruction, a spiritual conditioning. The later, higher development, looked back on the earlier development as something that was imperfect in relation to the more perfect. The later stage then established itself as an absolute beyond which the enlightenment process could not go. It was the final, full, perfect enlightenment of man, the only true way of man's salvation. That Mahayana Buddhism assumed this status and denied the independent efficacy of the earlier Buddhism is an event of singular importance. It introduced a sense of historical development within Buddhism. The unifying element in Buddhism is the personality of Buddha, who is central to both its earlier and later development, although in a more sublime evaluation of his identity; whereas in the Christian tradition the human appearance of the savior personality is found in only the second, higher phase of the tradition. The eternal divine reality, Yahweh, the Lord, is the unifying element.

When the basic outlines of the Buddhist process are examined, the fundamental objective of Buddhism is found to have always remained a very simple one: transition out of the world of sorrow into the world of no-sorrow. There is, then, in the beginning, this world and the other world, Samsara and Nirvana. All mankind is so immersed in Samsara and its turmoil that no one is able to make the transition to Nirvana. All men are in darkness, no one is enlightened. All men are in a stupor, no one is awakened. All are under the spell of Mara; no one has broken out of this confinement. This status of mankind remains unaltered until someone comes who of himself attains enlightenment, who finds a ford across the stream of Samsara, who breaks the spell of Mara. This person, the Tathagata, the enlightened, awakened, the Buddha, victorious over Mara, finder of the ford, appears upon the earth with unique ability to set up what is thrown down, to reveal what is hidden, to point out the right road to those gone astray, to bring light into the darkness. The total hope and expectation of mankind is centered on this person, this teacher, guide, savior. With this guide a beginning is made, the work of salvation, transformation, enlightenment, awakening can proceed. The higher destiny of mankind is initiated.

But there is need for understanding on the part of mankind. How is the vision to be communicated? Is man truly capable of the vision he needs, of the goal to which he aspires? Enlightening mankind is an extremely delicate process. Plato understood this. He pointed out that a person who saw the true realities of the higher order and then came and spoke to men about them would not be believed and might even be thought a madman. Socrates, who brought such a sublime message to the Greek world, was executed by those to whom he brought a vision higher than any they had yet known. The prophets of Israel had no easy time. Among the accusations made by the spiritual leaders of Israel in the later period was that they had consistently opposed and even stoned their prophets. Jeremiah was in this manner a tragic figure who presented a message that the community would not or could not receive.

India was more willing to listen to its spiritual personalities, but the prophetic difficulty remained, the difficulty of communicating a vision beyond that to which men are accustomed. Buddha had experienced difficulty in attaining his own enlightenment. He was aware of the difficulty in guiding others. Thus his original hesitancy, thus also the limitations he imposed upon his teaching. Men could absorb so little! Too much illumination would blind rather than enlighten, would disturb rather than calm the minds of men and still them into wisdom. Much had to be left to the developmental processes of time. The conviction with which his teachings were received and the enthusiasm Buddha evoked indicate that his followers had some awareness, even at this early period, of the extraordinary spiritual process that was taking place. The cosmic-human order was undergoing a "sea-change." This is indicated with extraordinary vividness in the scriptures. They are so strong in their assertion of the magnitude of the spiritual events taking place as to seem utterly extravagant. Yet in looking back from the present and seeing just how powerful has been the spiritual impress of Buddhism on the life of man, these writings and early expressions seem only a calm enunciation of evident fact.

Yet the details were hidden. Mankind was not yet capable of the more glorious details of the spiritual communication being made to it. But once the doctrine of the eternity of the Buddha, the doctrines of Tathata and Sunyata, of the threefold body of Buddha, of the Buddhahood of all men, of vicarious suffering and salvation by faith and grace had been explicated there was needed an explanation of doctrinal development itself in order to hold together the fullness of the tradition, to keep it from being dispersed, fragmented, and rendered ineffective. That Buddhism attained a clear, reflexive consciousness and enunciation of the inner dialectical evolution of Buddhist doctrine is among the very highest achievements of its later development. A full sense of the developmental process in human history was not achieved, and a sense of spiritual development was achieved only imperfectly. But even in the West this has remained one of the central issues of our own religious and cultural traditions. Only in the twentieth century are we attaining any full appreciation of the historical developmental processes to which mankind and his spiritual and cultural traditions are subject. Buddhism did not and evidently could not of itself evolve the historical insights that have been attained in the West, but it did evolve a doctrine of development within its own scriptural tradition that is one of the most distinctive elements of the tradition. This is contained in the *Lotus Sutra*. By the first century of the Christian era the unfolding of Buddhist teaching had extended so far that a declaration had to be made concerning the relation of the later teaching to the earlier teaching, for doctrines were being taught that were not presented at an earlier period, doctrines, in part at least, opposed to earlier teaching.

There were two alternatives: one was to emphasize identity and continuity of the tradition from its earlier to its later stage; the other was to emphasize difference and discontinuity. By mitigating the differences an easy solution could have been reached, yet neither alternative was fully satisfactory. By insisting on identity it might be concluded that nothing should be done except to repeat the earlier teaching, made into a norm beyond which Buddhism could not go. By insisting on difference it might be concluded that the earlier teaching had little or no relation with the later teaching. The first solution was a conservative-traditional solution which would stiffen and destroy the living Buddhist process and leave it flat and undeveloped. The second was a liberal-modernist solution which might cause the tradition to disintegrate from lack of self-identity over a period of time.

Buddhism took the most difficult decision of all but the most fruitful. It chose to affirm strongly both the difference and identity in a dialectical process by which alone mankind could be adequately enlightened, awakened, transformed, and brought to complete salvation from the sorrows of the human condition. This dialectical process demanded a two-stage movement toward illumination. Man was that deep in darkness, his stupor so heavy, the farther shore so distant; also the glory was so great, illumination so radiant, the salvation experience so sublime. By emphasis both on the tragedy of the human condition and on the exalted nature of its healing, later Buddhism attained a depth dimension of wonderful proportions in its survey of Buddhist development. Yet there was less a depth dimension than a height dimension, for the *Lotus Sutra* relates little of the tragic aspect of the human condition and much of the sublimity of the destiny to which man is called. The real tragedy of the human condition is simply that man does not appreciate the high nature of his own calling. He fails to understand the higher realities that should be obvious. Man complicates what is so utterly simple.

In Buddhist revelation, then, the first stage required a bending down of the eternal Buddha far into the realm of time and matter and human limitation. He must be seen as a man among men, suffering as others suffer. He must walk the earth, rest upon it, be nourished as all men are nourished. He must teach in the words men know, speak to children in words they understand, not in words adults understand. This was the Buddha of the early Buddhism. He spoke to men in their words, taught them according to their capacity. There were no other words that man could understand. There were indeed no words at all in which the higher reality could be expressed. Thus the twofold disadvantage of Buddha as teacher. Yet he did reveal to men the real nature of their human problem, the problem of sorrow, and the eightfold path whereby they might be released from sorrow and attain Nirvana. These were presented with such lofty insight that men awakened from their stupor, were cured to some extent of their blindness, and moved toward the healing of sorrow.

Although men did not realize it fully, this was only the first step. The eternal had entered so intimately into the time, had expressed itself so perfectly in the forms and expressions of time, had veiled its absolute status so totally that men did not really understand what was happening. Nor did men appreciate the extent of divine transformation to which they themselves were called. There awaited them a great surprise. Their true destiny was not Nirvana but Buddhahood. They were to be not merely men entering into the Nirvana experience, they were themselves enlightenment-beings, Buddha-beings; their destiny was realization of their own Buddhahood. This was the startling discovery awaiting man but which man could not at all comprehend at this early period. The salvation experience had in it higher implications than they could possibly imagine. Nor was this status of Buddhahood reserved for an elite, even a spiritual elite. It was for all men, to be attained by the simplest means. The initiative which carried man over into this new order was not individual human initiative but initiative from a higher source, from the eternal Buddha in his transterrestrial reality. If men could not at first understand this, now they must appreciate this mystery in its full range if they were to enter into the high calling that is theirs. The excitement of the *Lotus Sutra* is its teaching that there are spiritual treasures awaiting man that man cannot conceive of in his most vivid imaginative efforts or in his most attractive dreams. Only by a gradual evolutionary process could mankind be led into this wonderworld beyond. Until the *Lotus Sutra* spoke of this depth and time dimension in the program of man's salvation no one could really understand the message of Buddha.

The second and third chapters of the *Lotus Sutra* present one of the most significant tenets in Buddhist teaching, that man's destiny is more sublime, yet more easily attained than man thinks. There is a higher being, the Buddha in his eternal nature, whose providential care of man is more compassionate and more effective than man can imagine. It took Buddhism five centuries of development before the Parable of the Burning House could be written. If there is any doubt as to the spiritual grandeur of Buddhism this section of the *Lotus Sutra* should be sufficient to convince a person. It might also be said that anyone who fails to appreciate the second and third chapters of the *Lotus Sutra* will fail to understand the very heart of Mahayana Buddhism. The teaching there is one which the Theravada Buddhists cannot understand or accept. This, the supreme moment in the differentiation process between the Mahayana and the Theravada, is even more important in the spiritual life of Buddhism than the moment when the doctrine of Sunyata was first expounded in the Wisdom Sutras. In both instances, however, Buddhism opens out into infinite horizons.

The first chapter of the *Lotus Sutra* presents an apocalyptic vision of the eternal Buddha in all his splendor, radiant as the sun, illumining the entire cosmic order and about to make the most solemn pronouncement that mankind has ever heard. The expectation is built up with the description of the presence there before the Buddha of the entire company of the Blessed Ones who have gained release from sorrow, the Bodhisattvas; there is a vast company of Arhats, the perfect ones; there are a multitude of monks; and finally there is the presence of all living creatures extending into an infinite distance. The great and famous Bodhisattva, Maitreya, is there, as well as Manjusri. Announcement is made to the assembly that Buddha, the Tathagata, the Blessed One, is about to set forth a grand exposition of his teaching.

In the second chapter there is first a solemn declaration by Buddha of the basis on which he teaches, a presentation, as it were, of his credentials as the one with supreme knowledge. The question is asked by Sariputra, the wisest of Buddha's followers, as to why Buddha insists so much at this time on the importance of his knowledge. Sariputra says that he has never before heard the Buddha placing such emphasis on his knowledge or the skill of his own teaching. "Why do you repeatedly say, 'Profound is the truth discovered by me; it is difficult to understand the mystery of the

Buddhas'?" The answer given is that the message he wishes to convey is of such a nature that the world, including the gods, would be frightened if this were expounded. Sariputra begs the Lord to say what he has to say because there is a great multitude of people present, many of whom, capable of understanding, would value and accept his words. But again Buddha resists, saying that this is a matter too subtle, too difficult; that many would scoff at the revealed truth. Then in response to a third entreaty of Sariputra, Buddha answers: "Be attentive, then, listen well and take to heart what I say: There is only a single way of salvation, the way of being a Buddha, an enlightenment-being." The way of the earlier teaching concerning Nirvana is inadequate. "I show Nirvana to the ignorant, to those of low capacity, to those who have not been disciplined through the teaching of the many Buddhas, to those bound to continual rebirth and wretchedness." To those Buddha can speak only of Nirvana, and not of Buddhahood. To these he cannot yet say: "You shall become Buddhas." But to those who have led good and noble lives, who are prepared to receive his message he announces: "You will become yourselves Buddhas, benevolent and compassionate" (Lotus Sutra, II, 31–50).

Constantly the refrain is repeated in this section of the Lotus Sutra: "There is in truth only one way, the way of the Buddha-being." There is no other way, neither that of the follower of the earlier teaching, nor that of one who of himself has attained a certain spiritual perfection. There is only the way of "Buddhazation," of participating in the eternal being of Buddha.

Yet the problem occurs: Why was this not taught from the beginning? The answer given is that men were not originally well disposed. "They are difficult to correct, they are proud, hypocritical, dishonest, evil, ignorant, dull-witted; hence they do not hear the good Buddha-call: Not once in many rebirths." Buddha must deal with these in a special way. He must first lead them in the direction of Nirvana. This they can understand; they cannot understand or respond to the attraction of Buddhahood. Yet this alone is the true way of salvation, the true destiny of mankind. It is also the only really gracious way, the only way in conformity with the Buddha reality which is infinitely generous and wills that all men attain the supreme experience of Buddhahood, an experience identical with his own. "I would be guilty of envy, should I, after reaching the spotless eminent state of enlightenment, establish any one in the inferior way. That would not be proper." As there are certain trees which blossom but seldom in the course of many years, but then are most beautiful, so this truth revealed by Buddha is something mankind has awaited for a long while, but now has blossomed in its full splendor. Now it can be said: "Forsake all doubt and uncertainty: you shall become Buddhas, Rejoice!" (*Lotus Sutra*, II, 56–144).

This is the teaching, the high teaching of Mahayana Buddhism. Then comes the series of parables in which this teaching is illustrated with exceptional brilliance: the Parables of the Burning House (chap. III), the Prodigal Son (chap. IV), the Good Physician (chap. XV), the Rain Cloud (chap. V), the Hidden Jewel (chap. VIII). All of these exemplify the truth that men do not really know the treasures that are theirs; they mistake their true nature and destiny; they carry within themselves a splendor much greater than they realize. Nor do they appreciate the goodness of the trans-earthly Providence that wishes to bring mankind to the experience of total enlightenment.

This Providence is illustrated most vividly in the Parable of the Prodigal Son. A young man leaves his father's house at an early age to seek his fortune in the world. The fortunes of the father prosper, while the fortunes of the son decline. The father moves to a distant city, becomes a wealthy man with treasure and a great house, his barns filled with grain. He is served by many servants and owns extensive territory. The son, on the other hand, is impoverished through the years and roams through the countryside and through the cities seeking employment. After some thirty years have passed, the son in his wanderings comes to the region of his father's house. During the long years the father has been pining for his son. He says repeatedly, "Oh how happy I would be if only my son were here to enjoy all these possessions!" Finally, when the wandering son arrives in the neighborhood of the estate, the father is sitting at the door of his house on a throne, surrounded and waited on by many attendants. Many friends and acquaintances are there as in a court setting. The son, not recognizing his father, seeing such majesty and so many great people, is suddenly terrified. Thinking that they will seize and imprison such a wretch as he feels himself to be, he quickly leaves.

The father, however, recognizes his son. Filled with joy that now his son will be able to enjoy the great treasure he will give him, he gives orders that his servants go and bring back the son. They go, take hold of the son, and bring him back. But the son remains frightened. He cannot recognize his father in such splendor and thinks that he is being taken captive and might be imprisoned, punished, or even executed. So overcome, he falls to the earth in a faint. The father, seeing this, tells the servants to release the son, to revive him, and let him go. He then calls two of his most wretched-looking servants to go and approach the son and offer him employment on the estate, menial work such as the son might think appropriate to himself. The son agrees and begins working there.

The father, seeing his son through the window, then takes off his ornaments, his princely attire, puts on soiled clothes, smears himself with dirt, and then goes to his son and addresses him as someone addresses a laborer telling him to do this and that and to remain at work on the estate and he will be given double pay and anything he needs. The father also tells the son that he has an old cloak that the son can have if he should need it. Gradually becoming acquainted with the son, he later tells him to look upon him as a father. "I am an older person and you are a younger man and you have done excellent service here." This father-son relationship is developed and strengthened over the years. When the father begins to fail with age and is near death, he calls an assembly of his household and the people of the region and in their presence he tells them: "This is my son." He identifies to the son the town where they originally lived, how he was called as a boy, how he left home, how he as a father had been seeking his son for so many years. Then he announces: "I declare to you all that this is my son. I leave all my possessions to him." The poor man is, of course, shocked and utterly amazed that so suddenly and unexpectedly he has received such wealth and such territory and has recovered his father. This story of the *Lotus Sutra* then ends: "Even so, O Lord, do we represent the sons of the Tathagata, and the Tathagata says to us: 'you are my sons,' as the householder did. . . . We were content with the Nirvana we had obtained and considered that we gained much. But now the Tathagata has revealed to us that we are his heirs . . . we have obtained unexpectedly and without longing the jewel of omniscience, which we did not desire, nor seek, nor search after, nor expect, nor require; and that in as much as we are the sons of the Tathagata" (*Lotus Sutra*, IV).

There are several significant things accomplished by this story. Above all it provides an explanation of the relationship between the earlier and later teaching and the skillful means whereby men are brought to a destiny beyond their understanding or desire by a goodness and skill of transterrestrial origin. There is another story in the *Lotus Sutra* which explains all these things in slightly different fashion, the Parable of the Burning House, the most famous of all the Mahayana parables.

There was a householder, a man of wealth, who had a mansion of many rooms in which dwelled his large family and relatives. The entire building was old, unsteady, falling to pieces. One day the entire house was suddenly caught up in flames. Inside children were playing in one of the rooms. The householder, an old and venerable man, was faced with the problem of how to rescue the children. He calls to the children, tells them that the house is on fire, to come out. But the children cannot understand what he is talking about. They have never seen a house on fire and so are not aware of any urgency. They are not afraid or alarmed. He calls them several times. Still they do not heed. What is the father to do? There is but one door. He must bring them safely out of the flames. He must not frighten them by telling them of their disastrous situation, for then they would rush off in every direction and be destroyed. As a wise man he thinks of a stratagem. He tells the children that there are toys outside that he wishes to give them, among which are toy ox carts and goat carts. "Come, quickly, leave the house and I will give you these things," he cries. Such promises the children can appreciate. They all run toward the door and escape from the burning house. But once they have arrived outside, their father, the householder, gives them not toys, but true realities; not toy carts, but real ox carts adorned with bells and jewels, decorated wtih flowers, carpeted and with cushioned seats. The carts are drawn by white oxen, alert and swift (*Lotus Sutra,* III).

Thus goes the story. The interpretation is this: The burning house is the phenomenal world, the world of Samsara which is on fire with destructive forces, especially with desire which is destroying it and all who dwell in the world. All things are subject to change and thus are in process of certain destruction and decay. Such is the human condition from which there is no escape except through the one opening, the great way of Buddhahood. But no one goes toward salvation through that means of escape, men are occupied with their trifling play within the world and do not understand that they are in a desperate situation. But the eternal Buddha, householder of the world, knowing that the world is on fire, seeing that men do not respond to the simple exhortation to leave the house, promises mankind that he will give them Nirvana. Men understand the promise. Attracted by the hope of release from sorrow they rush to this end and escape the burning house. But once they have responded to the guidance of Buddha he grants them not the toy carts of Nirvana, but the real, the gorgeous carts of Buddhahood, for there is in reality only the one path to release from sorrow. The Buddha says to all men: "You are my children, I am your father who has brought you safely away from suffering in the world in which you have been immersed for such a long period. I teach you Nirvana although you have not as yet reached the true goal, but are on your way to Buddhahood."

While this parable emphasizes the temporary, instrumental, and pedagogical function of the Hinayana Buddhism and its objective of Nirvana, the Parable of the Hidden Jewel emphasizes the possession of great treasure which man does not realize. This parable is related in the following manner: There was a certain man who visited a friend who was quite wealthy and who, receiving his friend with affection, dines with him and then gives to his visitor a jewel of great value. He ties it in a knot in the upper robe of his visitor and is pleased that he is able to give such a valuable gift to his friend. But the visitor, a poor man, is not aware that the jewel has been placed in his robe. He wanders on through the world and meets with great misfortune and becomes a beggar and is not at all aware of the jewel that he has on his person. One day the two friends meet. The wealthy man reveals then to his friend that there is a jewel tied in his robe. The poor man discovers it and becomes extremely happy for the jewel is of such value that he now becomes himself a rich man who can obtain all that he wishes. "In the same manner, O Lord, we were not conscious of our former situation placed in us by the Tathagata in previous lives and we were here in the world dull and ignorant, for we were satisfied with Nirvana and sought nothing better, but the great friend of mankind has revealed to us our greater destiny: Nirvana is not the truly blessed rest repose; the full insight of the highest spiritual beings, that is the true repose, the supreme bliss" (Lotus Sutra, VIII, 43–44). This is the course of human life, the story of man's torpor and of the divine awakening, of man's ignorance and the manner of his illumination, of man's wretchedness and the revelation of his splendor.

Chapter Nineteen

Conclusion: The Creative Present

Hinduism, Yoga, and Buddhism are no longer merely Indian traditions, they are world traditions. India has lost forever its exclusive claim on these traditions. Now they are part of the universal human heritage; even the creative aspect of these traditions is no longer an exclusive concern of India. Mankind is now an integral part of the Indian spiritual process. What happens to these traditions in the future will be as much a product of forces outside of India as of forces within India. Already an extensive influence is felt on Hinduism from without the country. To a corresponding degree the Indian religions are affecting the religious-spiritual thought and emotions of mankind. Study of these traditions is a part of these traditions. We as Westerners have ourselves entered into the Indian religious process by the very fact of our study and our effort at understanding these traditions and giving expression to them within the context of our own present. Thus the Indian traditions are occupying the world even as the other world traditions are now occupying India. The Indian traditions are now a part of our own intellectual and spiritual life as we become a part of its historical development. We can no longer live adequately without the Indian spiritual traditions, nor can these traditions do without us.

There is an urgency in our understanding these traditions, for we are involved in the spiritual shaping of the world universal, not simply in the study of this world. This shaping of a world in the present requires continuity with the past. We are determined by these traditions even while we are determining these traditions. The past itself is an aspect of the present. For the first time we are bringing the world spiritual traditions into a common human heritage. This is not only a study; it is a creative spiritual process. Those studying the religions of mankind are themselves creating this common spiritual heritage. One of the great tasks to which our age is called is that of giving spiritual shape and substance to the world society now in the process of formation. This new vision of the past is a creation of the present with infinite consequence for the future.

In every phase of life, in the intellectual, artistic, and spiritual aspects of life, the total human past is now the past of each people and each individual person. We do not live only in the West or even primarily in the West; we live in the world, the total world of man. The achievements of India and China are now available to us and form part of our own heritage, as do the cultures of Japan and Persia and Africa. This is the period of the worldwide expansion of the mind in all areas of life. The global spiritual past is the only adequate context for present understanding of man even though this effort at universal awareness is thwarted by exclusivist attitudes that still exist in the world. Even now, however, the futility of such exclusivism is widely recognized. All live currents of thought seek to encompass the full human dimensions of man.

Within this larger world of mankind the multiple spiritual and humanist traditions implicate each other, complete each other, and evoke from each other higher developments of which each is capable. These traditions implicate each other, for each has a universal mission to mankind. Each is panhuman in its significance. None can be fully itself without the others. Each has a distinctive contribution to make to human development that can only be made by itself. Each must therefore be kept distinctive even as it reaches a universal diffusion among men. For any tradition to withhold itself from the other societies of mankind or for any to exclude the other traditions is to vitiate and stultify its own tradition and development, to condemn itself to sterile isolation from the only forces that can give it life and creativity. All human traditions are dimensions of each other.

This brings up a most significant aspect of the entire human and spiritual development of man, the secular and scientific development in these past few centuries in the West and its diffusion throughout the entire world. The awareness of this universal context of human experience, the drawing together of the nations of the world, man's knowledge of the past and his way into the future—all these are the direct result of contemporary secular and scientific development of man. This secular development has generally been considered as the destruction of the human and religious qualities of man's life. At the time when the secular movement arose and our new scientific and technological mastery of the natural world came about, the spiritual traditions of mankind were all in a state of decline. It seemed rather obvious that this new movement in man's life had caused the de-spiritualization of human culture. This judgment has lingered until the present. Yet now it can be clearly seen that secular development did not itself destroy the spiritual vitality of any people. The spiritual vitality in the West and elsewhere throughout the world of the higher civilizations had already declined from within at the end of the eighteenth century if not earlier. The spiritual forms of life had remained but the inner life had already withered. The new secular development manifested this inner situation; it did not cause it. It has been rather a purifying element in the spiritual life of mankind. It has everywhere given man a new type of spiritual honesty. It has revealed many of the superstitious attitudes and practices that had sprung up. In association with modern social movements it has brought about in India recognition of the evils inherent in the caste system. It has also restored to India many spiritual treasures of the past which had become confused, distorted, or neglected through the centuries. It has also fostered a more healthy human development throughout the entire world. The greater human sense that has awakened in the world through secular forces and the sense of social injustices everywhere are effects that religion, even the highest religions and spiritualities of the past, could not, or at least did not, bring about.

It is not surprising that secularism itself should have its own corruptions and that through pride in its accomplishments it should overreach itself at times and destroy many precious human and spiritual values. But now a purification has taken place within this secular development. Having established a more human form of secularization mankind can now proceed on its course with the inestimable benefits that have come from these secular movements. In looking back over the past centuries men find themselves spiritually much better off than men of former centuries, certainly than the people of the past two centuries. Men can now be spiritually more creative, religiously more real, and humanly more helpful than they ever were in previous centuries. In this meeting of the nations men are confident that the human process will be fostered, the religious traditions of mankind will all be fulfilled, and a world humanism will emerge. The coming world spirituality will be the product of the distinctive callings and gifts of all the various peoples of the world. Each brings its treasure, its living experience, its human creativity. As this remarkable spiritual converse begins we find that a significant feature of the manifold traditions of mankind is an awareness that man must be born again in a higher spiritual way if he is to be truly human and to fulfill his higher destiny. This second birth is symbolized in Hinduism by imposition of the sacred cord, and in spiritual initiation ceremonies the world over. Man is not truly himself until this second, this higher birth, has taken place, and has brought man into the order of eternity, the order of reality transcendent to the phenomenal world. It is the beginning of a higher spiritual illumination and transformation that reaches beyond the world of change into a final infinity, into the realm of the Hindu Brahman, the Buddhist Nirvana, the Yoga Kaivalya. This awareness and experience of the transtemporal, transhistorical, transhuman is a human heritage that is once again claiming the attention of men. After the discovery of the human values of secularism man is returning to a more complete wisdom with this transphenomenal dimension. The future of man is a drawing together and a moving forward of all traditions. It is a gathering in of all man's human and spiritual attainments in a world-embracing tradition.

As we enter into global expansion of our spiritual vision we are faced with a higher spiritual development of man than we might have expected. Especially in the case of India one of the disconcerting aspects of study is that the spiritual discipline found there is overwhelming with its high mystical qualities. The West, too, has its mystical traditions. In its high moments the West functions in a way as mystical as that of any tradition. But the West is religiously oriented more to the acceptance of the world, the rational, the human, the material, and to a spiritual world dominated more by sacramental rituals, authoritative doctrines, institutional directives, and by simple prayer and congregational worship than by intense efforts at inward concentration leading to some spiritual experience of a transcendent nature. The Indian world appears to us overintense in its spiritual concerns, too negative in its attitude toward the rational processes of thought, neglectful of the social aspect of religious worship, susceptible of distortion by subjective imagination and emotion. Thus there are differences of modality in the spiritual levels on which India and the West function. In recent centuries at least, much of Western religious development has been socially oriented, has seen high spiritual value in establishing justice in the distribution of the wealth of the earth among men. Thus there is an activism in the West that tends to overshadow the contemplative aspect of the spiritual tradition. The mystical elements were more highly developed in an earlier period of Western religious life, in the days of the great monasteries and the foundation of contemplative religious institutes dedicated to contemplation, the reading of sacred texts, the cutting of ties with the material and social orders.

Just what brought about the Western religious preoccupation with the social to the partial exclusion of the mystical would not be easy to identify. There is an inherent concern in the tradition for the corporal works of mercy. This sense of the justice on earth as a prerequisite for the high spiritual destiny in heaven is no doubt largely responsible for the change that took place. But more than that there is the current of gnosticism in the West that produced, by way of reaction, a profound suspicion of enlightenment unless this was controlled by established canons of authenticity associated with defined doctrines, unless there was preserved some direct contact with the sacraments, and unless the whole religious-spiritual life was integrated into the wider life of the Church, the basic spiritual community. All of these things tended to the view that the true Christian did not commit himself to intense individual effort at contemplative religious experience. It was considered too dangerous an exercise, something in which too many had gone wrong. The safe, the more authentic Christian way, the approved way, was to center attention more on moral perfection than on contemplative experience. Even a person as authentic in his mystical experience as John of the Cross lived under a cloud insofar as the official ecclesiastical establishment was concerned. Yet even John himself recognized the need and value of such guidance and such a disciplined approach to the spiritual life in its higher phases. There were many valid reasons for the attitude adopted in the West, and it would be difficult to say that the total effect of the Western spiritual discipline has not been on the whole the healthiest context for Western spirituality. Indeed it may be the only context in which Western spiritual development can take place effectively. It fits more with the total culture of the West and most likely no other course has really been open to us.

It is clear, however, that differing spiritual disciplines are needed to provide for the differing needs of peoples and traditions. But now as the

peoples and traditions come together and begin communicating their spiritual vision and spiritual disciplines to each other, the differences cause each
tradition to see its own distinctive qualities more clearly, both in its ad-
vantages and disadvantages. The important thing is to recognize the higher
achievements of each and to enter into a new understanding of the total
range of the spiritual heritage of mankind. Each can be inspired by the
other. Indian spiritual personalities in modern times have learned much
from the West and have incorporated aspects of Western spirituality into
their own traditions. The entire nineteenth century and well into the
twentieth century has been a period when the social work of Christians has
been an inspiration to India. This is especially true of the great follower
of Ramakrishna, Vivekananda, who worked long to assist in the alleviation
of the poor of India on a basis of religious dedication, and of Gandhi, who
brought to bear on the total political and economic life of India a new
spiritual vision. This was derived from the ancient spiritual traditions of
India as well as from the West, but it functioned in a new way, a new
modality, a way that made it effective in transforming the society. In a corresponding way the West has now an opportunity to learn from the high
forms of spiritual insight of the Indian traditions. India offers an intensity
of dedication to the interior life that the West has recently neglected.
After a period of secularization the West is again feeling a deep need for
the inner serenity and contemplative experience so highly developed in
India. This does not mean that we can ever adopt the Indian way in its
totality. We are a different people. It is not likely nor is it necessary that we
imitate the technical side of Indian spiritual disciplines. We can be inspired
by them to live more deeply in the contemplative traditions that we ourselves possess and that these be further developed in the light of the Indian
experience. Above all this experience must be appreciated, understood, and
accepted as part of the larger human heritage. Beyond this there is the
inspiration of the religious life expressed in the Vedic Hymns, of the grand
vision of Brahman found in the Upanishads, of the devotional expressions
of the Bhagavad-Gita and the saints of later Hinduism, of the spiritual
discipline and contemplative life of the Yogins, of the Buddhist awareness
of the transient nature of all things in time, of the great doctrine of Sunyata
expressed by the Wisdom Sutras and Nagarjuna, of the wonderful sense of
a higher Providence expressed in the Lotus Sutra. Everywhere there are
magnificent expressions of the spiritual foundations of the life of man. All
these form a significant part of the universal spiritual heritage of man

which now becomes, in its totality, the heritage of each human person upon the earth.

The present generation is the first that is able to take part in this most fascinating spiritual venture with a full and direct understanding of the basic issues and their significance, for this is the first generation that is able to study the spiritual formation of man as it should be studied, within a universal-cultural-historical context. For the first time the materials are adequately prepared for study; the scriptural languages are being taught; the basic scriptures themselves are available in sound translations; the proper interpretation is making itself known. This is a new and difficult, but, at the same time, an extremely satisfying endeavor. From now onward this universal context will be the only satisfactory context in which any spiritual tradition can rightly be studied and understood—even in its own distinctive import for man.

These traditions of the past are intensely alive in the present. They are not dead but living traditions. Although they are ancient, they are also modern. This can be seen especially in India where the most vital currents of modern life have been brought into intimate association with the past through men such as Aurobindo in the Hindu-Yoga tradition, Tagore in the cultural order, Gandhi in the political, Nehru in the political and economic orders, and Radhakrishnan in the realm of philosophy and contemporary religious development. Numerous others could be mentioned. Of the three traditions dealt with in this study, Hinduism is represented most strongly, for the modern development of India took place within the Hindu tradition more than in any of the others. Buddhism has not been an active force within India for almost a thousand years. During this time, however, it has spread across all of Asia east of India as the most dynamic and all-embracing spiritual force known to this entire region. And, finally, Buddhism is returning to India as a vital force in the intellectual and social life of the society. Its modern phase is still quite limited, but Ambedkar, the author of the Constitution of Independent India, became a Buddhist and brought Buddhism back into the social and political life of India, especially in the service of the Untouchables. Yoga has always been strong in India and its influence can be seen everywhere, even though its discipline in the more rigorous sense finds less expression in the modern centers of India's development. Even so, Yoga is absolutely and thoroughly alive and spreading powerfully over the world as a basic spiritual discipline available for men of every continent and every tradition. The most impressive exponent of Yoga in modern times is Aurobindo Ghose. Through his writings particularly, the tradition in its higher spiritual expression is widely known among the scholars of the world.

In studying these spiritual traditions of India it is important that they be considered as in a state of constant development rather than as fixed realities. There is hardly anything so deadening to those traditions or to their understanding than to consider them as fixed, integrated realities that have attained now, or at some time in the past, a definitive expression that can be used as the fixed basis on which to identify them. There is indeed some primordial experience that is striving for expression in each of these traditions, yet they have never attained and apparently never will attain definitive expression. They are themselves part of the historical process even though they seek transhistorical objectives. Thus when one speaks of the Hindu religious or spiritual tradition it is important that a person think of the tradition as a continuing process, not as already determined. The process is still alive, still changing, still seeking to express a vision which is indeed primordial but which has also developed considerably over the centuries and is presently undergoing one of its most vital and significant changes in the entire history of its existence.

The process is something that can be described in its various stages, but one cannot say that this phase of the process is the authentic stage and that the other stages are unauthentic, even when apparent contradictions arise within a tradition. One cannot say of Hinduism that a sense of the Impersonal Absolute is the basic spiritual and thought orientation of the tradition, for later the entire tradition underwent a transformation that led to a dominant devotional expression. And with Yoga, one cannot say that the earlier expression of Yoga which led to a termination of the spiritual process in the indwelling of the Self apart from any personal theistic attitudes is the "true" Yoga rather than the Yoga of the *Bhagavad-Gita* or the later developments within Yoga which led to a mystical experience of the divine. And with Buddhism one cannot say that the early exclusive emphasis on personal effort at liberation is the basic attitude of the tradition, for later an extensive commitment was made to salvation by grace. All phases of development belong to these traditions and must be accepted, not as alien to the tradition, but as historical developments within the tradition, as integral elements in the specific spiritual process under consideration.

The doctrine of constant change and development establishes the basis on which the present vital changes can take place within these traditions.

One could say that at the present time these traditions are developing more profoundly and more soundly than they have developed for centuries. They are entering into a new phase of their existence, a new phase of significance not only for the societies that have in the past been associated with and guided by these traditions but for the entire world of man. All can now benefit from these traditions and can give to these traditions both a new challenge and new strength to fulfill a wider role than they have thus far envisaged for themselves.

Bibliography

General

Charria-Aguilar, O. L., ed. *Traditional India*. Englewood Cliffs, N. J., Prentice Hall, 1964, pbk.
A series of short studies on the main aspects of Indian spiritual and cultural development by recognized scholars, quite readable, excellent for the non-specialist.

de Bary, William T., ed. *Sources of Indian Tradition*. New York, Columbia University Press, 1958 (available in pbk, 2 vols).
A rich collection of materials on Indian spiritual development. Last section especially good on leading personalities of modern India.

de Bary, W. T., and A. T. Embree. *A Guide to Oriental Classics*. New York, Columbia University Press, 1964. pbk.
A valuable guide to basic sources and reading materials covering the entire Asian world. The India section is of great help to student, teacher, and general reader in pursuing the trends of thought suggested in this book.

Garratt, G. T., ed. *The Legacy of India*. Oxford University Press, 1937.
A book of essays on Indian cultural development by experts who possessed exceptional competence.

Hiriyana, M. *Outlines of Indian Philosophy*. London, Allen and Unwin, 1932 (available in pbk).
A standard guide to India's thought development. While not profound in its presentation of the material, it does outline basic traditions with clarity.

Radhakrishnan, S. and Charles A. Moore, eds. *A Sourcebook in Indian Philosophy*. Princeton University Press, 1957 (available in pbk).
This is the best source book for intellectual development of India. Advanced students with some philosophical competence will find this work particularly satisfying.

Hinduism

Dasgupta, S. N. *Hindu Mysticism*. New York, Ungar, 1927, pbk.
A clear presentation of the various phases of Hindu religious development written in simple, direct fashion, easily understood by the general reader.

203

The author is the most learned Indian scholar in modern times in his acquaintance with the historical development of Indian thought.

Embree, Ainslee T., ed. *Hindu Tradition*. New York, Modern Library, 1966.
A fine selection of readings from the earliest period of Vedic hymns to twentieth-century writings of Gandhi, with brief but valuable introductory sections. Probably the best book for the general reader or the college student.

Hume, R. C., tr. *Thirteen Principal Upanishads*. New York, Oxford University Press, 2d ed., 1931.
Accurate and readable translation of the whole series of greater Upanishads; a standard English translation with complete texts.

Mascaro, Juan, tr. *The Upanishads*. Baltimore, Penguin Books, 1965, pbk.
A good presentation of the Upanishads containing most of the important sections; a number of the Upanishads are given in their entirety. Recommended especially for those students using inexpensive paperback books for their study.

Renou, Louis. *Religions of Ancient India*. New York, Schocken Books, 1968, pbk.
Simple, brief, well written introductory study by one of the finest of contemporary India scholars.

Zaehner, R. C. *Hinduism*. Oxford University Press, 1962, pbk.
Best and most readable general study of the main ideas of Hinduism for the reader who wishes to obtain a deeper understanding of the main doctrines of Hinduism.

—— *Hindu Scriptures*. New York, Dutton (Everyman's Library), 1966.
New translation of the basic scriptural texts given in full or at least in substantial sections: especially good for translations of *Upanishads* and the *Bhagavad-Gita*.

Yoga

Eliade, Mircea. *Yoga, Immortality and Freedom*. New York, Panthenon, 2d ed., 1969.
The most penetrating study available and quite readable, it is concerned with the spiritual significance of Yoga rather than with its specific techniques for spiritual development. Excellent on the entire spiritual orientation of India.

Mishra, R. S. *Textbook of Yoga Psychology*. New York, Julian Press, 1963.
An effort at understanding the psychological processes in the Yogic advance to spiritual insight; somewhat imaginative, but helpful in understanding the Yogic terms and procedures.

Sivananda, Swami. *Practise of Bhakti-Yoga*. Amritsar, 1937.
A good presentation of what traditional Yoga can mean to modern man.

Vivekananda, Swami, tr. *Raja Yoga or Conquering the Internal Nature*. New York, Ramakrishna Center, 1956. (Contained also in Lin Yutang's collection *The Wisdom of China and India*, New York, Modern Library, 1942.)
A clearly written translation of entire text of the original classic written by Patanjali at the end of the pre-Christian era. Quite accurate.

Wood, Ernest. *Yoga*. Baltimore, Penguin Books, 1959, pbk.
Detailed presentation of such Yoga techniques as posture, breathing, and the gradual attainment of control over mental, emotional, and bodily functions of man in order to lead him to the interior quiet needed for a higher liberating insight.

Woods, J. H., tr. *The Yoga-System of Patanjali, or the Ancient Hindu Doctrine of Concentration of Mind Embracing the Mnemonic Rules, called Yoga-Sutras of Patanjali*. Harvard University Press, 1927.
A translation more literal than readable, but of special value for study of the early explanatory writings of Veda-Vyasa and Vachaspati-Mishra. A book that will mean more for the advanced student with philosophical background.

Buddhism

Burtt, E. A. *Teachings of the Compassionate Buddha*. New York, Mentor, 1955, pbk.
A good selection of Buddhist texts which cover both Hinayana and Mahayana phases of development. Introductory paragraphs are too brief and lack depth. Still this is a convenient and useful book.

Conze, Edward. *Buddhism; Its Essence and Development*. New York, Harper (Torchbook), 1959.
A good presentation of the basic ideas of Buddhism, along with the story of its early divisions and doctrinal development. Requires careful attention. Can be used as a small reference book by beginners.

——— *Buddhist Thought in India*. London, Allen and Unwin, 1962 (available in pbk).
A more substantial survey of the subject written with personal understanding of the Buddhist experience and its basic thought orientation. Especially good for the reader with some philosophical background.

de Bary, William T., ed. *The Buddhist Tradition*. New York, Modern Library, 1969.
Probably the best single volume to guide a beginner through the vast course of Buddhist development; extensive selections of basic scriptural texts, each introduced with a few clear sentences placing the selection in context and indicating its significance.

Foucher, A. *Life of the Buddha*. English tr. by S. Boas. Wesleyan University Press, 1963.
Well-written account of Buddha's life as this is presented to us in the art, legends, and scriptural compositions from the earliest period.

Murti, T. R. V. *The Central Philosophy of Buddhism*. London, Allen and Unwin, 1955.
A basic text for understanding the development of Buddhist thought in the Mahayana Tradition—for those interested primarily in the speculative insights of Buddhist thinkers.

Rhys Davids, T. W., tr. *Questions of King Milinda*. New York, Dover, 1963, pbk.

A Hinayana Buddhist text from the beginning of the Christian period ex-
plaining the entire Buddhist experience of reality and the way of liberation;
written as a catechetical treatise, it is thoroughly readable and enjoyable to
this day; has many good passages on the Nirvana experience.

Thomas, E. J. *History of Buddhist Thought*. New York, Barnes and Noble 1951.
A basic presentation of Buddhist thought development.

Warren, Henry Clarke. *Buddhism in Translations*. Harvard University Press,
1953.
An extensive collection of early Pali scriptures arranged topically and with
many selections also from Buddhaghosa's *Path of Purity*.

Zurcher, E. *Buddhism: Its Origin and Spread in Words, Maps and Pictures*.
New York, St. Martin's Press, 1962.
A brief, informative work of special help to the general reader in locating
Buddhism in its origin and its stages of expansion throughtout the far Asian
world.

Glossary

Adhyasa A false imposition by the mind of the nature and characteristics of one thing on something else, especially the imposition of characteristics of phenomenal reality on the absolute reality of Brahman.

Advaita Vedanta Non-dual Vedanta; the thought system of Shankara in which true reality is considered absolutely unique, beyond all multiplicity.

Agamas In Hinduism, writings that guide the devotional and ritual life of the sectarian traditions; in Buddhism, the Chinese translations of the early Buddhist scriptures.

aham I; the phenomenal personality.

ahamkara Egotism; undue attribution to the secondary cause of what is due to the primary cause.

ahimsa Non-injury; a negative term with connotations of a positive and profoundly human relationship with others, indeed with all living things.

Ajanta The site in central India of some twenty-nine caves excavated and occupied by Buddhist monks in the early Christian centuries and used as monasteries and shrines, containing splendid remains of early Buddhist art.

Ajivika A spiritual sect of the followers of Gosala, who taught a doctrine of absolute determinism (sixth century B.C. to A.D. thirteenth century).

Akbar (1542–1605) A Mogul ruler of northern India 1556–1605.

Alvars Poet-saints who sang praises to the god Vishnu (sixth to tenth century A.D.).

Amida, Amitabha The Buddha of infinite light who saves by compassion and grace those who have faith and manifest devotion to him.

Ananda The cousin and favorite disciple of Buddha.

Appar A poet-saint who composed songs of praise in honor of Shiva (seventh century A.D.).

Aranyaka Forest Meditations; Vedic scriptures concerning sacrifice and its higher meaning.

Arhat A perfect one; in the Buddhist monastic tradition, one who had surmounted all the bonds keeping man within the endless cycle of phenomenal change.

Arjuna One of five brothers, sons of King Pandu, who fought in the wars described in the epic *Mahabharata*; one to whom the revelation of Krishna is given in the *Bhagavad-Gita*.

Arya Samaj The Holy Society; a group formed by Dyanand Sarasvati to re-
vivify the spiritual traditions of ancient India (nineteenth century A.D.).
Aryan Noble; specifically, the Indo-European peoples of India.
asana Sitting posture; a main aspect of the meditative spiritual disciplines of
India.
asavas Inner defilement, in Buddhism.
asrama A place of retreat and meditation in Hinduism; also asramas, the four
stages in the ideal pattern of Hindu life: student, householder, forest dweller,
homeless wanderer.
Ashvaghosa The Buddhist author who wrote the life of Buddha entitled Buddhacarita (first century A.D.).
asmi, asmita I am, I-am-ness; assertion of the phenomenal ego, a supreme
obstacle to spiritual liberation in both Hinduism and Buddhism.
Asoka Emperor of India, a most capable and most humane ruler (third century
B.C.).
asteya Non-stealing.
Atharva-Veda The last collection of Vedic Hymns, which pertains more than
the other three to popular religous devotion, charms, and superstitions
and which contains as well hymns of high intellectual and spiritual significance.
Atman The Supreme Self; the absolute support of the phenomenal order and
of the individual man, experienced inwardly as the true reality of everyone.
Aurobindo See Ghose.
Avalokitesvara A savior figure in later devotional Buddhism, venerated especially in China and Japan.
Avatamsaka A great Buddhist Mahayana scripture which presents the doctrine
of cosmic identity, the basis of the Hua Yen school of Buddhism.
Avatar The appearance of deity in earthly form, especially in human form,
the most venerated of whom are Krishna and Rama.
Bhagavad-Gita Song of the Lord; a sacred poem in the Mahabharata, con-
sidered the gem of Hindu religious literature.
Bhagavat The Blessed One; a term of address, in Hinduism to deity and in
Buddhism to Buddha, which also refers to distinguished human persons.
Bhagavata Purana The most influential and best written of the eighteen Puranas,
and one of the latest (probably tenth century A.D.).
Bhakti Devotion, love; a name given to the devotional tradition of India; this
became the supreme way of liberation in the sectarian Hindu traditions
after the time of the Bhagavad-Gita.
Bharut An ancient shrine of India containing much of the earliest Buddhist
art.
Bhutakoti The highest point of being; the Supreme Reality; a term much used
in later Mahayana Buddhism for the Buddha reality.
Bimbisara A ruler in northern India at the time of Buddha.
Bodhisattva An enlightenment-being; the supreme ideal of spiritual perfection,
as conceived in later Mahayana Buddhism, that replaced the earlier ideal
of Nirvana; also Bodhisattvas, Buddist savior figures, such as Maitreya.

brahmacariya Continence; a basic requirement for attaining spiritual liberation in Indian traditions.

Brahma Samaj The Society of God; a society founded by Ram Mohan Roy to purify and elevate Hinduism and to give it a vital place in the spiritual and social development of modern India (nineteenth century A.D.).

Brahman The Supreme Reality in Hinduism, identical with Atman.

Brahmanas Ritual Books; the ritual literature of the Vedic period.

Brihadaranyaka One of the earliest and greatest of Upanishads, notable especially for its doctrine of the all-pervading presence of the ineffable Brahman within and yet above all phenomenal reality.

Buddhaghosa The greatest Theravada Buddhist writer, the author of the *Path of Purity* and extensive commentaries on the Theravada scriptures (fifth century A.D.).

Buddhacarita The life of Buddha written by Ashvaghosa (first century A.D.).

Buddhi The intuitive faculty of the mind; sometimes used for the mind itself.

Carvaka An unorthodox materialist school of Hinduism.

Chandogya An early and important Upanishad identifying the inner self, the Atman, with the absolute reality of Brahman, "Thou art that."

Chanhu-Daro A significant site of Indus Valley civilization of the pre-Aryan period.

Chu Hsi A Chinese neo-Confucian philosopher of the twelfth century A.D. who composed commentaries on the early classics, especially on Mencius, and was later established as the authority of Confucian orthodoxy during the Ming Period.

Chuang Tzu A Chinese Taoist philosopher (fourth century B.C.).

cittam Mind, thought, mind-stuff; a term of special importance in the Yoga Sutras of Patanjali.

Das See Tulsi and Ram.

dharana Concentration of mind.

Dharma in Hinduism, the religious-social class structure of society; in Buddhism, the teachings of Buddha; also in Buddhism, the elements which constitute the phenomenal world.

Dharmakaya The Truth Body of Buddha; the absolute reality of Buddha, or Buddha considered as the ontological truth of things; the main element in the doctrine of the Threefold Body of Buddha, the others being the Bliss Body and the Transformation Body.

dharma-megha Cloud of truth; the sudden penetrating experience of the Yogin when he attains liberating knowledge.

Dhammapada Path of Perfection; one of the earliest and best known works of Buddhism; a guide to spiritual perfection.

dhyana Mental concentration; the interior discipline of mind whereby an experience is attained leading to liberation from the binding and painful aspect of the phenomenal world.

Dipamkara One of the forms in which Buddha appeared in a former life.

Dravidian Southern; a term designating the non-Aryan peoples of central and southern India.

Duhkha (Sanskrit), dukkha (Pali) Sorrow. In Buddhism, the primordial experience man has of the world and the human condition as unsatisfactory, as sorrowful of its very nature.

Durga One of the names of the feminine consort of the god Shiva.

dvandva Duality; a main obstacle to man's transphenomenal experience.

Dyanand See Sarasvati.

Gandhara A region northwest of India, now in Afghanistan; the center of Hellenic culture in the post-Alexandrian period and where the first Buddha images were made around the first century A.D.

Ghose, Aurobindo (1872–1950) An outstanding Yogin of India, a contemporary of Ramakrishna. Aurobindo is distinguished for his intellectualism; Ramakrishna, for his devotion.

Gosala A wandering spiritual teacher with many disciples at the time of Buddha, taught a doctrine of absolute determinism in both cosmic and human orders.

Grihya Sutras The official guide to proper conduct of the household religious rituals in the Hindu tradition, especially concerning personal sacraments from birth to marriage.

Guadapada Author of a commentary on the Chandogya Upanishad, a predecessor of Shankara who was significant in establishing the Vedanta tradition of Indian thought (sixth or seventh century A.D.).

Gupta A dynasty which ruled in northern India during the golden age of Hindu culture (320–544).

Harappa A significant site of the pre-Aryan Indus Valley civilization.

Hinayana The Little Way of early Buddhism, as contrasted with the Great Way of the Mahayana Buddhism; a designation imposed by Mahayana writers, especially in the Lotus Sutra.

Indra The most prominent deity in the Rig-Veda; a storm deity of special significance for slaying Vitra, the symbol of evil in Vedic mythology.

Isa A short but important Upanishad of the later Vedic period; containing in eighteen verses a precise summary of Hindu theology as it existed at the time (c. sixth century B.C.).

Ishvara The Lord; the personal deity.

Jainism The tradition of extreme asceticism founded by Mahavira, who taught a doctrine of souls in all things (sixth century B.C.); also an extreme doctrine of non-injury (ahimsa).

jhana The Pali spelling of the Sanskrit dhyana, meaning mental concentration.

jivan mukta Liberated while living; indicating that the salvation experience does not take place after death, but is an immediate and lasting experience that takes place in life.

Kabir (1440–1518) A poet-saint of Hinduism, much influenced by the Islamic Sufi tradition.

Kaivalya Isolation; in Yoga writings, the experience of liberation from the bonds of the phenomenal world.

Kali One of names of the feminine consort of Shiva.

kalyana mitta Beautiful friend; in Buddhism, the spiritual teacher and guide of a person still in the learning stage.

Kami Deity or spiritual being; a Japanese term for the spiritual presence perceived in natural phenomena.

Kannada A language of southern India.

Kapilavastu Buddha's birthplace, on the border of India and Nepal.

Karma The determining consequences of a deed already done on what follows —good deeds have good consequences; evil deeds, evil consequences.

karma-phala The fruit-of-action; in Hinduism, especially in the *Bhagavad-Gita*, the principle of doing an action simply because it is *Dharma* (prescribed by the religious-social structure of the society) and not because of any quest for gain.

Katha A philosophical and popular Upanishad, known especially for its depth of inquiry into life after death.

Kaurava The adjective derived from Kuru, that is, pertaining to the Kuru tribe.

Kena An Upanishad in verse which treats especially the ineffable nature of Brahman.

Keshub See Sen.

Khuddakapatha The last of the five collections of the discourses of Buddha.

kirtan A highly devotional and popular group religious expression through ecstatic song and dance, often led in the past by the saint-singers of the sectarian devotional Hindu traditions.

Krishna A human appearance of the god Vishnu; the prominent figure in the *Bhagavad-Gita* and the *Bhagavata Purana*; in both, the main doctrine is the love relationship between God and man.

Lalitavistara The life of Buddha written in the Sanskrit language at the beginning of the Christian period, containing many highly legendary episodes.

Lalla A woman poet-saint of the Shaivite sect of Hinduism in Kashmir (fourteenth century A.D.).

Lankavatara A principal Mahayana Buddhist scripture which presents the doctrine of mind only and thus prepared the way for the Yogacara school of Buddhist thought.

Lotus Sutra An early, well-known Mahayana Buddhist scripture of great influence in China and Japan which presents the doctrines of the eternal existence of Buddha, salvation through faith and grace, and Buddhahood as the final goal of man.

Madhva The founder of the dualist school of Vedanta (fourteenth century A.D.).

Madhyadesa Middle Region; the central part of northern India in the Ganges Valley to which the Aryans migrated after 1200 B.C. and where much of early Hindu culture developed.

Maghavan The term of address to Indra, the dominant deity in the *Rig-Veda*.

Mahabharata The *Great Bharata*; the massive epic account of the wars of early Hindu India. Expanded through the centuries, it became an extensive collection of Hindu traditions, thought, laws, customs, social behavior, and spiritual ideals.

Mahasanghika One of the eighteen sects of Hinayana Buddhism which exalted the Teaching of the Great Council over the Teaching of the Elders (Theravada) and thus prepared the transition from Hinayana to Mahayana.

Mahat The Great One; the first emergence of the determined phenomenal world from the primordial cause in nature (Prakriti).

Mahavastu A Sanskrit scripture of the Mahasanghika sect of Hinayana Buddhism which presents Docetist doctrine that Buddha only appeared to live and function in a human body within the phenomenal order, while in reality he remained in an eternal and unchanging status.

Mahavira (died c. 470 B.C.) Considered the founder of Jainism.

Mahayana The Great Way, or the Great Career; sometimes called neo-Buddhism, an advanced form of Buddhism characterized by intensive intellectual and devotional development; proposed Buddhahood instead of Nirvana as final goal of man.

Maitreya The future Buddha who will save through mercy and faith, of special significance to devotional Buddhism in East Asia.

manas Mind.

Manikka A poet-saint of the Tamil region of southern India who wrote and sang in praise of the god Shiva (eighth century A.D.).

Manjusri A Buddha with special qualities of wisdom, especially prominent in the Vimalakirti Sutra.

mantra A formula with special spiritual efficacy used especially in the Tantric form of Buddhism; also used to designate the Vedic Hymns.

Manu The first man; the sage who gave to Hindu India its basic law codes governing the entire structure of Hindu society.

Maya The phenomenal world considered as not truly real but as an ephemeral appearance or illusion.

Mimamsa Enquiry; one of the six dominant thought traditions of Hinduism, especially significant for its search into the meaning of Vedic ritual.

Mohenjo-Daro A site of the Indus Valley, pre-Aryan civilization which existed approximately from 2800 to 1700 B.C.

Moksha Liberation from the bonds that keep man within the phenomenal world of ceaseless and meaningless change, the supreme spiritual ideal of Indian traditions.

Mundaka A principal Upanishad with special clarity in its presentation of the two ways of knowing: the higher way of knowing the supreme reality of Brahman, the lower way of knowing the phenomenal world.

Muni A silent one; a wandering ascetic mentioned in the Rig-Veda but apparently derived from the non-Aryan traditions of India.

Nagarjuna Founder of the Middle Path School of Mahayana Buddhism, who taught particularly the doctrine of emptiness (Sunyata) as the highest expression of transphenomenal reality (second century A.D.).

nama-rupa Name and form; a designation of the phenomenal world in both Hinduism and Buddhism.

Nayanars Poet-singers in praise of the Hindu god Shiva in southern India (mainly sixth to ninth century A.D.).

niyama Spiritual discipline.

Nyaya One of the six main thought traditions of orthodox Hinduism; a philosophical school especially concerned with the logical processes whereby the mind arrives at an understanding of things.

Nimbarka The founder of a Vedanta school that teaches that identity in difference is a more acceptable doctrine than the non-dualism of Shankara (twelfth century A.D.).

Nirguna Brahman See Saguna Brahman.

Nirvana The act of extinction, or blowing out; in Buddhism, supreme spiritual attainment, total release from the sorrow of temporal existence. Nirvana is a term used also in Hinduism, a term for final bliss in union with Brahman.

Pali The language of Hinayana Buddhist scriptures.

Pandavas The sons of King Pandu, opposed to the Kauravas in the wars recounted in the *Mahabharata*.

Pandurang A name of God in the Marathi language.

Panna Ultimate wisdom; the Pali spelling of the Sanskrit *prajna*, the saving wisdom of those who attain a state of spiritual blessedness.

Paramartha Supreme reality; in Indian traditions, absolute being.

Parvati One of the names of feminine consorts of the Hindu god Shiva.

Prajapati Lord of Creatures; a Hindu deity of special importance in the sacrificial aspect of the tradition.

Prakriti Matter or Nature; one of the two primordial principles of the entire order of things (the other being Purusha); the dynamic creative force of the world, according to the Sankhya tradition.

Puja Worship of a personal deity, especially through images and symbols, which developed with special intensity in the middle of the first millennium A.D.

Puranas Ancient things; the popular scriptures of devotional sectarian Hinduism.

Purusha Spirit, person; in Hindu thought, especially in the Sankhya tradition, the transcendent spiritual principle opposed to Prakriti.

Purusottama The Supreme Spirit; the highest divine reality, Brahman, often used in the *Bhagavad-Gita*.

Radha The milkmaid especially beloved of Krishna, considered a symbol of every human person beloved by God.

rajas Passion; one of the three strands or qualities found in everything within the phenomenal world according to Sankhya teaching.

Rama The hero of the epic *Ramayana*, popular in Hinduism as exemplifying the man of perfect virtue; a human appearance of the god Vishnu.

Ramakrishna (1836–1886) The most revered of modern Hindu saints, a man of extraordinary devotion to God throughout the entire course of his life.

Ram Das (1608–1681) One of the five great Maratha poet-saints of this period.

Ramananda A devotee of Rama from southern India, whose teachings had great influence on the devotional life of Hinduism (fifteenth century A.D.).

Ramanuja (1050–1137) A teacher of modified dualism in the Vedanta tradition, the greatest of Vedanta philosophers after Shankara, a devotee of Vishnu, and the first of the sectarian theologians of the later Hindu tradition.

Ramaprasad (1718–1775) A poet-saint of Bengal who composed hymns of praise to Shiva and especially to the consort of Shiva, Kali.

Ramayana The Story of Rama; one of the two great epics of India, composed in final form perhaps two centuries before the Christian era.

Rig-Veda The first and most valuable collection of Vedic Hymns.

Rishi Seer; name given those whose spiritual experience and religious vision is recorded in the Vedic literature.

rita The immanent principle of order governing the universe, a word much used in early Vedic literature, but less used later on.

Roy, Ram Mohan (1772–1833) A reformer of Hinduism from Bengal, sometimes called the father of modern India, the founder of Brahma Samaj.

Rudra A lesser storm deity in the Vedic Hymns, perhaps a prototype of the god Shiva who was later much venerated.

Sadhana Spiritual discipline leading to liberating vision.

Saguna Brahman The absolute reality considered as possessing attributes, known also as qualified Brahman, in distinction to Brahman without attributes, known as Nirguna Brahman.

Samadhi The highest intuitive experience in Hindu, Yoga, and Buddhist traditions whereby liberation is achieved.

Sama-Veda The collection of Vedic Hymns which contains the chants used by the priest presiding at the Soma Sacrifice.

Sambandar A poet of the god Shiva who wrote in the Tamil language (seventh century A.D.).

Samdhinirmocana Sutra Explication of Mysteries Sutra; an important Mahayana Buddhist scripture (probably late second century A.D.).

Samsara The phenomenal world endlessly changing in a cycle of life, death, and rebirth.

Sannyasi One who has gone forth into the homeless life, the fourth final stage in the Hindu pattern of spiritual development.

Sanskrit Well made; the language of India which derives at an early period from the same Indo-European language out of which Western languages, including Greek, Latin, Slavic, and Teutonic languages, have evolved.

Sankhya The earliest of the six thought traditions of Hindu India, a school of philosophy that provided the terminology and context for much of Hindu speculation.

santosa Inner spiritual serenity.

Sarasvati, Dyanand (1824–1883) An Indian reformer who sought to restore the prestige and influence of the Vedic Hymns in the modern period, a main figure behind modern Indian nationalism.

Sariputra The most capable disciple of Buddha, often mentioned in Mahayana Buddhist writings.

sattva Goodness; one of the three strands or qualities found in all phenomenal reality according to the Sankhya teachings.

Savitri A lesser solar deity of the Vedic Hymns.

Sen, Keshub Chunder (1838–1884) A leading figure in the nineteenth-century revival of India. Having a deep appreciation of Christianity, he sought to establish a common basis of religious belief for mankind.

Shaivism The cult of the Hindu god Shiva.

Shakti The feminine creative principle; considered as the consort of a deity, often worshipped independently.

Shankara The spiritual and intellectual reformer of Hinduism at the end of the Buddhist period, the first to give extensive scholastic exposition of the doctrines taught in the earlier Vedic compositions, especially in the Upanishads; the founder of Advaita Vedanta (eighth century A.D.).

Shinto Way of the Gods; the traditional Japanese religion.

Shiva One of the two principal deities of sectarian devotional Hinduism (the other being Vishnu).

Shudra The fourth and lowest of the four traditional classes into which Hindu society is divided.

Siddhartha The personal name of Buddha.

Sigalovada Suttanta A discourse of Buddha addressed especially to lay persons.

Sila Virtue, morality; the first division of the spiritual path leading to liberation in Buddhism and in Yoga.

Smriti What is remembered; the later part of the religious literature of Hinduism, of less import than the Vedic literature itself.

soma The juice of a milky plant extracted and offered as libation to deity; also Soma, the sacrifice itself, the most common of the Vedic sacrifices.

Sruti What is heard; the canonical Hindu scriptures composed of hymns, sacrificial prescriptions and liturgical directions, forest meditations, and interpretive compositions concerned with the nature and attributes of Brahman.

stupa A dome-shaped shrine in which the relics of Buddha are kept.

Sufi The highly spiritual tradition of Islam.

Sukhivativyuha Sutra Land of Bliss Sutra; a Mahayana Buddhist scripture which shows that the paradise of Amida is granted to all who manifest faith and devotion to Amida Buddha.

Sunyata Emptiness; the highest concept of Mahayana Buddhism, expounded in the Wisdom Sutras and in the Madhyamika school of Nagarjuna.

Surangama Sutra A Mahayana Buddhist scripture containing idealist doctrine of special influence in China.

Surya A sun deity of the Vedic Hymns, mentioned frequently in later Hindu literature.

Sutra In Buddhism, a scriptural work of canonical status; in Hinduism, generally a basic collection of aphoristic statements concerning Hindu belief, practice, or thought.

Sutta Nipata An early canonical scripture of Buddhism belonging to the fifth collection of the discourses of Buddha.

svayambhu Self-existence; the final reality of things in both Hinduism and later Buddhism.

Svetasvatara A later theistic Upanishad which prepared the way for the *Bhagavad-Gita*.

Tad Ekam That One; in Hinduism, the supreme divine reality.

Tagore, Rabindranath (1861–1941) The first modern literary figure of India to attain world recognition, a deeply religious and humanist personality with an extraordinary range of interest in the cultural and political development of the modern world.

tamas Darkness; one of the three strands or qualities found in all phenomenal reality, an important concept in the Sankhya thought tradition.

Tantra A literature and spiritual method in both Hinduism and Buddhism which makes extensive use of signs and symbols to assist in attaining spiritual identity with the cosmos and eventually spiritual liberation.

Tao In Chinese thought the ultimate principle of reality immanent in all things.

tapas Asceticism.

Tat tvam asi Thou art that; an expression much used in Upanishadic compositions.

Tathagata The "one thus come," or the "one thus gone"; a significant name given to the Buddha.

Tathata Thusness; the supreme reality in Buddhism.

Theravada Teachings of the ancients; the only school of Hinayana Buddhism, that has survived as a living tradition, found in Ceylon and in much of southeastern Asia.

T'ien Heaven, God, nature; much used in Chinese thought in all its varied meanings, which must be discovered in context.

Tukaram (1598–1649) The Maratha saint of the Krishna cult.

Tulsi Das (1532–1623) The composer of the poem *Ramacarita*, which profoundly influenced the devotional lives of the Hindu people of northern India.

Uma One of the feminine consorts of Shiva.

Upanishad The highly mystical intuitional treatises of the Vedic revelation, concerned primarily with the nature and attributes of Brahman as transcendent and immanent in all things, comprising some fourteen principal works, some two hundred including those written later and of lesser significance.

Vaishesika One of the six thought traditions of Hinduism, a school of philosophy primarily concerned with the structure of the cosmic and natural worlds, advocating a doctrine of primary elements.

Vaishnavism The cult of the Hindu god Vishnu.

Vallabha (1479–1531) A Vedanta theologian, strongly theistic, who taught a doctrine of identity in difference.

Vasanas The impression of past deeds in the subconscious regions of man's being.

Vasubandhu A Buddhist writer who with his brother, Asanga, developed the Yogacara school of Mahayana Buddhism (fifth century A.D.).

Vayu Wind; an atmospheric deity in the Vedic Hymns.

Vedanta The most influential theological tradition of Hinduism, a school of philosophy endeavoring to explain the Upanishadic writings concerned with the nature and attributes of Brahman and the way to attain liberating knowledge. The basic writings, begun by Badarayana, in his *Brahma Sutras* composed apparently in the first centuries of the Christian era.

Vedas The religious compositions accepted as infallible divine revelation by the Hindu tradition comprising the Hymns, Brahmanas, Aranyakas, and Upanishads.

Vimalakirti A Mahayana Buddhist scripture that presents the high spiritual attainment of the layman, Vimalakirti, most influential in East Esia.

Vinaya Pitaka The first part of the Buddhist canon; sacred writings that contain directions for the monastic life.

Vishnu The most significant deity of devotional Hinduism, generally worshipped in one of his human appearances, either as Rama or as Krishna.

Vishnu Purana A basic scripture of sectarian Hinduism expressing the basic beliefs of the worshipers of Vishnu.

Visvakarman Maker of All Things; a deity in the *Rig-Veda.*

Vivekananda (1863–1902) A disciple of Ramakrishna, who spread the teachings of his Master throughout the world, presented these teachings at the Parliament of Religions held at the Columbian Exposition in Chicago in 1893, and introduced a modern social consciousness in modern Hinduism.

Yajna Sacrifice; especially, the Vedic sacrifices which dominated the religious life of early Hinduism.

Yajur-Veda A collection of hymns taken mostly from the *Rig-Veda* which were used by the priests in offering sacrifices.

Yoga The spiritual discipline derived from primordial pre-Aryan India outlining an interior spiritual discipline which leads to isolation of the supreme spiritual principle in man from its confinement and frustration due to its apparent association with the natural world of Prakriti.

Yogacara The idealist school of Mahayana Buddhism (begun in fourth and fifth centuries A.D.).

Zen Mental concentration; a Japanese word derived from the Chinese *ch'an,* in turn derived from the Sanskrit *dyana,* meaning meditation or withdrawal of the mind from the external world; in China and in Japan, a special school of Buddhism that sought to attain a sudden saving illumination of mind by the use of special methods.

Index